RICHARD OF CORNWALL

Photographed by B. Hutchings, Winchester

CORFE CASTLE

RICHARD OF
CORNWALL

BY

N. DENHOLM-YOUNG

Formerly Fellow of Magdalen College, Oxford
Author of *Seignorial Administration in England,*
Collected Papers on Mediaeval Subjects, etc.

NEW YORK
WILLIAM SALLOCH
142 SEVENTH AVENUE SOUTH
1947

CONTENTS

ILLUSTRATIONS

INTRODUCTION

ALL my notes towards this book and a draft of about a third of it were stolen from the Zürich-Chur express in the winter of 1938-1939, with the rest of my personal luggage. I had at that time far too much on hand to make use of this misfortune in the now almost traditional way. I no longer regret it, however, as I had not yet learned enough of the composition of the chief chronicles of the period, particularly the works of Matthew Paris and Thomas de Wykes, nor had I made up my mind on some important constitutional topics, some of which I have now dealt with in other publications.

Richard, Earl of Cornwall and King of the Romans, is far more important as an English magnate than as King of Germany — though he is still the only Englishman who has attempted to rule that country as a unity. He lived to be sixty-three, but spent less than four years — about a quarter of his reign — in Germany, and the records of his rule are scanty. Moreover, the interest of his reign, apart from the history of diplomatic relations with the Papacy, France, and his rival Alfonso X of Castile, lies rather in the double election itself, the cultural advance and the political disintegration of Germany. But a biography is not the place for a detailed history of that dismal Interregnum between Hohenstaufen and Habsburg in which Richard's reign forms three-quarters of the whole. His excursions to Germany are baffling to the student and heart-breaking to the biographer. The tangle of English politics in the mid-thirteenth century is difficult enough to unravel if the task is pursued without distraction. The added complication of four journeys to the Continent, so timed that they coincide with periods of desperate confusion in this country, makes it difficult to thread one's way to the end of the story.

These difficulties have no doubt been felt by other scholars. For this obviously important theme has been undertaken by some well qualified to deal with it who have — perhaps with more discretion than the present writer — not proceeded to the point of publication. I allude to these works because other scholars have mentioned them to me: I have not had the good fortune to see them. The lack of any modern biography in any language is my own justification for this book. There are, in German, three small but valuable dissertations which between them cover the whole life and much (though not all) of the activity of Richard of Cornwall, namely the works of Koch, Bappert, and Lemcke. These, and the old-fashioned *Leben und denkwürdige Thaten Herrn Richards* of Gebauer, with its valuable appendices of documents, I have had constantly at hand.[1] Taken with Professor Tout's long article in the *Dictionary of National Biography* they comprise the only connected accounts of the subject. Of the three German dissertations that of Koch extends only to 1257. It is thorough and accurate, though loaded with undiscriminating references to the chronicles, whose study when he wrote had not progressed very far. His work was continued, a little less accurately and with less sureness of touch, for the period 1257-1272 by Bappert. It may be noted that half, and half only, of this thesis formed the original publication. The London Library copy is of this shorter version. Lemcke's *Beiträge* are an exhaustive study of the few known events of the period of the double election with special reference to the inaccuracy and duplicity of Matthew Paris, upon whom his judgment is too severe (cf. p. 96 *infra*). I have not found it necessary to cite these works, or even the more ponderous Gebauer, at all frequently, though in the early stages of my work I used them much. Apart from the fact that they are almost unobtainable, it was my intention by going behind them to the sources to make reference to them unnecessary. The diplomatic history of the years 1257-1272 might have been traced, perhaps, in greater detail, but the life of Richard of Cornwall is not really a suitable peg upon which to hang it.

I have to thank the President and Fellows of Magdalen College, whose archives I have been permitted to use,[2] for the Fellowship which enabled me to undertake this work, and Mr. J. E. A. Jolliffe of Keble College for providing the facilities which made possible its completion as well as for his illuminating comments on many of the problems arising out of its composition. To Mr. Antony Thompson I am grateful for supervising the preparation of the plate of coins and for providing me with the description that accompanies it.

Mr. Sherborne has very kindly supplied the map, which is chiefly

[1] I am indebted to Mr. A. L. Poole of St. John's College, Oxford, whose authoritative survey of German history in the thirteenth century is the only work of its kind in English, for allowing me to impound for a long period his copies of the works of Koch, Bappert, and Lemcke.

[2] See pp. 162, 171.

of castles, Cornish boroughs, and country seats. Other places from which Richard of Cornwall drew rents or over which he had rights are enumerated in the alphabetical directory on pp. 165-70, and that in turn I should not have had the courage to attempt had not Miss Midgley edited two invaluable volumes of Accounts of the Earldom of Cornwall for the Camden Society.

MANUSCRIPTS USED

The manuscript sources used have not yielded as much as might have been hoped. P.R.O. Exch. K.R. Misc. Book 37 (now referenced as E. 36/57) is a transcript of deeds relating to the Earldom of Cornwall, made temp. Ed. I. The description in the P.R.O. *Guide* conceals the fact that a large number of the deeds are grants to Earl Richard, not to his son Edmund. Unfortunately for our purposes the book does not contain any of Richard's charters, but only grants to him. It is merely a collection of title deeds. Miss Lucy Drucker very kindly made an analysis of the chartulary for me, thus greatly facilitating my examination of the MS., which contains nearly three hundred charters. Miss Drucker also examined for me the early Memoranda Rolls, which contained nothing to my purpose. A few points were gleaned from the Ancient Correspondence (p. 125, n. 4).

The most important Record Office source used was the Pipe Rolls for the period during which Richard of Cornwall contracted to make new money. These became available to me too late for a full use to be made of them in the text. I therefore subjoin a note of the six occasions on which there was a division of the profits on the recoinage. The amount given on each occasion is Richard's portion. In estimating how far the profits were due to Richard's intervention at the Exchequer it will be noticed what happened after he had gone to Germany in April 1257.

1 November,	1252	£5,513
1 November,	1255	2,339
4 June,	1257	1,821
1 October,	1257	231
	1259	618
	1261	489

I may add that William of Gloucester, who became Warden of the Mint in October 1257, had till then been the king's goldsmith. He had had the new gold pennies in his keeping. It seems a probable deduction from this and what else is known about William that he was the designer of the gold penny. This fits in with the view expressed in the text, that Richard makes rules and regulations for the Mint, but the king has a gold coin made outside the contract, and probably outside the Mint.

The plate of coins is enlarged to approximately one-and-a-half times the actual size.

N. DENHOLM-YOUNG

St. Nicholas House
25 Devon Close
Perivale
Middlesex

BIBLIOGRAPHY

Ann. Berm.=*Annales monasterii de Bermundeseia* in *Annales monastici*, vol. III (Rolls Series).

Ann. Burt.=*Annales monasterii de Burton* in *Ann. mon.*, vol. I.

Ann. Dunst.=*Annales prioratus de Dunstaplia* in *Ann. mon.*, vol. III.

Ann. Hales.=*Annales monasterii de Hales* in *M.G.H.*, XXVIII.

Ann. Lond.=*Annales Londonienses* in *Chronicles of the Reigns of Edward I and II* (Rolls Series).

Ann. Osen.=*Annales monasterii de Oseneia* in *Ann. mon.*, vol. IV.

Ann. Theok.=*Annales monasterii de Theokesberia* in *Ann. mon.*, vol. I.

Ann. Wav.=*Annales monasterii de Waverleia* in *Ann. mon.*, vol. II.

Ann. Wint.=*Annales monasterii de Wintonia* in *Ann. mon.*, vol. II.

Anct. Deeds.=*Descriptive Catalogue of Ancient Deeds* (P.R.O.).

Auvray, L., *Registres de Grégoire IX*.

Ballard, A., and Tait, J., *British Borough Charters*, vols. I-II (Cambridge, 1913, 1923).

Bappert, J. F., *Richard von Cornwall seit seiner Wahl zum deutschen König, 1257-1272*.

Bémont, Charles, *Simon de Montfort*, Eng. trans. by E. F. Jacob (Oxford, 1930).

Berger, E., *Registres d'Innocent IV*.

B.F.=Böhmer-Ficker-Winkelmann: *Regesta Imperii 1198-1273* (1881-1894).

B.F., Acta=*Acta Imperii Selecta* (1870).

Blaauw, H., *The Barons War* (2nd ed., 1871).

Bliss, W. H., *Calendar of Entries in the Papal Registers relating to Great Britain and Ireland*, vol. I (1893).

Boase, T. S. R., *Boniface VIII* (1933).

Book of Fees=*Liber Feodorum. The Book of Fees: commonly called 'Testa de Nevill', 1198-1293*. Edited by Sir H. Maxwell-Lyte. 3 vols. (P.R.O.).

Botfield, Beriah, *Manners and Household Expenses of England in the XIIIth and XVth Century* (Roxburghe Club, 1841).

Breakspear, Sir Harold, 'Corsham' in *Wilts. Arch. and Nat. Hist. Mag.*, vol. xliii, pp. 511-39.

Cal. Ch. R.=*Calendar of the Charter Rolls*, especially vols. I and II, 1226-1300 (P.R.O.).

Cal. Lib. R.=*Calendar of Liberate Rolls*, 1226-1252 (P.R.O.).

Cam, H. M.='Studies in the Hundred Rolls' in *Oxford Studies in Social and Legal History*, vol. VI, 1921.

Chaytor, H. J., *Savaric de Mauléon* (Cambridge, 1939).

Cl. R.=*Close Rolls*, 1227-1272 (P.R.O.).

C.P.R.=*Calendar of Patent Rolls*, 1232-1272 (P.R.O.).

Coggeshall, Ralph of, *Chronicon Anglicanum*, ed. J. Stevenson (Rolls Series).

Darby, H. C., *An Historical Geography of England before 1880* (Cambridge, 1936).

Davidsohn, R., *Forschungen zur Geschichte von Florenz*, vol. IV (1908).

Denholm-Young, N., *Collected Papers on Medieval Subjects* (1947). 'Thomas de Wykes and his Chronicle' in *E.H.R.*, lxi, 157-79. 'The Merchants of Cahors' in *Medievalia et Humanistica*, Number 4, 1946.

D.N.B.=*Dictionary of National Biography*, especially 'Richard of Cornwall' in vol. xlviii (1896), by T. F. Tout.

Doüet D'Arcq, L., *Collections de sceaux. Archives de l'empire. Inventaires et documents*, 3 vols., 1863-1868.

Dugdale, W., *The Baronage of England*, 1675-1676. *Monasticon Anglicanum*, old ed., 3 vols., 1655-1673; ed. Caley, 7 vols., 1817-1830.

Edwards, J. G., 'The *Plena Potestas* of English Parliamentary Representatives' in *Essays in Medieval History presented to H. E. Salter*.

E.H.R.=*English Historical Review*.

Excerpta e Rot. Fin. 1216-1272. Ed. Charles Roberts, 2 vols. (Record Commission, 1835-1836).

Flores=*Flores Historiarum* (Rolls Series).

Flor. Wig. Cont.=*Florentii Wigorniensis Monachi Chronicon ex Chronicis*, ed. B. Thorpe, 2 vols., 1848. The Continuatio is in vol. II.

Foed.=Rymer, *Foedera, Conventiones*, etc. (Record Commission).

Foss, E., *The Judges of England*, 9 vols., 1846-1864.

Fournier, P., *Le Royaume d'Arles* (Paris, 1891).

Gavrilovitch, M., *Étude sur le Traité de Paris de 1259* (Paris, 1899).

Gebauer, G. C., *Leben und denkwürdige Thaten Herrn Richards, erwählten römischen Kaysers, Grafens v. Cornwall und Poitou* (Leipzig, 1744).

G.E.C.=*The Complete Peerage*, by G. E. Cokayne, new ed., V. Gibbs and others, 1910 ff.

Gerv. Cant.=*The Historical Works of Gervase of Canterbury* (Rolls Series).

Grousset, R., *Histoire des Croisades* (Paris, 1934-1936).

Hampe, Karl, 'Ungedruckte Briefe zur Geschichte Richards von Cornwall' in *N.A.*, vol. xiv, 675; 'Reisebericht aus England' in *N.A.*, vol. xxii, 337.

Harcourt, L. W. Vernon, *His Grace the Steward and Trial by Peers*, 1907.

Hist. MSS. Comm. Rep.=*Historical Manuscripts Commission Reports*.

Jacob, E. F., *Studies in the Period of Baronial Reform and Rebellion* in *Oxford Studies in Social and Legal History*, vol. VIII, 1925.

Kantorowicz, E., 'Peter de Vinea in England' in *M.I.O.G.* (1937-1938), 43-88.

Koch, Hugo, *Richard von Kornwall. Erster Theil, 1209-1257* (Strassburg, 1888).

Lacomblet, T. J., *Urkundenbuch für die Geschichte des Niederrheins* (Düsseldorf, 1846).

Lanercost, Chronicon de, ed. J. Stevenson (Bannatyne Club, 1835).

Lemcke, G., *Beiträge zur Geschichte König Richards von Cornwall* (Berlin, 1909).

Lewis, F. R., 'Beatrice of Falkenburg the Third Wife of Richard of Cornwall' in *E.H.R.*, vol. lii (1937), 279-82.
'The Election of Richard of Cornwall as Senator of Rome in 1261, *ibid.*, 657-62.

Lewis, G. R., *The Stannaries* (Boston, 1908).

Lib. de Ant. Leg.=*De antiquis legibus liber: Chronica maiorum et vicecomitum Londoniarum* (Camden Society, 1846).

Liebermann, F., *Ungedruckte anglo-normanische Geschichtsquellen* (Strassburg, 1879).

Little, A. G., 'Friar Henry de Wodestone and the Jews' in *Collectanea Franciscana*, vol. ii, 150-7.

Lloyd, J. E., *History of Wales* (2nd ed., 1912).

Lunt, W. E., *Financial Relations of the Papacy with England to 1327* (Medieval Academy of America, 1939).

Madox, T., History of the Exchequer (ed. 1711).

Mat. Par.=*Matthaei Parisiensis: Chronica majora*, ed. H. R. Luard, 7 vols. (Rolls Series).
Historia Anglorum, ed. Sir F. Madden, 3 vols. (Rolls Series).

Maxwell-Lyte, Sir Henry, *Historical Notes on the Use of the Great Seal* (1926).

Melrose Chronicle=The Chronicle of Melrose with an Introduction by Allan Orr Anderson and M. O. Anderson, and an index by W. C. Dickinson (London, 1936).

Midgley, L. M., *Ministers' Accounts of the Earldom of Cornwall, 1296-7*, 2 vols. (Camden Society, 1942, 1945).

Mitchell, S. K., *Studies in Taxation under John and Henry III* (1914).

M.G.H.=*Monumenta Germaniae Historica.*

Mon. Ang.=*Monasticon Anglicanum*, see Dugdale.

Morris, W. A., *The Medieval English Sheriff to 1300* (Manchester, 1927).

N.A.=*Neues Archiv.*

Norgate, K., *The Minority of Henry III* (1912).

Oliver, G., *Monasticon Diocesis Exoniensis* (Exeter, 1846).

Oxenedes=*Chronica Johannis de Oxenedes*, ed. H. Ellis (Rolls Series).

Painter, S., *Studies in the History of the English Feudal Barony* (Baltimore, 1943).

Pasquet, D., *Essay on the Origins of the House of Commons*, translated by R. G. D. Laffan, 1925.

Pat. R.=*Patent Rolls*, 1216-1232 (P.R.O.).

Poole, A. L., 'The Interregnum in Germany' in *Cambridge Medieval History*, vol. vi, chap. iv.

Powicke, F. M., 'The Oath of Bromholm' in *E.H.R.*, vol. lvi, 529 *f.*
'Loretta, Countess of Leicester' in *Historical Essays in Honour of James Tait.*
'Guy de Montfort' (1265-1271) in *Transactions of the Royal Historical Society*, 4th ser., vol. xviii, pp. 1-23.

P.R.O.=Public Record Office.

Raine, J.=*Letters from Northern Registers* (Rolls Series).

Ramsay, Sir James, *The Dawn of the Constitution* (1908).

Red Book= *The Red Book of the Exchequer*, ed. Hubert Hall, 3 vols. (Rolls Series).

Registres des papes, publiés par l'école française de Rome. Innocent IV, 1243-1254, ed. Berger; Alexandre IV, 1254-1256, ed. Bourel de la Roncière; Urbain IV, 1261-1264, ed. Dorez et Guiraud; Clément IV, 1265-1266, ed. E. Jordan.

Registrum epistolarum fratris Johannis Peckham, 3 vols., ed. C. T. Martin (Rolls Series).

Rish., *Chron.*=William Rishanger: *Chronica et Annales, 1259-1309*, ed. H. T. Riley (Rolls Series).

Rish., *de Bellis*=*Chronicon de duobus bellis apud Lewes et Evesham, 1263-1267*, ed. J. O. Halliwell (Camden Society, 1840).

R. L.=*Royal and other Historical Letters illustrative of the Reign of Henry III*, 2 vols., ed. Shirley.

R.Lit.Cl.=*Rotuli litterarum clausarum*, ed. T. D. Hardy, 1204-1227, 2 vols. (Record Commission).

Robert of Gloucester's Chronicle, ed. T. Hearne, 2 vols. (Oxford, 1724).

Rogers, J. E. Thorold, *History of Agriculture and Prices*, vols. I-II (1866).

Rot. Hund.=*Rotuli Hundredorum tempore Henrici III et Edwardi I* (Record Commission).

Roth, C., *A History of the Jews in England* (Oxford, 1941).

R.S.=Rolls Series.

Ruding, R., *Annals of the Coinage* (ed. 1819).

Salter, H. E., *The Boarstall Chartulary* (Oxford Historical Society).
The Oseney Chartulary (Oxford Historical Society).

Salzman, L. F., *English Trade in the Middle Ages.*

Sandford, Francis, *Genealogical History* (ed. 1707).

Sternfeld, R., *Karl von Anjou als Graf der Provence* (Berlin, 1888).

Stubbs, W., *Select Charters*, 9th ed., by H. W. C. Davis.

Teulet, A., J. de Laborde and E. Berger, *Layettes du Trésor des Chartes.*

Treharne, R. F., *The Baronial Plan of Reform* (Manchester, 1932).

Turner, G. J., *Select Pleas of the Forest* (Selden Society, 1901).

V.C.H.=Victoria County History.

Wagner, A. R., *Historic Heraldry* (Oxford, 1939).

Weber, F. P., in *Numismatic Chronicle*, 3rd series, vol. xiii (1893) on
  Richard of Cornwall's coins as King of the Romans and *ibid.*, vol.
  xiv (1894), 85, on his shield of arms.

Wend.=Roger de Wendover, *Flores Historiarum* to 1235 as embodied in
  Matthew Paris.

White, A. B., 'Some Early Instances of Concentration of Representation
  in England' in *American Historical Review*, vol. xix, 735-50.

William of Newburgh, continuation of, vol. II (R.S.).

Wright, Thomas, *The Political Songs of England from the Reign of John to
  that of Edward II* (Camden Society, 1839).

Wurstemberger, J. L., *Peter II, Graf von Savoyen*, 4 vols. (Bern and
  Zürich, 1856).

Wykes=*Chronicon vulgo dictum Chronicon Thomae Wykes* (R.S.).

ADDENDA

p. 34. Business as usual. Add that on April 22nd, 1237, Richard was enjoined by the king to set out on a treasure-hunt in the Isle of Wight and Cornwall, by digging up the barrows (*hogas*) there. It appears that either Richard or the inhabitants had been excavating for treasure in the island when the king heard of it and intervened. The record is not quite explicit (*Close Rolls*, 433-4). Richard had the island at that time by reason of the custody of young Baldwin de Redvers.

p. 51. In Richard's renunciation of 1243 note (i) that there had been a claim to lands in the possession of King John, when he was count, in England, Ireland and beyond seas. I do not know on what this claim was based. (ii) Richard was to receive 1,000 marks a year until £500 p.a. worth of land had been received, and for every £100 worth of land assigned 200 marks was to be deducted from the fee.

p. 95. I have implied a total lack of evidence for charges of extravagance in Germany. Against this may be set two small points: Richard gave the city of Worms 1,000 marks on July 25th, 1258 (Ann. Wormat. 60), and on September 12th, 1260, promised 400 marks to the Bishop-elect of Strassburg (B.F. 5375-6).

COINS. A find in 1843 at Marburg of thirty-four deniers of Richard of Cornwall is described in *Numismatic Chronicle*, 3rd series xiii (1893), by F. P. Weber, who thought it likely that they were minted in 1257 at Aachen. The coins, which are heavily clipped, are inferior in workmanship and design to the contemporary English silver penny.

CHAPTER ONE

EARLY YEARS: GASCONY
(1225-1227)

RISING OF THE EIGHT EARLS
(1227)

RICHARD OF CORNWALL was Henry III's younger brother, son of King John and Isabella of Angoulême. For nearly half a century he influenced, and at times of crisis dominated, his brother's policy. At an early age he won an international reputation and led a Crusade which successfully continued the work of his brother-in-law, the Emperor Frederick II. He was the only Englishman to become King of the Romans, a position which he maintained for fifteen years (1257-1272). He financed and supervised the great recoinage of 1247-1248, and was still sharing the profits of the Mint when it issued its first gold coin since the Conquest. As Regent in 1254 he has a real but not always acknowledged place in the history of Parliament, holding the first full assembly to which there was a general summons of knights of the shire. He was universally believed to be the richest man in England: how he acquired his wealth is shown in the following pages.

There has been no book in English on Richard of Cornwall, and only portions of the subject have been discussed by German writers since 1744, when Gebauer produced a work which for its period was well done. The present biography is not written in support of any theory of history. It is simply an attempt to build up a picture of the man by considering afresh everything that may be known about him from sources printed and unprinted.

From the loss of Normandy until the Treaty of Paris in 1259 England and France were not at peace. The intervening years saw a series of truces, some renewed just in time, some broken, some allowed to lapse through negligence. While Pandulf, the papal legate, had been in England he had impressed upon the government the urgency of renewing the truce, and this was done. By 1224, when the term was again running out, Hubert de Burgh was in power. Foreign policy was not his strong point: it may be doubted whether he had one. So it came about that while Hubert was destroying Falkes de Bréauté, the Norman adventurer raised to power by King John, the truce with France was allowed to expire and the new French king, Louis VIII, walked into Poitou.[1] The English lost everything north of the river Garonne, retaining only Bordeaux, Bayonne, and Gascony. Repeated appeals for help from the communes of Poitou and Gascony were backed by the report of an English agent stating that the towns were prepared to defeat the king's enemies, if only they had money, and adding, 'I believe they would if they had with them the king himself or his brother Richard.'[2] To prevent further losses and with the object of recapturing Poitou, the council at length took heed of these appeals and decided to send an expedition. In 1225, in return for a confirmation of the charters, the barons granted a fifteenth on movables, yielding some £57,000, much of which was applied to the maintenance of the little army in Gascony, 1225-1227. The nominal leader of this expedition was Richard, the king's brother, who had just been knighted at the age of sixteen and was now styled Count of Poitou.

Richard, fifteen months younger than Henry III, was born on January 5th, 1209, at Winchester.[3] He was named, somewhat ironically as it turned out, after his uncle, Cœur de Lion, who had died ten years before he was born. The perversity of his father, King John, has thrown a mist over his childhood, for John had amongst his numerous illegitimate progeny another son Richard, born well before 1200. This man had his scutage for Poitou in 1214,[4] was married by 1215 to Roese of Dover,[5] assumed knighthood the same year,[6] and was much occupied in administration, chiefly as constable of Wallingford Castle, from at least June 1216 to at least March 1218.[7] Consequently there are a number of references in the records which may refer to either, as well as a few which have become firmly attached to the biography of Richard of Cornwall.[8] To clean the picture before we attempt to restore it, we must deprive our Richard

---

[1] For the situation in France see C. Petit-Dutaillis, *La Vie et le Règne de Louis VIII*, chap. iii.

[2] *R. L.*, i, 239.

[3] *Ann. Wav.*, 264; *Ann. Marg.*, 29. See also *Gerv. Cant.*, ii, 107.

[4] *R.Lit.Cl.*, i, 201.

[5] *Ibid.*, 168, 242b.

[6] *Ibid.*, 268b.

[7] *Ibid.*, 289, 353b and *passim*; *R.Lit.Pat.*, i, 185.

[8] Dugdale (*Baronage*, i, 761), appears to have started this confusion, which is reflected in numerous modern works (e.g. Morris, *The Medieval English Sheriff*, p. 181; the *Chron. Melrose* (facsimile edition), index *s.v.* Richard.

at the age of seven of the constableship of Wallingford Castle, or of Chilham in Kent.

When Richard of Cornwall was three years old there was a rumour that he and the queen's household had been murdered in Marlborough castle.[1] He was probably taken to the north with John in January 1213 and left at Durham, as in September there is an order to the custodian of the bishopric to send him to court in the care of Robert de Vipont.[2] John went to Poitou in February 1214 and wrote home on June 19th to the Abbot of Beaulieu and others for the queen, Isabella of Angoulême with her children Richard and Joan, and the Beauchamp children, Andrew and Elyas, to be sent out to him.[3] After this Richard cannot have seen much of his mother, who went to France in 1217. When he was six, just below the usual age for children to be placed in other households, he was sent to Corfe castle to be educated by Sir Roger d'Acastre under the care of Peter de Mauley. He was taken there with his master, two trumpeters and his washerwoman in or about April 1215.[4] It has been assumed, and nothing is known to the contrary, that he spent much of his time there until at least 1220, when he was brought to London by Peter de Mauley for his brother Henry's coronation.[5] In 1221 there was a nominal grant to him of the honour of Eye[6] and in 1223, though part of the time he was lying ill at Lambeth,[7] he went on pilgrimage to Canterbury with Alexander II of Scotland.[8] The credit of taking part in a campaign against the Welsh in October of the same year might equally be ascribed to his namesake.[9]

[1] *Ann. S. Edmundi*, 153, in Liebermann *Ungedruckte anglo-normanische Geschichtsquellen*, Strassburg (1879).

[2] *R.Lit.Pat.*, 104. The other references in this volume (except 117, 197) are to Richard the bastard.

[3] *Ibid.*, 117; Coggeshall, 168: 'ducens secum reginam suam, et Ricardum filium suum, et Alienor sororem Arturi'.

[4] *R.Lit.Pat.*, i, 197. To Peter de Mauley. 'Mittimus ad vos dilectum filium nostrum Ricardum mandantes quatinus bonam curam et diligentem de eo habeatis et necessaria ei inveniatis et Rogero Magistro ejus et duobus trumpitoribus et lotrici ejus et inter nos bene computabimus.'

[5] *Foed.*, i, 160. In July 1221 Peter de Mauley was allowed 7,000 marks for his expenses at Corfe, including the care of Richard (*R.Lit.Cl.*, i, 466). At Christmas 1220 Richard was given a grey pélice. This and other details are in *ibid.*, i, 444, 460, 497b.

[6] July 3rd, 1221, grant of the honour of Eye during pleasure, with Falkes de Bréauté as steward to answer to him (*Pat. R.*, 294). At the same time Richard received half the estates of Henry de Pagham, a follower of Falkes (*R.Lit.Cl.*, i, 605, 621). The appointment of Falkes as steward makes it certain that this is the prince and not the other Richard.

[7] *R.Lit.Cl.*, i, 540, a writ of *liberate* for 10 marks expenses.

[8] *Ibid.*, i, 554b. A similar writ. Whether or not the prince had a household and no matter how it accounted, these writs for sums payable to 'Richard' and not *ad opus Ricardi*, etc., suggest the bastard not the prince.

[9] *Ibid.*, i, 605.

From 1215 until 1223 Roger d'Acastre is styled Richard's master,[1] until at least 1220 Peter de Mauley is responsible for him, and when he is granted an honour in 1221 a steward is imposed upon him. It seems therefore fairly safe to assume that if he already has his own household its independence is purely nominal. On King John's death, shortly after Richard had been sent to Corfe with Eleanor of Brittany and Isobel of Scotland, an invitation was received from Geoffrey de Marisco offering Isabella of Angoulême and her son Richard an asylum in Ireland.[2] The Council, however, declined this, finding no doubt that John's state prison was safe enough. Richard reappears at the coronation of May 1220, and the next event about which there can be no shadow of doubt is when he is knighted by his brother at Westminster on February 2nd, 1225, shortly after his sixteenth birthday.[3] A few days later he was given the county of Cornwall during pleasure.[4]

On March 25th, 1225, a commission of three was appointed for the recovery of Gascony, fast slipping out of control, and the reconquest of Poitou. The patent was issued to Richard as the king's brother, his uncle William Longsword, Earl of Salisbury, and Philip d'Aubigné, sometime tutor to Henry III, to assist the Gascons and Poitevins against the French.[5] The relations of these three to one another or to the king are not specified, but the Gascons and Poitevins are, in the common form, ordered 'to be intendent' to Richard, and in this context the other two are not mentioned. Richard can only have been a figurehead, set up as emblem of a loyalty and an allegiance yet to be won, for he had only just been knighted and we have repeated assertions that he was far from warlike. The military leader was Salisbury, an old soldier of some distinction. These men formed the nucleus of the council sent out to look after the young count.

The expedition set off on Palm Sunday, the day that they were commissioned. As not infrequently happened, there was no exact computation of the number of ships needed, so that this time far

---

[1] There are two Acastres near York. Roger and Robert d'Acastre appear in the list of knights who accompanied Richard to Gascony in 1225. They held of the honour of Plympton in Devon (*Book of Fees*, 612, 760, 773, 787), and Roger in 1217-1223 received lands elsewhere (*R.Lit.Cl.*, i, 325b, 495).

[2] *Foed.*, i, 145.

[3] *Oxenedes*, 137-8; *Gerv. Cant.*, 114; Wend. in *Mat. Par.*, iii, 92. Ten other young men who were knighted with him were assigned to his household.

[4] *R.Lit.Cl.*, ii, 16; *Pat.R.*, i, 507 (February 13th, 1225). The Cornish tin-mines were added on November 27th (*Pat. R.*, 3).

[5] *Pat. R.*, 516.

more than necessary were requisitioned and many had to be sent
home.[1] The list of those who went with Richard bears out the
rough estimates of the chronicles that forty to seventy knights
accompanied him.[2] Among them were Henry de Turberville, who
became seneschal of Gascony next year, Hugh de Vivonia, who had
already filled that office and was now acting as the Earl Marshal's
deputy with the army,[3] and Roger d'Acastre, Richard's tutor. It
is not said that the original contingent contained any infantry, but
later five hundred Welsh footmen were sent out as reinforcements.[4]

From at least August 14th, 1225,[5] Richard styled himself Count
of Poitou, and was so officially styled hereafter.[6] Matthew Paris
refers to a secret charter of this year by which he was also enfeoffed
with Gascony, but that is another story. As Richard never had
effective possession of his county of Poitou in the whole course of
his life, the exact date at which he assumed the title is only of importance for dating undated documents in which it occurs. He retained
the style, however, until after Henry III had disappointed him by
a grant, immediately revoked, of Gascony in the summer of 1243.
He probably dropped the title Count of Poitou when he renounced
his claims on Gascony in December of that year. That there were
limitations set upon his authority in Gascony, as distinct from Poitou,
may be seen from the arrangements whereby two at least of the commissioners were required for giving receipts for money received
from home.[7] Much of the money was sent out in bulk, through the
wardrobe rather than the exchequer, with Caorsins or merchants of
Bordeaux as bankers. Sometimes it was sent in the king's 'great ship'
commanded by a Templar, and sailing, for greater safety, in a large
convoy. In this and other ways about £36,000 was sent out to
Richard or paid on his behalf, thus consuming the greater part of
the fifteenth.[8] Reinforcements in men were on a less generous scale.
Though Hubert de Burgh was virtually supreme at home the country

---

[1] *Ibid.*, 514-15.
[2] *Ibid.*, 573-4, cf. *Ann. Wint.*, 84; Wend. in *Mat. Par.*, iii, 92; R. L., i, 239.
[3] *R.Lit.Cl.*, ii, 38.
[4] *Pat. R.*, May 1226, p. 35; *R.Lit.Cl.*, ii, 110, 117b.
[5] *R. L.*, i, 262.
[6] *Foed.*, 179, 182; *R.Lit.Cl.*, ii, 59 (August 18th). *Mat. Par., Hist. Angl.*, ii, 270, has 'Dederat
ei namque rex, ante recessum suum ab Anglia, comitatum Cornubie cum tota Pictavia; unde
ab omnibus comes Pictavie vocabatur, titulusque literarum suarum "comes Pictavie et
Cornubie".' There is added in the margin, 'Clam dederat ei *Wasconiam* et incartaverat'. See
infra, p. 48, n. 4.
[7] *Pat. R.*, April 28th, 1225, pp. 523-4, cf. 534-5.
[8] Mitchell, *Studies in Taxation*, 168-9.

had not yet fully emerged from the period of uncertainty ushered in by the rebellion against John and the invasion of Prince Louis. The Earl of Salisbury before he sailed for Gascony had felt sufficiently anxious to make an agreement with the government whereby six knights were to be put in charge of Salisbury castle for him if war broke out in England while he was away.[1]

About a month after they had landed at Bordeaux Richard sent home a brief but exultant letter, dated May 2nd, announcing the conquest of all Gascony except La Réole,[2] the siege of which lingered on through the summer and autumn.[3] Its fall in November marked the pacification of Gascony. In spite of this early success there had been no serious attempt to reconquer Poitou. The lack of royal demesnes, castles or towns, and its fickle and turbulent baronage, had made Poitou always the weak spot in the Angevin empire. The barons were led by Hugh de la Marche, Count of Lusignan, first love and second husband of Isabella of Angoulême, Richard's mother, and he was ready to change sides at any moment. Secondly, Savaric de Mauléon, the troubadour and soldier, though long faithful to John, had deserted Henry's cause through lack of English support and admitted the French into La Rochelle. He was in a position to cut communications by sea, and his depredations impeded the free flow of men, money, and materials from England to Gascony.[4] Thirdly, any lasting effects that the campaign had were probably due to old Salisbury. It was his last effort. He did not live to see Richard reap the reward of his labours, but fell ill, came home in October and died six months later.[5] He had returned to England at the express wish of the government. It is likely that Hubert de Burgh realized that something was amiss in Gascony, for as late as September 21st an appeal had been issued to all Salisbury's tenants to go and help him.[6] One of the reasons for his recall may have been that he had not prevented Richard from seeking to marry the King of Laon's daughter. When this was reported to the council in England they — that is, primarily, Hubert de Burgh — refused to sanction

[1] *Pat. R.*, 514.
[2] *Foed.*, i, 178.
[3] When Hugh de la Marche attempted to relieve La Réole the English hurried north to meet him. The armies were separated by the Dordogne and probably never came to blows, though Wendover (in *Mat. Par.*, iii, 93) reports a crushing victory over the French.
[4] *Pat. R.*, ii, 25. The little that is known about Savaric is brought together by H. J. Chaytor in his *Life* (C.U.P., 1939). Savaric had a considerable reputation as a troubadour, but few of his poems have survived.
[5] *R.Lit.Cl.*, ii, 83.
[6] *Pat. R.*, i, 550.

it on the ground that they hoped to negotiate a marriage nearer home.[1] So Richard had to wait another six years.

Without Salisbury Richard's council disintegrated and no further military progress was made. From October 1225 there was no outstanding man until Henry de Turberville was appointed seneschal in October 1227.[2] Henry III, who was less than two years older than Richard, was personally worried and in spite of a severe and recent illness he seriously proposed to go to Gascony himself. From this he was dissuaded by his council. The anxiety felt at home for the success of the expedition after Salisbury's recall and the French attack on Toulouse is reflected in Wendover's story of how Henry was much comforted by one of his counsellors, Mr. William Perepund, a skilful astronomer, who assiduously read in the stars confusion and death to the French and their king. More substantial grounds for optimism were received in a letter from Richard (which has not survived) saying that all was well. Henry was therefore persuaded to drop his policy for a time and follow the counsels of Hubert de Burgh. The decision not to reinforce Richard was a right one. With the forces likely to be at their disposal the English could not have hoped to reconquer Poitou, and all the wiles of Richard's diplomacy were wasted on the Poitevin barons. Richard's position was made much more difficult by Louis VIII's crusade against the Albigensian heretic, Raymond, Count of Toulouse, with whom Richard was in alliance. Louis VIII took the cross in January 1226 and until his death near Avignon in November continued to embarrass England's diplomacy by making war on her heretical ally. He also successfully outbid the English for the favour of Pope Honorius III, who as politely as he could made it quite clear which side he supported.

The death of Louis on November 8th, 1226, and the accession of a boy of twelve to the French throne set all the political weathercocks spinning. Savaric de Mauléon admitted Richard to La Rochelle, which momentarily gave us much of Poitou, Hugh de la Marche and the Vicomte de Thouars changed sides, Raymond of Toulouse made an open treaty with Richard,[3] and a truce was made with France.[4] But negotiations for a full peace, carried on concurrently

---

[1] *R.Lit.Cl.*, ii, 83. *Maritagium propinquiorem.*
[2] *Pat. R.*, ii, 149, wrongly dated 1226 in *Foed.*, i, 182.
[3] *Foed.*, 183; *Ann. Dunst.*, 98-102; Wend. in *Mat. Par.*, iii, 110-11.
[4] Teulet, *Layettes*, ii, no. 1926. The date is between April 11th and 30th, 1227 — *Foed.*, i, 187. In the sealed copy of his truce with France Richard is simply styled *Ricardus comes, frater domini regis.*

with those for the truce, fell through.[1] In February 1227 the Archbishop of Bordeaux and Savaric de Mauléon accompanied Richard
to Thouars in an attempt to win over the Counts Theobald of Champagne (another poet) and Henry of Bar,[2] who promised much but
quickly deserted to the French. In March Peter of Brittany and
Hugh de la Marche followed their example.[3] Thus the attempted
coalition dissolved and in April Richard sailed for home.

For the last eighteen months of his stay in Gascony Richard had
had no prominent adviser except Philip d'Aubigné. After suffering
the attacks of Louis VIII for nearly a year, Raymond of Toulouse
had on November 12th, 1226, written to implore Henry III to send
out someone who should be more powerful than the rest on
Richard's council, both to advise him and to rule his court for him.[4]
The letter is unfortunately mutilated, but it is important as one of
the few pieces of evidence that point convincingly to what was
happening in Gascony after Salisbury's departure, and to assess
Richard's responsibility for it. The sum total of achievement or
failure is not in doubt. They had regained Gascony, but they had
not made, and hardly attempted to make, any advance across the
Garonne into Poitou.[5] Still Richard was only eighteen when he
left Gascony, and Raymond of Toulouse's letter reads as if it were
fully understood in Languedoc that he could not be expected to
control his own council. The few surviving details of Richard's rule
in Gascony cannot therefore be made to yield many clues to
Richard's character or policy. But he had two impressionable and
not unsuccessful years in this land of flexible and adroit politicians
and it is clear that already he preferred making treaties to making war.[6]

On landing in May Richard was warmly welcomed by his
brother,[7] but their hitherto harmonious relations[8] were soon to be
broken. Henry had come of age in January, and one of the immediate results was the enfeoffment of Hubert de Burgh with the

---

[1] *Foed.*, 186, 190-2. The best account of these events is in Miss Norgate's *The Minority of Henry III*, pp. 250 *et seqq.*

[2] *Foed.*, 184.

[3] Koch, 23-4.

[4] 'Qui . . . in regimine curie sue possit plenius providere.' The letter is wrongly dated 1228 in *R. L.*, i, 338.

[5] Koch, 21 citing *Chron. Tur.*, 316-17, states that Richard tried to take La Rochelle and failed miserably, in the spring of 1226.

[6] For his alliance with Auvergne in 1225 see Petit Dutaillis, *Louis VIII*, p. 268, and with Toulouse, *ibid.*, *piéces justificatives*, no. ix, pp. 518-20.

[7] *Mat. Par.*, iii, 123.

[8] The evidence for this consists of a few small gifts, but these are usually valuable indications of personal regard.

earldom of Kent. The industrious Hubert richly deserved this reward, but the creation of an upstart as an earl, and his unblushingly acquisitive habits, led to increasing unpopularity and eventually to the alienation of all parties. After the fall of Falkes de Bréauté (1224), the departure of Peter des Roches on Crusade, and the death of Stephen Langton in 1228, he ruled England practically alone. He had exposed himself to further criticism by presuming to marry in 1221, as his fourth wife, Margaret, sister of Alexander II of Scotland, a lady intended by King John for Henry III or Richard.[1] Hubert was beginning to behave towards his colleagues and to Henry too much like a schoolmaster, and the barons complained more and more that they were excluded from the inner councils of the king.

Hubert de Burgh's elevation was followed by that of Richard of Cornwall, who already held the county during pleasure and was Count of Poitou. He was officially styled earl on August 4th, 1227,[2] and it is commonly said that no precise date can be given for his creation. Nevertheless, one was given by Dugdale and it is difficult to see why it should have been ignored. Dugdale states that 'upon the third day of Pentecost (*id est* 3 Cal. Junii 11 H 3) [Richard] was advanced to the style and dignity of Earl of Cornwall at Westminster with great solemnity'.[3] This useful synchronism for May 30th is convincing, and is given almost word for word in the *Annals of Waverley*.[4] The creation comes just when it is expected, as soon as might be convenient after the termination of his work in Gascony, and shortly before the official use of the style. There is no reason to reject this.

Richard, however, was still unprovided for. He still held his lands 'during pleasure',[5] and he was dissatisfied with the amount of his endowment. To maintain his position as the king's brother and as heir to the throne he was entitled to more liberal treatment. He had not been an earl for many weeks before a violent quarrel with Henry over his Cornish estates led him to associate with the discontented

---

[1] *Mat. Par. Addit.*, 71.

[2] *Pat. R.*, 137.

[3] Dugdale, *Baronage*, 762, citing 'Annal. S. August.', probably Thomas Sprot's chronicle, which was partly burned in the Cottonian fire of 1731. The Close Roll shows that Henry III was at Westminster on May 30th, 1227. This piece of evidence, which did not find its way into Thorne or Elmham, is ignored by *D.N.B.* and *G.E.C.* (new ed.). The latter under Cornwall (iii, 430-2) contains some nine distinct errors in two pages. This, however, is not a criticism of the later work in that great enterprise.

[4] *Ann. Wav.*, 303, 'Henricus rex Anglie fecit Ricardum fratrem suum comitem Cornubie, in die Pentecostes, iii, viz., kal. Junii apud Londoniam.' Cf. *Ann. Dunst.*, 104.

[5] It is not known on what terms he was made Earl in 1227.

barons. Only once again did he rise in arms against his brother, and never again to right his private wrongs.

The real leader of the opposition at this time was Ranulf de Blundeville, last of the great earls of Chester of the Norman line, whose vast territorial wealth gave him control of the north-west midlands. As the Earl of Richmond was an absentee and there was no earldom of Yorkshire, Ranulf and the Count of Aumale ruled much of the north country between them. Ranulf, at first a supporter of the régime, had quarrelled with the justiciar in 1222, and lost much power by the wholesale resumption of castles next year. He and the disaffected barons had in 1224 even sent envoys to Rome, in order to force their way into the inner councils of the king with papal support. But their plans were foiled by Hubert de Burgh's emissaries. They remained excluded from the council, and government fell more and more into the hands of a small clique of officials.

Richard of Cornwall had been too young to be associated in these conspiracies, but on his return from Gascony in 1227 he soon showed his hand. The story is well told in a naive way by Roger of Wendover, who wrote only a few years after the event and had, as will be seen, special opportunities of hearing what took place.

Wendover tells us that the quarrel arose on July 9th because on his return Richard seized 'a certain manor' which King John had given to Waleran le Tyes (or Waleran the German) one of his mercenaries, as belonging to the Earldom of Cornwall.[1] Waleran complained to the king who wrote to his brother ordering him to make immediate restitution. Richard hastened to court and pleading 'without any advocate' that the manor was his by right, put himself on the judgment of the king's court and the magnates. 'The king and the justiciar were highly indignant at hearing him mention the magnates' and Henry in an imperious and indiscreet tone ordered his brother to give up the manor or quit the realm.[2] Richard replied that he would do neither without the judgment of his peers, and went straight home. The justiciar then, 'as is reported', advised the king to have Richard seized by night and to keep him in close confinement. Warned of this plot Richard secretly left the city accompanied by only one knight and did not draw rein till he came to Reading. His household followed him in the morning and the company proceeded to Marlborough, where they met William Marshal,

---

[1] Wend. in *Mat. Par.*, iii, 123-5.
[2] *Loc. cit.*, 'rex voce tumultuosa et nimis festinata [*al.* indiscreta]'.

ARMS OF RICHARD, EARL OF CORNWALL

Argent a lion rampant gules crowned or within a bordure
sable bezanty

From *Historic Heraldry of Britain* by Anthony R. Wagner,
reproduced by courtesy of the Oxford University Press

eldest son of the late regent, his friend and sworn ally.[1] When
Richard had told his story the two went together to the Earl of
Chester and made a pact with him. A large force was collected at
Stamford, joined now by five other earls — Gloucester, Warenne,
Hereford, Ferrers, and Warwick — with many barons and a crowd
of armed men. They then wrote to the king threatening civil war,
blaming Hubert de Burgh, and demanding a reissue of the Charter
of the Forest 'which he had lately annulled at Oxford'. The king
appointed a day, 'the third of August', at Northampton. They met
and the king at the urgent request of the magnates gave Richard his
mother's dower, with all the lands of the Count of Brittany in
England, and the lands of the late Count of Boulogne. And so they
went home quietly.

So much for Wendover. In its essentials his story can be controlled by the records. The causes of the quarrel, the dates on which
it began and ended, the meeting between king and barons are all in
the main correctly reported. Wendover tells us that the quarrel
began on July 9th and the Patent Roll records a royal mandate dated
July 11th to the tenants of eight Cornish manors enjoining them 'to
be intendent' to Waleran Teutonicus, as they had been before the
king gave the county of Cornwall to Earl Richard his brother.[2]
Six of these manors, to a net yearly value of about £165, were in
1296-1297 or earlier demesne manors of the Earldom of Cornwall.
One small one was retained by Waleran or his kinsfolk, and one
has not been traced.[3] As none of the six demesne manors is in the
1228-1229 list for the scutage of Kerry,[4] it might be argued that
Richard had remitted his claim to them, leaving Waleran in possession for life, but the fate of the manors concerned between August
1227 and the later years of the century is obscure.

The second point at which Wendover's story can be checked is
the date of the meeting at Northampton, which he assigns to

[1] Sacramento confederatum.

[2] *Pat. R.*, 133; a similar mandate is in *R.Lit.Cl.*, ii, 191, dated *c.* August 10th.

[3] The eight manors granted by John to Waleran Teutonicus were Alverton in Madron
parish, Tybista in Creed parish, Braynel, Helston-in-Trigg, and Penmayn, Tamerton, Moresk
in St. Clement, and Rillaton. These, except Alverton and Tamerton, were held in 1297
by Edmund of Cornwall in demesne (Midgley, xxiii ff., 227-34). Alverton was retained by
Waleran or his relatives 'of the new enfeoffment of (*per*) Earl Richard' for half a small fee
(*Book of Fees*, 394, 437). I know nothing of the Earl's holding in Tamerton.
  The date of the second writ giving possession to Waleran is 'Tuesday the vigil of St.
Laurence' (*R.Lit.Cl.*, ii, 191). The feast of St. Laurence (August 10th) was itself a Tuesday
in 1227, but the writ is presumably meant to be dated August 9th. This may suggest a last-
minute arrangement (as in 1238) between Richard of Cornwall and Henry III.

[4] *Book of Fees*, 394.

August 3rd. It can be shown that he wrote iii non. Aug. for iii id. Aug., and that he meant August 11th, in the following way. Henry granted safe-conducts to Chester, the Marshal, and Richard, Earl of Cornwall, only on August 4th at the New Temple.[1] The meeting was therefore arranged for some day shortly after this, not for August 3rd, as the earls having threatened rebellion would hardly come to court before they had received their safe-conducts. On August 6th Henry was at St. Alban's, so that is how Wendover comes to have the whole story in such detail — and on August 10th-13th he was at Northampton.

Thirdly, there had been trouble in February over recent perambulations of the forest, when the king reafforested certain districts. In 1225 the forests had been perambulated in accordance with the provisions of the charter of the forest, and certain districts had been disafforested.[2] When Henry 'came of age' (January 9th, 1227) he at once challenged the decisions of the perambulators county by county, beginning with Shropshire (January 10th). Before the rising of the earls certain counties had admitted their error and been pardoned. This gradual 'correction' of the bounds of the forest was one of the grievances of the earls, stated in an exaggerated form by Wendover. Added to this, certain clauses in Magna Carta were in dispute between the counties and their sheriffs. At the petition of the magnates at Winchester, therefore, the king had summoned representative knights and the sheriffs from eight counties to come to Lincoln in September 1226.[3] But this assembly never met. When the Great Council of Winchester had broken up the king cancelled the meeting.

In 1227 the earls reiterate their grievances, backed by the heir to the throne who has just had a violent quarrel with his brother, and by a threat of rebellion. Immediately after an armed 'parliament' with the king at Northampton, the cancelled summons of the previous year was reissued (August 13th) to thirty-five counties for an assembly at Westminster on October 20th.[4] This extraordinary assembly[5] appears not as an attempt by Hubert de Burgh to broaden

---

[1] *Pat. R.*, 137, 160, 161.   [2] G. J. Turner, *Select Pleas of the Forest* (Selden Soc.), xcvii-ci.
[3] *R.Lit.Cl.*, ii, 153 — Stubbs *Select Charters* (9th ed.), p. 353.
[4] The constitutional significance of this first known general summons of popularly elected representative knights was pointed out by Professor A. B. White in *American Historical Review*, xix, 735-50.
[5] It was to consist of 140 knights, 35 sheriffs, plus all the foresters of fee, the perambulators of the forest, and all who claimed liberties in the forest from 17 of the 35 counties. The writs are in *R.Lit.Cl.*, ii, 212-13.

the basis of consent, but as an expedient adopted under baronial pressure. The king preferred to bargain with individuals. As soon as Richard of Cornwall had been pacified and the barons had gone home, the king resumed his policy of reclaiming the forests, and his action remained a grievance throughout the century. It is not known if the assembly of knights and sheriffs ever met.

Wendover does not, however, mention what may well have been another cause of dispute between Richard and Hubert de Burgh, namely, that the former had to surrender the honour of Berkhampstead to Hubert's nephew Raymond de Burgh on July 12th, 1227, and did not regain it until the marriage settlement of 1231.[1] How far the seven other earls were satisfied is not known. If we judged from Richard's later behaviour it might seem possible that he made his own bargain and left the others to make theirs. He may still have felt discontented, for he was in spite of lavish grants 'during pleasure' still unprovided for. By a decision of the council in 1218 Henry had been unable to make grants in perpetuity during his minority. When the young king emancipated himself in January 1227 his brother had an obvious claim upon his bounty. Yet Richard had to wait another four years until finally on the occasion of his marriage in 1231 he received a proper settlement — the Earldom of Cornwall and the honours of Wallingford and Eye in fee. It is not known if he ever received a formal charter for Poitou, or whether, in spite of his earldom, he had Cornwall in fee before 1231. He did not receive Isabella's dower in fee until her death in 1246. That Richard was in an unusual position seems to have been appreciated in official circles, as the safe-conducts of August 4th, 1227, speak of the Earl of Chester and his men (*suos*) coming with him, and the same formula is used to the Marshal, but Earl Richard, who appears to hold nothing in fee simple, is given protection for himself and those (*eos*) coming with him.[2] The reason is likely to be that Richard, though an earl, is not yet of age and so has received no homages.

The earls in this crisis were certainly, as Wendover reports, attacking the justiciar and the whole régime, but they seem to have had no constructive programme, and on Chester's death no obvious leader except the Marshal. Richard of Cornwall was still too young to take an independent line at court with any success and as his material

[1] *Pat. R.*, 134.
[2] 'Consimiles literas habet . . . R. comes Cornubie . . . excepto eo quod loco "suos" ponitur "eos".'

wealth had just been substantially increased he had no adequate
reason for continued opposition. For the next two years he received
not infrequent marks of favour, but his doings or whereabouts
cannot again be traced until the Breton campaign of 1230.[1]

Wendover's account of the territorial settlement of August 1227
calls for some comment. The grants to Richard, he says, comprised
his mother's dower-lands in England, the lands of the Duke of
Brittany in England and the honour of Boulogne.[2] But Berkhampstead (which was part of the dower) was immediately taken away,[3]
and he did not yet receive Wallingford or Eye. The lands of the
Duke of Brittany have no reference to the honour of Richmond,[4]
but mean the honour of St. Valery, which had been held by the
Count of Dreux, of Brittany.[5] There were here some five demesne
manors with Beckley (the *caput*) and Yarnton in Oxfordshire as the
most important. St. Valery had after 1231 the same steward as the
honour of Wallingford, but the distinction was long maintained in
the Account-Rolls. The honour of Boulogne which Wendover mentions as part of the grant, was treated as an escheat during the years
1227-1230, but it is not known if Richard held any portion of it
during this time.[6]

The blurred and shifting picture of Richard's possessions before
1231 makes it difficult to be precise about his gains in 1227. They
were chiefly financial, being worth about another £1,000 a year, and
in no way strategic. Hubert de Burgh was exercising his usual
caution over the custody of strategic castles. He had need to do so,
for immediately after the earls had secured Richard's settlement for
him a rising tide of discontent had swept the barons away to Chepstow 'for a tournament' which was prohibited on the ground that,
although not within the shire, Chepstow was nevertheless within
the realm.[7] So Richard was given little in demesne and no castles in
1227. What he really needed was somewhere of his own to live in
when not at court or down at Launceston. This settlement gave him
Isleworth, just outside London, and Beckley which, as he had not

[1] Richard may have been in the Kerry campaign of 1228 (*Cal. Lib. R.*, 144, 158).
[2] Wend., *loc. cit.*, and *Ann. Dunst.*, 104.
[3] *Pat. R.*, 145 (September 29th, 1227).
[4] *D.N.B.* is here in error. Cf. *Cl. R.*, 85, which shows that Richmond was in the king's hand in 1228.
[5] *Pat. R.*, 191 (June 17th, 1228); *R.Lit.Cl.*, ii, 198 (August 21st, 1228).
[6] See the detailed lists of fees of the honour in *Book of Fees*, 484-5, 489-90, 1428-36. Richard later held Glatton and Kirton of this honour.
[7] *Pat. R.*, 142-3 (September 8th-14th, 1227).

yet acquired Wallingford or Berkhampstead, were very desirable. For the most part his mother's dower meant to him an agglomeration of rents and farms of towns on ancient demesne.[1]

Richard's next important acquisition was on November 1st, 1229, when he received the honour of Wallingford 'during pleasure'.[2] He may have received Berkhampstead back again at this time, as he was granted the amercements of the tenants of the honour.[3] Other and smaller gifts were made to him at this time,[4] and indeed on an increasing scale in every year of his life in which he was not out of favour with the government. In 1230 when his support was really wanted for the Breton expedition that his brother had so much at heart, he was given seisin of the honour of Eye 'during pleasure',[5] a present of 1,000 marks,[6] and a lucrative wardship.[7] It might seem than an effort was being made — it was unsuccessful — to detach the young earl from the baronial party. This, however, is probably only half the truth. The grant of Eye and the 1,000 marks can just as naturally be regarded as presents on his coming of age (January 5th, 1230) and he might henceforward expect a reasonable share of whatever wardships were in the market. But he never held many wardships: we shall only hear of five in the next forty years. This was not due to any distaste for them. He wanted the Umfraville wardship in 1245 and was much annoyed because it was given to Simon de Montfort. Richard may have had a legitimate ground for complaint in that he managed to obtain so few custodies.

---

[1] *Ibid.*, 140-1, Order of September 4th, 1227, to the tenants to be intendent, with leave to tallage. It was not all acquired at once. Apart from Berkhampstead, the grant of Exeter and the Devon manors was made only on December 13th, 1228 (*Cl. R.*, 24). See further the Appendix.

[2] *Cl. R.*, 258, cf. *Pat. R.*, 313, 434. It was granted without the prebends of the chapel.

[3] *Cl. R.*, 181. The grant included amercements of the dower in Devon and of the last eyre in Hertfordshire. He was also given 400 marks (*Cal. Lib. R.*, 121, 141, 150).

[4] e.g. in 1228 he received 100 marks and the wardship of John de Montague's lands (*Cal. Lib. R.*, 121; *Cl. R.*, 56).

[5] *Cl. R.*, 287 (January 28th, 1230).

[6] *Cal. Lib. R.*, 172.

[7] Grant of the wardship of the lands and heirs of Theobald Walter in six counties and Ireland, July 26th, 1230 (*Pat. R.*, 388, 427, 428; cf. *Cl. R.*, 370, 422, 541-2). By October 1231 Richard had still not assigned dower to the widow (*Cl. R.*, 572). In 1232 he sold his rights to Richard de Burgh (*Cal. Ch. R.*, i, 166).

CHAPTER TWO

BRETON EXPEDITION
(1230)

FIRST MARRIAGE, WITH ISABELLA
MARSHAL (1231)

RICHARD IN OPPOSITION

THE second foreign expedition of the reign, which Richard was thus induced to join, had in February 1229 been foreshadowed in a foolish and mysterious letter inviting the earls, barons, and knights to set out with the king at an unspecified date for an unknown destination.[1] In July, when the truce with France expired, the usual measures were taken to requisition a fleet and to control the movements of all incoming or outgoing foreign merchants.[2] On July 27th a general summons was issued for October 15th at Portsmouth.[3] But in October ships were lacking, for which Hubert de Burgh has won a reputation as a bad quartermaster. It was hardly the work of a justiciar to solve problems in logistics: the chamberlains should have seen to it, or possibly the stewards. However, when Henry realized that the expedition would have to be postponed the violent Angevin temper blazed out and he was only prevented from trying to kill the 'old traitor' on the spot by Ranulf de Blundeville. It was very late in the year to start a campaign and Hubert may possibly have delayed purposely, thinking that if Henry must have one, it had better be as brief as possible. So they tried again in the spring, and this time there were far too many ships. Henry was determined to do things on a grand scale: he had a new regalian suit for the occasion sent to Portsmouth, 'of white diaper or white cloth of silk, a crown, sceptre, and staff of silver-gilt, with sandals and gloves'.[4] They sailed at the end of April 1230 with four hundred and fifty men of knightly rank.[5]

The professed object of this expedition, and its only achievement,

---

[1] *Cl. R.*, 232. At the same time the Cinque Ports were warned, as they had to collect much of the fleet (cf. 245).

[2] *Ibid.*, 245, 247.   [3] *Ibid.*, 248.   [4] *Ibid.*, 323.   [5] *Pat. R.*, 357-62.

was to restore Peter Mauclerc to the Duchy of Brittany. But this was merely a pretext for an attempt to recover the Angevin inheritance. The time was thought to be opportune because Blanche of Castile, ruling France in the name of her young son Louis IX, had forced Raymond VII of Toulouse, who had been confirmed in his hopes of English support in March 1229,[1] to come to terms in the treaty of Meaux in the same year. The northern and western barons of France, fearing a similar fate, had invited Henry's aid.

In comparison with Richard of Cornwall's campaigns of 1225-1227, the much more imposing effort of 1230 achieved less from the military point of view, but its political repercussions were far more important. The Earl of Chester now played the part allotted to Salisbury in 1225: he did the fighting, both while Henry was in France and after he had left. Henry merely marched from St. Malo to Nantes, spent the whole of June there in feasting and entertainments because Hubert de Burgh would neither let him attack the French nor send for a papal legate to advise him, and then marched down through Poitou to Bordeaux. After this demonstration they marched back again.[2] Richard of Cornwall's little force of seventy knights had, in 1225, at least reconquered Gascony, and made some hostile motion towards Poitou. The royal force, six times the size, and with active support from the north-west of France, did nothing at all. If any hopes had been cherished that Henry III would prove the warrior that he always imagined himself to be, they must have been shattered in the lamentable gaiety of his progress through France.

The importance of this pathetic failure was that it led directly to the downfall of Hubert de Burgh, for he quarrelled again with the king. It was also the first time that Richard of Cornwall had had to work side by side with his brother. If he had not already formed his opinion he can hardly have failed in 1230 to realize Henry's incompetence in military matters, and his constant need for someone on whom he could lean. As soon as Richard had landed in France (May 2nd) he wrote home to Walter, Bishop of Carlisle, the Treasurer, in a dull but business-like letter, that all was well with him. It is a letter very different in tone and composition from the epistles sent from Gascony in 1225 or Palestine in 1242, which were

---

[1] *Cl. R.*, 233.

[2] This was only made possible by the dispersal of the French army at the end of its forty days' service. Apart from the siege and capture of Mirambeau on the way to Bordeaux and a repulse from Saintes the royal army, it seems, saw no fighting.

meant for public consumption.[1] We know that John Morin and Roger d'Acastre, his old tutor, were with Richard,[2] but he is not otherwise mentioned until September, when he was one of the plenipotentiaries to treat for peace with France and a little later for a further alliance with Brittany.[3] The free living at Nantes had exposed the army to an unspecified disease, which also attacked Richard and Henry while they were at Redon (dép. 1. et V.), and was put forward as an excuse for coming home in October.[4] So Richard did not distinguish himself by any feat of arms. He probably abetted Hubert de Burgh in his policy of avoiding battle.

The importance of this year to Richard lay in the death of Gilbert de Clare, Earl of Gloucester, in October. The widowed countess Isabella was daughter of William Marshal I, Earl of Pembroke, and her mother was daughter and heiress of Richard de Clare, also Earl of Pembroke. Five months after Gloucester's death Richard of Cornwall had snapped up the widow to whom he was married on March 30th, 1231, at Fawley near Marlow in Buckinghamshire, by the Abbot of Tewkesbury, much to the annoyance of Henry III.[5]

Isabella Marshal, like all Richard's wives, was a woman of wonderful beauty,[6] but she was older than Richard, for she had already been married to Gilbert de Clare for fourteen years and had borne him six flourishing children. Her marriage with Richard of Cornwall produced another four, of whom the ill-fated Henry, who was murdered at Viterbo, alone survived childhood. Of the others, John the firstborn lived and died in 1232, and the second, Isabella, barely living out the year died in the autumn of 1234.[7] These unhappy events created a problem for Richard, who after four years of marriage had a wife who was no longer young and was still without an heir. On the pretext that Isabella's former husband was connected with him in the

---

[1] *R. L.*, i, 362.

[2] *Pat. R.*, 362.

[3] *Pat. R.*, 395, 399, with Hubert de Burgh, the Marshal, John de Lacy, and Ralph Fitz-Nicholas.

[4] *Ibid.*, 450 (September 30th) 'Que nuper eum cepit et nondum convaluit'.

[5] Oseney-Wykes, 72; *Ann. Theok.*, 78. Marlow belonged to the honour of Wallingford. Fawley was on the Marshal's fee (honour of Giffard), the tenant in 1234 being Bartholomew de Sackville (*Book of Fees*, 880, 1450). Their first son died at Marlow in September 1232 (*Theok.*, 89).

[6] Wykes, 72.

[7] Richard of Cornwall had four children by his first wife: (1) John, *b.* January 31st, 1232, *d.* September 22nd, 1232 at Great Marlow, buried at Reading Abbey (*Theok.*, 81, 89; *Dunst.*, 130); (2) Henry, *b.* November 2nd, 1235, murdered at Viterbo, 1271; (3) Isabella, *b.* about September 9th, 1233 (*Theok.*, 92), *d.* October 6th, 1234, buried by the side of her brother at Reading (*Theok.*, 93); (4) Nicholas, *b.* and *d.*, January 1240 at Berkhampstead.

fourth degree, Richard consulted the pope on the advisability of a divorce. He probably wrote early in 1235, as Gregory IX's reply is dated June 15th.[1] The pope enjoined him to lay aside all doubt and remain in lawful matrimony with his wife, but the problem solved itself when Henry was born on November 2nd, 1235. When Isabella died in childbed at Berkhampstead on January 17th, 1240, her body was buried at Beaulieu and her heart interred in a silver-gilt urn in front of the high altar at Tewkesbury. The Tewkesbury annalist, perhaps out of domestic piety, asserts that she had wished to be buried beside her first husband at Tewkesbury, but that Richard of Cornwall would not allow it.[2]

There is no indication that the marriage was secret, and the reconciliation was swift, so Henry's anger may have arisen from his not being consulted. Perhaps he, or Hubert de Burgh, had been planning a marriage for Richard with someone more closely connected with the court — the *nearer* alliance mentioned in 1226 inevitably comes to mind. The marriage with Isabella Marshal meant that Richard was likely to be drawn into the circle of his brothers-in-law (the Marshal, Norfolk, and Derby) and his stepson (Gloucester). He was already bound to William Marshal II as a sworn ally — a pact, which, if Wendover is right, had been made before the rising of the eight earls in 1227. But he had not been married to his friend's sister for more than a week before the Marshal died (April 7th, 1231), as a result of an illness contracted at the wedding.[3] His death produced a crop of problems, because his younger brother and heir was, as his father the Regent had been, a man of double allegiance. The old Marshal, starting as an almost landless knight-errant, had handed on to his son Richard a full share of his ruthless, sometimes even unscrupulous energy. On William Marshal II's death Hubert de Burgh, ever watchful for the fate of castles, at once had the English and Welsh castles handed over to professional administrators — knights attached to the royal household by Exchequer retaining-fees. Richard of Cornwall received, about April 11th, the custody of the Braose lands in England and the estates of the late Theobald Butler in Ireland, both of which had been held by William Marshal II. He at once obtained authority to take an aid from them.[4] This perhaps

[1] *Reg. de Grég. IX*, ii, nos. 2631, 2632 — Bliss, *Cal. Pap. Lett.*, 147.
[2] *Theok.*, 113-14, with details of her legacies to the Abbey, Richard's arrangements for the celebration of her obit, and the steps taken by Isabella to commemorate her first husband.
[3] *Ann. Theok.*, 78.
[4] *Supra*, p. 15, n. 7.

marked the reconciliation of the royal brothers, for Richard never quarrelled with Henry without coming away a richer man. He was also commissioned to guard the Welsh marches as best he could, and Henry wrote to each of the marcher lords enjoining them to assist Richard and protesting that he himself was coming as fast as he could.[1]

These measures, directed against Llewelyn, were only partially successful. The chancery enrolments are silent about Wendover's story that Richard Marshal went to Ireland and threatened war against the king. They reveal, however, that the ports were closed against the Marshal or anyone else of the power or counsel of the King of France.[2] Nineteen ports were told to arrest him if he tried to land. An attempt to treat the Marshal's Irish castles in similar fashion to those in England was not successful. Waleran Teutonicus was put in nominal charge of the nine castles in Ireland,[3] but the Marshal's Irish constables continued to hold out.[4] It seems likely that by the middle of May Richard of Cornwall was implicated, or at any rate that his loyalty was in doubt. His sworn alliance with the dead Marshal, whose sister he had married, and his friendship with Richard Marshal must have suggested the possibility. He is not known to have taken any action himself, but on May 12th-15th he was ordered, no doubt as a precaution, to give up the honour and castle of Wallingford and the manor of Watlington to a steward of the household, and on May 20th Hubert de Burgh at Hereford took back the Braose lands for himself.[5] Thus Richard did not have to guard the marches for more than three weeks, which was probably just as well, as Llewelyn had taken advantage of the Marshal's death to ravage the borders in a particularly savage manner, and a feeble campaign was begun against him during the summer. Hubert de Burgh seems to have remained almost inactive in the south, while the king went to Maud's castle near Radnor and spent two months rebuilding it. It was there in August that he admitted the new Earl of Pembroke to his estates, gave Simon de Montfort the honour of Leicester,[6] and made a handsome territorial settlement upon Richard of Cornwall.[7] In the middle of what should have been a hard-fought

---

[1] *Cl. R.*, 585. This letter is dated October 27th on the roll, but is placed between one of April 20th and another of May 3rd. It must surely be an error for April 27th, just after Richard had been given the Braose lands and when the king really was, as he says in the letter, coming as fast as he could (*cum quanta potest festinatione est in veniendo versus partes illas*).

[2] *Ibid.*, 582.   [3] *Pat. R.*, 430.   [4] *Cl. R.*, 496.   [5] *Pat. R.*, 434; *Cl. R.*, 510.

[6] *Cl. R.*, 541, 543.   [7] *Cal. Ch. R.*, i, 129, 139.

campaign, or at least a brisk punitive expedition, Henry characteristically found time to settle the fate of three earldoms. It is conceivable that he was taking advantage of the justiciar's absence, and
that these three creations mark a step in his emancipation from
Hubert de Burgh.

The treatment of the new earls was not ungenerous. Pembroke
had been a liege man of the King of France for the last eleven years,
taking a considerable part in public life and marrying a Breton
heiress. In a manifesto to Ireland in May 1231 Henry had professed
that he still did not know whether the Marshal wished to renounce
that allegiance. He also complained that the Marshal had not come
to do homage as he should have done.[1] Their subsequent relations, as
will appear, were embittered by this unpromising start, but he got his
earldom, and Richard of Cornwall who had also given the government some excuse for delaying grants in fee, received his settlement.

The charters that Richard of Cornwall had from the king this
year were four in number. The first, dated February 4th, 1231,
before his marriage, confirmed him in possession of his mother's
extensive dower-lands which he 'previously held of the king's bail,
to hold until the king restore them to his mother', or until they
made peace, in which case Richard was to be compensated.[2] He
also received the little honour of St. Valery, south of Thames in
Berkshire, that is, the lands of Count Robert of Dreux, and the
lands of the Duke of Louvain, being a regrant of the honour of Eye
in Suffolk. After his marriage Richard obtained, on August 10th,
his other and more vital charters which granted him (i) the honour
of Wallingford and the manor of Watlington the only demesne
manor of the honour, for three fees;[3] (ii) a confirmation of the
charter of February 4th; (iii) the county of Cornwall and the stannaries, for five fees.

Thus for the first time in his life, at the age of twenty-two,
Richard, Earl of Cornwall and titular Count of Poitou, found himself in possession of wide estates held in fee. From time to time
they were added to, e.g. by estates in Devon and by the honour of
Knaresborough, but henceforth his territorial wealth was securely
based on Cornwall, Wallingford (with which St. Valery was soon

---

[1] *Pat. R.*, 435. This is a weak point in Henry's argument. For he had closed the ports
against the Marshal in April and did not give him a safe-conduct until June (*ibid.*, 438).

[2] He only received the dower in fee simple on his mother's death in 1246. See Appendix.

[3] This charter had to be exemplified in 13 Ed. I because the manner in which the seal was
attached rendered it suspect (Exch. T. R. Misc. Bk., no. 57, fol. 54).

merged), and Eye, together with the scattered lands of Isabella of Augoulême's dower. Of these the most important was the honour of Berkhampstead which vied with Wallingford as his chief residence, and where he now appears as a patron of the Jews.[1]

There is a temptation in writing of the reign of Henry III to label people as royalist or baronial partisans, which simplifies the story but does violence to the truth. Richard of Cornwall's marriage had undoubtedly linked him with the most important baronial families, and so for the next seven years we find him more in the baronial than the royal camp. In the most important crisis since 1215, the rebellion of Richard Marshal, the Earl of Cornwall's behaviour has been stigmatized as displaying 'great weakness'. This is a harsh judgment, for Richard until the birth of Edward in 1239 was heir-presumptive to the throne, and cannot fairly be called weak because he hesitated to rebel against his elder brother. As in 1227 the rebels put forward no constructive programme, and the Marshal rebelled very hastily over a quarrel that was only in part his own. Only the fact that he supported the cause of some friends who had been dismissed without trial gave to his action any semblance of justice. Consequently there is no indication that the Earl of Cornwall intended to support the Marshal after the latter had become openly rebellious. But the events of this rebellion and of the next few years revealed to him fully the political wrong-headedness of his brother, and he evinced a growing impatience with Henry's government culminating in his own abortive rebellion of 1238, after which Richard was never again wholeheartedly on the baronial side. A notable point of all these fraternal disputes is the suddenness of the subsequent reconciliation, made easier no doubt by Richard's far more even temper, and because their clashes usually disclosed a substantial identity of interest. The quarrel of 1238 differed from all their other disputes in that Richard was for a moment prepared to impose a permanent check upon the king. In the earlier disturbances of 1227 and 1233 the leaders had been Chester or one of the Marshals. They were valiant soldiers, Richard was not, and should have known by then that he never would be. By 1238 Chester was dead, and the baronial demonstration of that year depended upon Richard of Cornwall for leadership. He was still young and handsome and great hopes were entertained of him.

[1] It is in this year that Richard is first heard of in connection with the Jews, when (in January) Abraham of Berkhampstead was shown favour at his instance (*Cl. R.*, 468).

In the summer of 1232 Hubert de Burgh's long rule came to an end. The complete failure of the expeditions to France and Wales, his quarrel with king and church owing to his supposed complicity in the anti-papal riots led by Robert Thwenge, were the most obvious reasons for his downfall. Henry had personal reasons for dismissing a minister who had deliberately thwarted him in his attempts to fight the French, and he had prepared a weapon against Hubert by adopting, while in France in 1230, the use of a Privy Seal. Henry struck at the justiciar in a despicable manner, by lulling the old man into a false sense of security. He loaded Hubert de Burgh with grants for life, fortified by a most solemn oath sworn by Henry at Bromholm priory, the then fashionable resort for pilgrims.[1] Six weeks later Hubert was cast aside, and replaced as justiciar by Stephen Segrave, 'a pliant man', while real power went to Peter des Riveaux and his kinsman Peter des Roches. To enable him to effect the desired reforms des Riveaux received an unparalleled collection of powers, giving him for a time complete responsibility for the household, the exchequer, and the local administration. Valuable work was done in reorganizing exchequer accounts and reducing the power of the sheriffs by making the office less lucrative.

But though Henry, by a palace-revolution, could give his faithful bureaucrats supreme authority, he could not finance their administration without calling upon the great council of barons. This meant concessions, for as soon as Hubert had been struck down the barons who had so long eagerly awaited his fall saw danger from another quarter and began to close their ranks. In the period 1227 to 1238 the manifold causes of baronial discontent found a focus in the Marshal family. After the death in 1219 of William Marshal the regent each of his five sons successively became Earl of Pembroke.[2] In 1227 William Marshal II, the eldest son, friend and sworn ally of Richard of Cornwall, had been the leader. The friendship sealed again shortly before William's death by Richard's marriage to Isabella Marshal, was maintained with William's brother Richard in 1232–1233, and renewed with Gilbert Marshal in the briefer but equally rebellious 'demonstration' of 1238. Not until the third of these occasions did Richard of Cornwall himself come forward as the leader of the baronage. On each occasion he withdrew his support,

[1] For Henry's action see F. M. Powicke, 'The Oath of Bromholm' in *E.H.R.*, vol. lvi.
[2] Since all the five sons died without issue, the estates descended through representatives of the five daughters.

twice at the last minute, but contrived in spite of this to maintain friendly relations with those he had deserted.

William Marshal II's support of Richard of Cornwall in 1227 had been by no means disinterested. The Marshal at that time was not *persona grata* with the king. In July 1226 Henry had written to him an odd letter suggestive of considerable friction. His heirs were asked to surrender Cardigan and Carmarthen castles if he went to Ireland: in mid-August he gave up Usk castle and received it back for four years.[1] This matter of Usk was again a point at issue in 1233. In the autumn of 1232 four earls — Richard of Cornwall, the Marshal, Warenne, and Lincoln — intervened to save Hubert de Burgh from the full weight of the king's ingratitude, by having him committed to their care in the castle of Devizes, each of the four providing one gaoler.[2] The Earl of Chester had already prevented the king from sending the London mob to drag Hubert out of sanctuary and would certainly have taken part in this arrangement had he not died in October at Richard's castle of Wallingford.[3] Throughout the winter the Earls of Cornwall and Pembroke were together in Wales. They defeated Llewelyn, who had broken the truce and threatened the Braose lands. Richard of Cornwall then fortified Radnor castle, leaving a strong garrison there in March 1233.[4] This is the last occasion that the two Richards are known to have been together before the Marshal's quarrel with the king.

Wendover traces the trouble to the Christmas court at Worcester in 1232, when one of the Marshal's deputies, Sir William de Rodune, was dismissed, and goes on to describe 'how the Marshal remonstrated with the king', alluding to some dispute in council between Richard Marshal as the spokesman of the baronage and Peter des Roches.[5] The barons then threatened to withdraw from the king's council, and made some kind of confederacy, refusing to attend a council at Oxford at midsummer. The records show that this confederacy was due to Henry's arbitrary action in disseising Gilbert Basset of the manor of Upavon in Wiltshire. The land was *Terra Normannorum*, but we do not know upon what terms Gilbert held it. He was allowed to take away his chattels, but he seems to have

---

[1] *Pat. R.*, ii, 81.

[2] The Earl of Cornwall sent Richard de Punchardun, one of his household knights, as his representative (*Cal. Lib. R.*, 190). For the arrangement see *R. L.*, i, 410; *C.P.R.*, 28-30.

[3] *Theok.*, 87.

[4] *Ibid.*, 88, 'About the feast of S. Gregory (March 12th) in Lent'.

[5] In *Mat. Par.*, iii, 240. The Close and Patent Rolls show the Bishop of Winchester at court and very active during the first few months of the year.

been surprised, as only the year before he was building a grange there. In February the king gave Upavon to one of his Poitevins, Peter de Mauley, who had held it a few years before.[1] Henry did this, as he afterwards confessed, *per voluntatem nostram*, and when peace was made had to hand it back *per consideracionem curie*.[2] Something similar, according to Wendover, happened in the case of Richard Siward, but Upavon was apparently made the test case, under cover of which the Marshal was prepared to raise rebellion. The Marshal was still high in favour in the middle of January, the first indication that he has quarrelled with the king being in June, when there is some evidence that they were disputing over the dower of Henry's sister Eleanor, widow of William Marshal II, soon to become the wife of Simon de Montfort, carrying with her the perennial problem of her dower.[3] In the middle of June, when the king was again at Worcester, and Richard of Cornwall with him, he reverted to John's detested habit of taking hostages for good behaviour from the barons.[4] Henry then returned for the Oxford council, from which 'the barons' abstained, even threatening to elect a new king unless the aliens were dismissed — a course said to have been urged upon Henry by a Dominican friar, Robert Bacon, in a sermon before the court.

By this time the state of the country was so unsettled that the council at Oxford made a provision to stop armed men from roaming about the country,[5] and a little later to prohibit all tournaments for a time.[6] If Wendover is right, it would be at this point, some time in July, that Gilbert Basset of High Wycombe and Richard Siward, who were perhaps already in alliance with the Marshal, were deprived by the king of certain manors. These men, with Philip Basset, Warin Basset, and Walter Clifford, were the heart and soul of whatever conspiracy there was. A further council called to Westminster for July 11th (mentioned only by Wendover) was similarly boycotted but a third at London on August 1st was better attended. Richard of Cornwall was present and Lincoln, Ferrers, and the Earl of Chester.[7] Wendover tells that Peter des Roches boasted of his experiences in the East and advised war, but that owing to the absence of the Marshal, Gilbert Basset, and others,

---

[1] *Cl. R.*, 17, 187, 194; *Book of Fees*, i, 381; *Flores*, ii, 208 has 'Netheravon' in error.
[2] *Cl. R.*, 437 (May 30th, 1234).   [3] *Ibid.*, 233, 310.
[4] But it was from the marchers only, not, as Wendover says, from all the barons (*ibid.*, 312).
[5] *Ibid.*, 317, 318; *R. L.*, 418.   [6] *C.P.R.*, 21.   [7] In *Mat. Par.*, iii, 247.

nothing was done. Nevertheless, the council decided on an expedition to Ireland and decided to summon foreign aid. A fleet was to be collected and on August 7th a general muster was ordered for Gloucester on August 29th.[1] The foreign mercenaries, under Baldwin de Guisnes, actually landed at Dover on August 16th.[2] The project of going to Ireland with an army was not abandoned until August 28th. While this was happening Henry thought to ensure the safety of the marches by granting the castles of Grosmont, Skenefrith, and Lentiliol to Peter des Riveaux.[3]

The Marshal on his way from Wales to attend this council came to Woodstock (according to one story) where he lodged with his sister, the Countess of Cornwall, and was warned by her of a royal plot to seize and imprison him like Hubert de Burgh. 'When night came he took the road, and did not draw rein until he arrived in Wales.'[4] This is graphic but not quite true. It would seem that the Marshal must have come to court, for on August 3rd-4th he and his nephew, the Earl of Norfolk, but no one else, received safe-conducts for going home.[5] Normally this would be quite unnecessary: it implies a breach with the king, either verbally or by letter. Next day the *jurati ad arma* or militia of five counties were called out. The counties selected and the places chosen for assembly suggest an intention of surrounding the confederates,[6] because the Marshal had not fled straight into Wales. He had drawn rein in the Basset country at High Wycombe and there collected his friends, so that it was afterwards accounted a crime to have ridden armed with the Marshal at Wycombe.[7] We do not know whether this prompt action of the government rendered the demonstration ineffective, for the militia were sent home almost as soon as they were called out,[8] or whether, as Wendover has it, the Marshal being forewarned had made good his escape before the net could close around him.

Speaking of these first weeks of August, and the part played by

---

[1] *Cl. R.*, 315-22 (detailed preparations for the fleet).

[2] Wend. in *Mat. Par.*, iii, 248. Wendover states that not only the royal household but the whole country was flooded with mercenaries, to the number of 2,000. On the basis of other such reinforcements in Henry III's reign we may safely assume a maximum of two or three hundred mounted warriors.

[3] *Cal. Ch. R.*, i, 185.

[4] Wend. in *Mat. Par.*, iii, 248.

[5] *C.P.R.*, 22.

[6] The counties concerned were Gloucester, Bucks., Worcs., Essex and Herts., and Oxon., to assemble at Camden, Aylesbury, Evesham, St. Albans, and Thame.

[7] *Cl. R.*, 253, 257, 258.

[8] *Ibid.*, 318 (August 6th).

Richard of Cornwall, Wendover relates that he at first adhered to the Marshal, but had long before returned to the king's side.[1] His position was bound to be difficult, from his friendship and kinship with the Marshal, and because Warin and Gilbert Basset were both his tenants.

The reward, or possibly the price of his loyalty, was the grant to him in demesne of Warin Basset's lands in Cornwall and the wardship of the rich estates of the young Baldwin de Lisle in Devon, Hampshire, and the Isle of Wight.[2] Gilbert Basset's holdings of the honour of Wallingford were committed to him during pleasure.[3] The other great men whose loyalty might be in doubt were similarly treated. The Count of Aumale had prudently been given the manor of Dartford in Kent;[4] Ferrers and Lacy were opportunely made Earls of Lancaster and Lincoln. These grants go some way towards justifying Wendover's assertion that the magnates were bribed.

After the fiasco at High Wycombe those barons who were suspected or convicted of supporting the Marshal were required to swear fealty and give hostages, the terms being embodied in charters. An exasperating entry on the Close Roll notes that the Marshal, too, gave a charter, but 'it was not like the other charters'.[5] Others surrendered their homage and withdrew from the king's allegiance.[6] The king then sent the Bishop of St. David's to defy the Marshal, who had retired to his own estates. Henry followed in person, travelling by easy stages, and still intent, apparently, on his Irish expedition. Continued resistance made this impossible: it was cancelled at the last minute, and by the beginning of September Henry was making himself ridiculous at the siege of the Marshal's castle of Usk.

But after keeping up a fierce assault on it for several days, the provisions of the besieging army began to fail, and the king, seeing he would be obliged to raise the siege, was ashamed of ever having come there; he therefore sent some of the bishops to the earl marshal and asked him, in his respect for the royal

---

[1] Wend. in *Mat. Par.*, iii, 248. 'Nam Ricardus frater domini regis diu ante ad regem reversus est, qui Marescallo prius adherebat.'

[2] *Cl. R.*, 252.

[3] *Ibid.*, 281 (October 18th, for Wilton in Wiltshire).

[4] *Cal. Ch. R.*, i, 186.

[5] *Cl. R.*, 321, 'Comes Ricardus Marescallus fecit cartam suam, set non qualem alii fecerunt'.

[6] *Ibid.*, 271, September 22nd, 'Ricardus Siward qui fuit ligius homo regis homagium suum reddidit et a fide regis penitus recessit'. He is therefore a manifest enemy and to be taken at sight. Cf. p. 324. Warin Basset did the same at Hereford, August 24th, 1233 (*ibid.*, 252).

person, *and that the siege might not seem to have been ineffectual*, to
surrender the castle, on condition that the king would restore
it to him within fifteen days uninjured [and that in the mean-
time he would] make all proper reformation in the kingdom.[1]

A truce was made early in September,[2] but it was allowed to expire
and Henry showed no signs of giving up the castle. The Marshal
was still in favour about the middle of October,[3] but by the 18th
the breach had become final, for on that day is recorded a grant of
half a dozen of his manors to Richard of Cornwall.[4] A few days
later Hubert de Burgh made his dramatic escape from Devizes and
was carried into Wales, where on October 30th 'about the first hour
of the day' he joined the king's enemies. The subsequent campaign
in Wales, where the king's forces, most incompetently led, were
routed by the Marshal now in alliance with Llewelyn, continued
throughout the winter, with the Marshal winning easily until he
allowed himself to be lured to Ireland. His tragic fate there need
not detain us.[5]

Just before the final rupture had taken place between Henry and
the Marshal that famous council at Westminster on October 9th was
the occasion for Peter des Roches to state that the peers in England
were not like the peers in France, and that the king could banish or
proscribe whomsoever he pleased after trial by his justiciaries. In the
end the king was forced to give way through the intervention of the
bishops, who played a decisive part in the later stages of the struggle.
The opposition of the Marshal and his followers appears to have been
based upon purely feudal principles, and it was in England itself
quite ineffectual to produce anything more than purely local disorder. But after a council of bishops had threatened to excommunicate him, Henry made one of his pilgrimages to Bromholm priory,
in the company of Peter des Roches, Stephen Segrave, and Peter des
Riveaux (February 16th). A few weeks later he dismissed them
from office, and all the rebels were pardoned, including Richard
Siward.

Richard of Cornwall, however, refused to be placated. Siward
was a presumptuous person who had married Gilbert Basset's sister,

---

[1] Wend., in *Mat. Par.*, iii, 249.   [2] *Cl. R.*, 258-9, 322.   [3] *Ibid.*, 262-3, 280.
[4] *Ibid.*, 281.
[5] Richard Marshal is eulogized by contemporary writers, the annalists of Tewkesbury and
Waverley and Wendover, as the *Estoire de Guillaume le Maréchal*. Like Simon de Montfort,
with whom there are a number of parallels, he was vociferously supported by the friars, had a
curiously popular appeal, and was highly esteemed by Grossetête.

Philippa, the dowager Countess of Warwick, without the king's consent. He held the manor of Headington by Oxford in her right, and had a dwelling there. He also held Stoke Basset of Richard of Cornwall, in the same right, and the manor of Beer in Dorset from the Marshal. He had been with William Marshal on the Breton expedition in 1230. Richard of Cornwall's withdrawal from the Marshal prompted Siward to destroy a favourite residence of the earl at Beckley, in Oxfordshire, the *caput* of his honour of St. Valery. Richard of Cornwall's pride was deeply wounded by this blow, and although Siward was reconciled to the king, becoming a royal official and a member of the council, Richard had him banished in 1236.[1] The earl's immediate reprisal was to obtain a grant of Siward's houses at Headington in order to carry them off to Beckley, to replace those that had been burnt.[2]

The Marshal received almost no English support, though he was in alliance with the Scots and Welsh. In England Norfolk was the only earl with him at High Wycombe, and he quickly made his peace with Henry by surrendering Framlingham Castle as a pledge of good behaviour.[3] This was fortunate, as the campaign in Wales illustrated the complete incapacity of Henry III as a soldier: his failure to take Usk and the success of the night attack at Grosmont were due to his inefficiency.

During this time Richard of Cornwall was in the background, absorbing one grant after another and quietly building up his resources. The first spectacular gift was at a decisive moment, in June 1233, when the Marshal seems to have quarrelled with the king. Richard at that time was given all the profits of a judicial eyre in Cornwall. This caused some comment, as it was the first eyre in Cornwall 'for thirty years or more' and at the coming of the justices all the inhabitants fled into the woods for fear of them.[4] Next year he was allowed to tallage his boroughs.[5]

During the brief period between the dismissal of the Poitevins in

---

[1] *D.N.B., s.v.* Richard of Cornwall refers to 'Richard Syward (*q.v.*)', but he is not in fact to be found in that work. See Dugdale, *Baronage*, 383; Farrer, *Fees*, ii, 17; *Mat. Par.*, iii, 363, 369 and index; Wykes-Oseney, 81; *Book of Fees*, i, 445, 449, 451, 851; *Close Rolls, passim.* As a turbulent marcher he appears in *The Normans in Glamorgan, Gower and Kidweli* by L. D. Nicholl (Cardiff, 1943), p. 86.

[2] *Cl. R.*, 363. A more puzzling gift was the manor of 'Hagenet' or Haughley, between Bury and Ipswich. It was the *caput* of the barony of Haughley, and had included a moated castle, but it was granted 'during pleasure' and without the fees appurtenant (*ibid.*, 385).

[3] *Ibid.*, 450.   [4] *Dunst.*, 135; *Theok.*, 90; *Cl. R.*, 227.

[5] *Cl. R.* 363, and in 1235 (*ibid.*, 215).

the summer of 1234 and the arrival of Henry III's Provençal kinsfolk
in 1236 Richard of Cornwall lived at peace with his brother. In
1234 he heads the list of seven earls and ten barons who are prohibited
from tourneying without the king's licence and are to prevent others
from so doing, at tournaments arranged for Northampton and Cambridge.[1] These events were often a focus for political intrigue, and
therefore discouraged. Sometimes the prohibitions, which were
very numerous in Henry III's reign, could be disregarded with im-
punity, but not on this occasion, for in 1235 certain people were
punished for flouting the order.[2] Richard was given a similar
responsibility, in 1245, with Simon de Montfort, who would be
more interested. The prohibition to Richard himself may be taken
as a matter of form, and no coolness between the brothers is indicated
by it. Richard was at court on September 26th, and there are a
number of grants to him in the course of the year.[3]

Peter des Roches and his son had not been gone many months
when negotiations were set on foot for the marriage of Henry's
sister with the Emperor Frederick II. Terms had already been discussed when in November 1234 Peter de Vinea was appointed as
imperial plenipotentiary to arrange the details. The contract of
marriage (February 22nd) and the safe-conduct for Isabella (May
3rd) were both attested by Richard of Cornwall, who with the king
saw the betrothed lady off to the coast on May 11th.[4] It was perhaps
for his good services during the negotiations that Richard was given
as a birthday present in 1235 the honour of Knaresborough, to be
held by the service of two knights' fees. This was worth a clear £300-
£400 a year to him.[5] He was also given the manor of Kirton-in-
Lindsey, for two fees,[6] and allowed to protect the Jews at Berkhampstead.[7] It is just possible that there is a connection between
this acquisition of his own Jews on February 7th and his sale of the
Braose wardship to Gilbert Marshal on February 10th for 3,000

[1] *C.P.R.*, 68.   [2] *Cl. R.*, 210, ct. 212.

[3] *C.P.R.*, 71. Richard was allowed to tallage his Ancient Demesne lands on January 7th
(*Cl. R.*, 363), to have the '$\frac{1}{40}$' of the Braose lands on February 6th (*Cl. R.*, 375), to have the
Braose castles back which Richard Marshal had seized (*C.P.R.*, 45), to have the honour of
Bergavenny restored to him (*C.P.R.*, 53), and the king was to make no peace with Peter des
Riveaux without saving to Richard the land which Peter held of Richard in Cornwall
(*C.P.R.*, 62).

[4] *Foed.*, i, 220, 223-4, 226; *Theok.*, 96.

[5] *Cal. Ch. R.*, i, 191; *C.P.R.*, 90, 94. It was at this time that Richard was seriously thinking
of a divorce, so he had the grant made out to him and the heirs of his *uxor desponsata*.

[6] *Cal. Ch. R.*, i, 193.

[7] *Cl. R.*, 46. In 1242 they moved with their chest to Wallingford, *ibid.*, 393.

marks.[1] For at this period of his career he was being loaded with grants and financial privileges of all kinds, and whatever the nature of his transactions with these Jews, Richard did not come to them as a borrower.

These facts go some way towards explaining why the Emperor Frederick was so anxious for Richard to be sent out to help him against the French. The invitation was received at, or about the time of, the council of Merton in 1236. Richard had had no opportunity of meeting the emperor: he had only twice left the country, each time going to the west of France. But the negotiations for this marriage must inevitably have brought Richard into contact with the imperial plenipotentiary, Peter de Vinea, who, we must assume, reported favourably to his master.[2] The intention, according to Matthew Paris,[3] was that Richard should attack the French, but if this was seriously meant, the plan was soon dropped, the emperor finding more than enough to do in Italy. In any case the barons were unwilling to let Richard go. Many excuses were proffered: he was heir-presumptive to the throne, and his presence in England was necessary because the truce with Wales was about to run out; Henry III was about to have a conference with the King of Scotland, and also proposed to go to Ireland, whither he had never been.[4] The most cogent reason is not alleged, namely that (as we may guess) high command under the emperor, though flattering, was likely to prove expensive. Henry III also sent a second letter, appointing William of Kilkenny, the later Bishop of Ely,[5] as his ambassador to Frederick, explaining that the barons were hostile to the proposal, and asking that as a necessary preliminary to a matter which he had at heart Richard might be granted an official safe-conduct by the emperor. The letter is undated and is ambiguous, but it looks as if at one point early in 1236 Richard had meant to go.

In this second letter, rather more private in tone than the first, there is mention of a meeting between the emperor and the King of France intended to be held at Vaucouleurs on the Meuse at

---

[1] *Supra*, p. 15, n. 7.
[2] For Peter de Vinea in England see E. Kantorowicz in *MIOG.*, li (1937-1938), pp. 43-88.
[3] From this point Paris becomes an original authority—for our purposes the best.
[4] The letter stating this is dated February 2nd, 1236, in *R. L.*, ii, 9. It is also in *Foed.*, i, 228-9, and in each case printed from the Close Roll.
[5] William of Kilkenny was later associated with Richard almost in the position of co-regent, while Henry was absent in Gascony in 1253-1254. Koch, p. 38, n. 2, and p. 39, n. 1, observes that this second letter must be after July 15th, 1235, as it refers to Isabella as Frederick's wife and places it after the invitation mentioned above. It is printed in *R. L.*, i, 474-5, where it is dated 'about June 1235'.

midsummer in 1237. Vaucouleurs was on the borders of France and Germany, and thither the King of France proceeded, to what Frederick II had intended to be an international peace conference, with a large army. Henry went so far as to appoint his ambassadors — the chronicler mentions the Archbishop of York as a third — and the Bishop of Winchester, Peter des Roches, had refused to go on the ground that the king had already denigrated him to the emperor. The embassy had even set off and was ready to sail when the emperor postponed the conference for a year, so they came home.[1] Though after a brilliant reception the emperor sent home all his wife's English followers, he continued to maintain the friendliest relations with her brothers.[2] But Richard did not intend to fight the emperor's battles for him, though he had every intention of going abroad.

In June 1236 he took the cross at Winchester and gave an earnest of his sincerity by cutting down his woods — we are not told where or to what extent — to pay for his expedition.[3]

Perhaps he felt freer to go as he now had in Henry a flourishing son and heir (born November 2nd, 1235),[4] a circumstance that made it easier for him to follow Gregory IX's advice and cast aside all doubts as to the validity of his marriage. His preparations continued — the Jews were 'asked' to grant him 3,000 marks in aid of his expedition[5] — but he did not start till the summer of 1240, since both pope and emperor had their reasons for wishing to postpone a crusade. Henry III, too, had a genuine reluctance to let him go because, in spite of their quarrels, Henry was growing more and more to depend upon Richard for counsel. The king did not always take Richard's advice, but he must usually have been sorry when he neglected it. It suited Henry as well as the pope when the latter sent a mandate ordering Simon de Montfort, Richard of Cornwall, and the Earl of Salisbury not to set out without special licence, as England was surrounded by enemies.[6]

A further reason for taking the cross in June 1236 may be found in

---

[1] *Mat. Par.*, iii, 393-4. G. E. C. refers to this embassy as if it had actually gone to the emperor.

[2] *Ibid.*, iii, 369.

[3] *Ibid.*, iii, 369. When Simon de Montfort adopted the same expedient he raised 'about £1000' (*ibid.*, iv, 7).

[4] *Ann. Theok.*, 98. From at least the age of five and until he was seven or older, Henry was brought up at Windsor with the Lord Edward (who was nearly four years younger) and others, in the care of Hugh Gifford and Mr. Walter le Brun de Dya (*Cl. R.*, 1240-1242, pp. 263, 269, 468). He was probably sent there at the time of his mother's death in January 1240.

[5] *Cl. R.*, 410; *C.P.R.*, 173 (January 1237).

[6] Bliss, 167 (February 25th, 1237).

Richard's dissatisfaction with the régime. Henry had married in January 1236 Eleanor of Provence, one of the four sisters all of whom became queens. The lady was brought to England by one of her numerous uncles, William of Savoy, Bishop-elect of Valence, who with astonishing rapidity so fascinated Henry III that within a few months of arrival he was made President of the Council. For the next eighteen months he was virtually Prime Minister, presiding over an efficient bureaucracy, which effected a number of administrative reforms. But it was almost immediately unpopular with the barons, who felt themselves excluded from the government by the failure of the king either to seek their advice or to take it when it was offered. This hostility was openly expressed at the April parliament of 1236, and the king made it worse by shutting himself up in the Tower of London when his barons tried to approach him. Henry seems to have realized that he had created (or at least was faced with) a difficult situation, for he quickly sent to Rome for a legate. His request was not answered at once, as Pope Gregory pointed out that the last time Henry had asked for this kind of moral support (namely in 1230) the petition had been countermanded as soon as it arrived. The barons probably knew of this embassy to Rome, which may have been linked in their minds with the concurrent resumption of alienated royal demesnes. This tense situation made it doubly difficult for the king to obtain a grant of money in January 1237. The aid was granted, through the efforts of William de Ralegh, but only on condition that the collection and expenditure of the tax was placed in the hands of baronial nominees. In return for this concession the charters were confirmed, and it was intended by the barons that they should be put into execution in all their details. The collection of the thirtieth was not due until towards the end of the year, by which time it had become a matter of some controversy. As a result Henry declared (November 28th) that he would store it in some safe place and spend it only by the advice of the legate, who had arrived in July. This in itself was a clear breach of the promise made by him in January. He in fact entrusted it to various household officials and spent it as he liked. Both the archbishop and Richard of Cornwall had rebuked the king earlier in the year for his dependence upon the aliens, but it is not to be thought that Henry and his brother were at loggerheads throughout the year, as might be imagined from Matthew Paris.[1] Richard, having had his say,

[1] *Mat. Par.*, iii, 411.

D

continued in his customary application to business. In June the negotiations with Wales about to take place at Worcester, under the terms
of a truce recently concluded by Thierry, Prior of the Hospitallers in
England, were delayed because Henry could not secure the presence
at short notice of Richard of Cornwall, William of Savoy, and
Simon de Montfort, without whom it was not expedient to treat.[1]
The meeting was postponed to August 1st, but Henry never reached
Worcester: the nearest he approached was Brill and then Wallingford, where he may have been with Richard, in mid-July. At the
end of September Richard was at York with the whole court, when,
with the help of the legate, an important treaty was made with
Scotland.[2] Again on October 26th, when the reversion of Richard
de Clare's marriage was granted to the Earl of Lincoln, it was done
expressly 'by the counsel of Earl Richard and others of the council'.
It seems possible that this phrase was inserted rather to guard the
king or his chancery against subsequent recriminations, than to
suggest that Richard of Cornwall was prominent in proposing the
match.[3] Even in December Richard was still serving on the council,
side by side with the unpopular Lacy and Simon de Montfort.[4] He
did not dislike them personally, but he sympathized with the barons
who were excluded from council, and with their grievances. A
week before Christmas the archbishop went to Rome ostensibly
upon his own affairs, but chiefly it may be thought, to procure the
recall of the legate. He may have wished also to oppose the marriage
of Henry's sister Eleanor, who had taken a vow of chastity in his
presence.

The resentment over the assessment, collection, and expenditure
of the thirtieth, hostility to the legate (in spite of its initial popularity), and the general dislike of the bureaucratic council over which
William of Savoy presided, combined to produce an explosion
which took place immediately after the marriage of Eleanor to
Simon de Montfort. The ceremony was performed on January 7th,
1238, without the consent of the baronage and by implication
against their wishes. The marriage of Richard de Clare and the Earl
of Lincoln's daughter had on the other hand been made with the
express consent of Richard of Cornwall and other councillors.
Thus Simon de Montfort's secret marriage provided a focus for the

---

[1] *Cl. R.*, 536.   [2] *Foed.*, i, 233.
[3] *C.P.R.*, 199. For this marriage see F. M. Powicke in *E.H.R.*, lvi, 544-5.
[4] *Cal. Lib. R.*, 299. £1,000 paid out of the wardrobe in the presence of the Archbishop
of York, Richard of Cornwall, Lacy, and de Montfort.

baronial discontent that had been gathering since April — if not January — 1236. For Simon was a foreigner, not even an earl, and his honour of Leicester was worth only about half what it had once been. Richard's sister suffered great disparagement, and everyone connected with the court, except Simon, 'lost face' over this marriage. Richard of Cornwall was particularly wounded. He was ill-fitted to battle physically with his enemies and all matters of dignity and appearances were more important to him than they would have been to a stronger man. He saw, too, with growing distaste as heir-presumptive that the natural resources of the crown to which he might hope to succeed were being squandered by his brother. Richard had had a number of children: Henry had been married two years and still had none. Richard had twice opposed his brother, each time with advantage to himself. On this occasion he was momentarily in open rebellion. A few days after Simon de Montfort's marriage he was in arms against the king with Gilbert Marshal, third of the brothers to become Earl of Pembroke, the Earl of Winchester, and others, at Kingston-on-Thames. His movements cannot be traced very closely. There may have been some parleying with his brother at Kingston, where Henry was represented by John Fitz-Geoffrey. The barons are also mentioned as being at Southwark on January 21st.[1] On February 3rd Henry wrote to the barons of the Cinque Ports enjoining them not to obey Richard of Cornwall if he tried to entice or bind them in the king's name.[2] The combined testimony of Matthew Paris and the Patent Roll leave little room for doubt that Richard was the prime mover in this rebellion. Matthew Paris was deeply interested in his cause, and bitterly disappointed by its failure. He relates how Henry tried to bargain separately with his opponents, and how, after the papal legate had negotiated in vain with Richard, he advised the king to yield. This Henry did on February 22nd, 1238. Provisions were written down and sealed by the legate and the magnates. According to these Henry agreed to abide by the decision of a chosen body of counsellors, but the Provisions never took effect because Richard of Cornwall, 'who had become the Captain of this rising',[3] deserted the baronial cause at the last minute (as he may have done ten years earlier) and so, says Matthew Paris, 'the reputation of Earl Richard was greatly blackened, and he became suspect who had been thought to be the staff

---

[1] *Flores*, ii, 224.   [2] *R. L.*, ii, 15 = *C.P.R.*, 209.
[3] *Mat. Par.*, iii, 477: 'Qui Capitaneus hujus impetus factus est'.

of their strength'.[1] Matthew Paris knew Richard personally and was indebted to him for much information, especially for documents concerning affairs of state,[2] but at this point in his narrative he is exceedingly emphatic without producing the evidence. He knew that there had been Provisions, but contrary to his habit he neither inserts them in his text nor refers to them as being in his *Additamenta*. By a long chain of argument it has been suggested that the Provisions of 1238 may be found in the so-called 'Paper Constitution' inserted by Matthew Paris or his reviser roughly and without comment under 1244.[3] There was no time to put these Provisions into effect and they were almost immediately forgotten, but Matthew Paris is the one person who might be expected to have a copy of them.

It is difficult to judge the scheme fairly from the incomplete, staccato, and sometimes fragmentary memoranda in which it has come down to us. It is clear, however, that real power is to be transferred from the king to the magnates, and that the Great Council is to meet only infrequently.

The essence of the scheme was to afforce the king's permanent council by four conservators of liberties who were to act as 'justiciars', to appoint five of the judges, and to have control over expenditure. These four were to be elected by 'all', i.e. by the baronage in the Great Council. The justiciar and chancellor, who might be conservators, were also to be elected, and not removed without the consent of the council. This was to put the monarchy into commission by giving a preponderance of financial and judicial control, with control of the seal, to the barons, of whom two at least were to be always with the king. One result of this would be to prevent arbitrary disseisin which had started the rising of William Marshal and Richard of Cornwall in 1227 and that of Richard Marshal in 1233. Whether or no this was their scheme, Gilbert and Marshal must have had the subject much in mind in drawing up their Provisions.

The king had yielded on February 22nd, 1238, and almost immediately Richard decided to throw away the fruits of his victory. He may have been encouraged to do this by a knowledge that 6,000 marks were shortly going to be carried to Paris for his use.[4] His

---

[1] *Mat. Par.*, iii, 479: 'famam comitis Ricardi in magna parte denigravit; et sic factus est deinceps suspectus qui credebatur baculus fortitudinis'.

[2] *Ibid.*, iii, 442, 471, 474-5, 612; v, 165-9, 347.

[3] See *E.H.R.*, lviii.

[4] *C.P.R.*, 222, dated May 30th. Secret bribes are mentioned in *Mat. Par.*, iii, 476.

reconciliation with Henry must have been recent when they met at the deathbed of their sister Joan, Queen of Scotland, at Havering. She died on March 4th in their arms and they buried her with the nuns of Tarrant.[1]

The real victory in 1238 lay with Henry, for he had won to his side the earl whose support was perhaps the most important single factor in delaying rebellion for the next twenty years. Richard was well rewarded for his change of sides, and may now be regarded as more or less permanently attached to the court party. The alliance was sealed by his second marriage to the queen's sister, Sanchia of Provence, in 1243. His later quarrels with Henry III were of brief duration and never pushed to the point of revolution.

---

[1] *Chron. Melrose* (facsimile edition), 86; *Mat. Par.*, iii, 479; *Theok.*, 106.

CHAPTER THREE

CRUSADE (1240); GASCONY (1242-1243)

SECOND MARRIAGE, WITH SANCHIA OF PROVENCE

FROM 1238 onwards Richard was much occupied with the thought of his crusade, but in March he received a request from Frederick II to delay his start until the ten-year truce expired towards the end of 1239. Frederick at the same time urged him to travel through Sicily.[1] Richard had opportunities, of which he obviously availed himself, of learning the truth about the Middle East from Baldwin, Emperor of Constantinople, who visited England in April-May,[2] for Richard believed in leaving nothing to chance. While he was in Cornwall in June a Saracen envoy arrived and Henry had him honourably confined in Canterbury castle, refusing him visitors that he might not spy out the condition of the land, there to be kept until the king had taken counsel with Earl Richard.[3] He kept in touch with Frederick, who sent him his boastful circulars about the battle of Cortenuova, the birth of his son (with suitable additions to give it a personal touch, as Richard was the uncle), and, in 1239, his diatribe against the pope.[4] Far more important to Richard were his dealings with the papal curia. In that quarter his advocacy must have been skilful and persistent, because though repeatedly urging him to delay his departure, Gregory IX at the same time granted him everything he could want. On April 20th Gregory wrote to Henry III urging him to delay Richard's crusade, on the ground that his presence in England was necessary for the safety of the kingdom, and stating that it would be better for the Holy Land if the magnates went in succession and not all together.

---

[1] *Mat. Par.*, iii, 471. Dated February 11th, 1238, at Vercelli. *Generalis terre*. (Cf. iii, 627, which may refer in error to this.)

[2] *Ibid., Hist. Angl.*, iii, 276; Richard gave him 200 marks, *Chron. Maj.*, iii, 481, 486.

[3] *Cl. R.*, 136 (June 12th).

[4] *Mat. Par.*, iii, 442. December 4th, 1237 (on Cortenuova, *Quanta audacia*); *ibid.*, iii, 474. March 3rd, 1238 (*Rem jocundam*, B.F., 2316, misses the point in calling the shorter version *blosse stylübung*); *ibid.*, iii, 590, April 20th, 1239 (*Levate in circuitu*, with the pope's answer, iii, 575-89).

But he added that he did not want to put obstacles in the way if Richard was really determined to go, and at the same time he wrote to Richard granting him whatever could be had in England from legacies to the Holy Land, or the redemption of crusading vows.[1] A grant of this kind to a private individual was quite unprecedented, and it aroused much comment. Immediately he had received this, Richard had 6,000 marks sent out in cash to the East by way of the Templars in Paris.[2] At the same time he was granted a general protection for his family and property, and a confirmation of Henry III's grant that if he died on crusade the issues of his lands until the following Michaelmas should be put to pious uses for his soul.[3] A few months later Gregory IX returned to the attack, urging Richard sharply to commute his vow to Constantinople and to divert his funds thither, alleging finally that he ought not to go at all, because the safety of England depended so much upon his presence.[4] The correspondence with pope and emperor, the sending of money abroad, coming so soon after the quarrel with Henry III, suggest that in the spring of 1238 Richard meant to set out in the course of the year, but little is known of his movements. He was at Berkhampstead on May 26th, when his old tutor, Roger d'Acastre, commuted his grants of land in Cornwall for a sum of a hundred marks,[5] and on June 15th was in Cornwall, where he settled a dispute between the monks of Tewkesbury and Richard de Grenville, in the presence of the itinerant justices.[6]

In May 1239 the birth of Henry III's son Edward settled many doubts and much reduced the chances of Richard becoming King of England. It also reduced the likelihood of disorder if Henry III should die during Richard's absence, so in spite of the opposition of pope and emperor, Richard made ready to start. With remarkable thoroughness his agent at Rome had another seven bulls sent off in

---

[1] *Reg. de Grég. IX*, ed. Auvray, nos. 4267, 4268. 'Legata in Terre Sancte subsidium, aut que de vicesima seu tricesima, vel pro redemptione votorum in eodem regno poterunt.' For the $\frac{1}{20}$ and $\frac{1}{30}$, and some further details, see W. E. Lunt, *Financial Relations*, 194-6, cf. 432-4, and *infra*.

[2] *C.P.R.*, 222. The money itself came from the king.

[3] *Reg. de Grég. IX*, no. 4276. Also 4277, permission to his chaplains and clerks to celebrate even where there is an interdict, and 4279, plurality of benefices allowed to four of his clerks.

[4] *Ibid.*, nos. 4608-9. 'Et nominato regno, *quod in tua providentia pro maiori parte subsistit*, personam tuam minime subtrahas, quin immo conceptum recedendi propositum omnino deponas.'

[5] Public Rec. Off., Exch. T. R. Misc. Bk., no. 57, fol. cxlix.

[6] *Ann. Theok.*, 108. On June 2nd Richard had been granted the amercements of William of York's eyre in Cornwall (*Cl. R.*, 58, cf. 70). Such grants indicate the temperature of the court. In 1236 and 1237 Richard received nothing at all from the king.

November, to add to the dozen or so that had already been issued in his favour, covering every manner of contingency, including his death, excommunication, or detention, and the observance of his will. It has seemed worth while to list these as an example of how the provident crusader would proceed.[1] Simon de Montfort contented himself with merely having his marriage regularized.

If Richard's anger against Simon had carried him to the point of rebellion, it did not last, or was cleverly concealed. Richard attested Amaury de Montfort's quit-claim to Simon of the honour of Leicester at Westminster on April 11th,[2] was godfather with him to Edward on June 20th,[3] and saved him from one of Henry's violent outbursts of temper in August.[4] It was through Richard's mediation, too, a factor that becomes increasingly prominent in English political history, that Gilbert Marshal, his brother-in-law, was reconciled with the king. He had wanted to join Richard's crusade, but being persuaded to stay at home was killed next year in a tournament at Hertford.[5]

The crusading barons met on November 12th, 1239, at Northampton, and made their oath to start the crusade, and not to be turned aside to Italy or Greece, about which there had been some misgivings since the pope had expressly advised Richard to go to Constantinople. Richard spent Christmas 1239 with Henry III at Winchester, when he persuaded the king to admit his ward, Baldwin de Redvers, to the Earldom of Devon.[6]

On the death of his wife Isabella on January 17th, 1240, Richard was in Cornwall, and he hurriedly returned to bury her at Beaulieu, in spite of the fact that she had herself wished to be buried at Tewkesbury.[7] He then went to St. Alban's to ask for the prayers of the

---

[1] The bulls of November 17th, 1239, are calendared by Bliss, 184-5, and may be summarized thus: protection for Richard, his wife, children, *familia*, and goods. If he dies overseas, his son Henry is to have the same protection until he is twenty-one; mandates to Canterbury, York, and Lincoln not to allow him or his son Henry to be molested; indult to Richard that no one shall issue any sentence of excommunication or interdict against him, his wife, or son, without special papal mandate; inhibitions (two) to anyone to seize or detain him after he has set out; indult that no one shall exact anything from the offerings made to his chaplains or clerks when they celebrate divine offices in his chapel; mandate to Canterbury, York, and Lincoln to cause his will to be observed, if occasion arises.

[2] *Layettes*, no. 2789.

[3] *Mat. Par. Hist. Angl.*, ii, 422; *Theok.*, 112.

[4] Bémont, ed. Jacob, *Simon de Montfort*, 61.

[5] *Mat. Par.*, iv, 56, 135; *Theok.*, 115; *Oseney*, 87; *Ann. Wav.*, 328. Richard and the king had probably been together at Wallingford on October 29th, when Henry granted ten oaks to Robert [? de Asthall], Richard's clerk (*Cl. R.*, 149).

[6] *Mat. Par.*, iv, 1.

[7] *Ibid.*, iv, 2.

convent for his crusade.[1] To the clergy assembled in council at Reading (May-June) he bade a tearful farewell, explaining to those who would have kept him that he would not stay in England to see the evils which they wrongly believed he could prevent.[2] His last public service before departing was as one of the 'dictators' of the agreement with David of Wales at Gloucester on May 15th.[3] Proceeding to London on June 5th, he left his son Henry in the care of Henry III, and handed over his ecclesiastical patronage to the Abbots of Wardon and Beaulieu, and his clerk, Robert of Asthall.[4] After some discussion Richard decided, on the advice of Thierry of Nussa, to travel overland to Marseilles and there take ship, neglecting the emperor's invitation to travel through Italy.[5]

The king and the legate saw him to Dover, where he embarked about June 10th, with a distinguished company. Besides Thierry of Nussa, his Chief of Staff, and the Earl of Salisbury, he had seven bannerets with him: his close friend Philip Basset, John de Beauchamp, Geoffrey de Lucy, John de Neville the Forester, Geoffrey de Beauchamp of Bedford, Peter de Brus, and William de Furnivall.[6] This implies fifty to seventy bachelors, whose names are not given. Others who went on this crusade and died in the Holy Land were Peter de Mauley, Robert Marmion, Eustace de Stuteville, Baldwin de Béthune, John Fitz-John, Richard's steward, and Eudo 'Fitz-Roy', one of John's natural children, who had an exchequer fee of £20 a year in 1237, and whose lands in Essex were granted to one of Richard's knights, Giles de Cancellis, in 1242.[7] The crusaders were not accompanied by Simon de Montfort. He had withdrawn from Richard's *familia* before they left England and went out independently through Italy.

Richard was in Paris by midsummer, and was royally entertained by Louis IX and Blanche of Castile. After renewing the truce between France and England, they provided him with a guide through their territory to the Rhône. At Lyons he was hospitably

[1] *Ibid.*, 43-4.   [2] *Ibid.*, 11.   [3] *Foed.*, i, 239 = *Cl. R.*, 241.
[4] *C.P.R.*, 248. Asthall, co. Oxon, was Richard's demesne of the honour of St. Valery. Robert was still in Richard's service in 1268, when he was Archdeacon of Worcester (*Cal. Ch. R.*, iii, 479).
[5] *Mat. Par.*, iv, 56. On June 3rd he was at Wallingford (Wykes, 86-7); June 5th, London (*Cal. Ch. R.*, 1337, p. 333); June 10th, Dover (*Dunst.*, 151-2: other chroniclers, of less authority, give conflicting dates for Dover).
[6] *Mat. Par.*, 44, 174-5.
[7] *C.P.R.*, 179, 270, 314. The land was 'Kanewedon' of the honour of Raleigh in Essex (January and August, 1242). Matthew calls him 'G. the earl's own brother' but *Flores*, ii, 249, has, correctly, Eudo.

received, but at Vienne, where he was to take ship down the Rhône, the citizens wanted to buy his *naviculas cursatrices,* offering three times their price. Protesting that he was not a merchant, the earl refused to sell, whereupon they stole the boats. Richard proceeded to Arles as best he could, and the now repentant citizens restored his boats to him at Beaucaire. The Count of Toulouse, in whose territory this outrage had taken place, was distressed, but seems to have done nothing. However, this led to Richard meeting his future father-in-law, Raymond, Count of Provence, who came from Tarascon to meet the earl, hoping for help against the Count of Toulouse.[1] At Marseilles, where Richard left a rent of twenty marks for prayers for himself, he was met by the papal legate, and the archbishop, John Baussan of Arles, who tried to persuade him to turn back. Having failed in this they tried to induce him to sail from Aiguesmortes instead of Marseilles. This, too, they refused to do, on account of the unhealthiness of the place. To emphasize their decision they sent a notorious anti-papalist, Sir Robert de Twenge, the 'William Wither' of the 1231 riots, as ambassador to the emperor. They then embarked at Marseilles (September 8th-15th), having spent three months on the journey from Dover to the Mediterranean, and landed at Acre on October 8th, 1240.[2]

Richard of Cornwall's crusade followed immediately upon that of Theobald IV, Count of Champagne and King of Navarre.[3] Theobald was a poet and no statesman, and his crusade, undertaken without any diplomatic preparations, considerably embarrassed the emperor. He had, we are told, a large force of knights with him, but the battle of Gaza in November 1239 — not to be confused with the more famous battle of 1244, which finally lost Jerusalem to the West — reduced 'Le Royaume sans Roi' to a state of hopeless confusion. The Syrian barons were divided among themselves, the Templars allying with Damascus, the Hospitallers (more prudently) with Egypt. Theobald hastily left for Europe, but not before he had recovered the important fortresses of Beaufort and Safed. At the same time Hugh, Duke of Burgundy, had begun to rebuild Ascalon.[4]

When Richard arrived he refused to be drawn into the quarrel between the Templars and the Hospitallers and went to assist the Duke of Burgundy in the reconstruction of Ascalon. On the advice

---

[1] *Mat. Par.,* iv, 45, where 'Avignon' as Koch (p. 51) points out, should be Lyons.
[2] *Mat. Par.,* iv, 47.   [3] *Ibid.,* 79.   [4] Grousset, *Hist. des Croisades,* iii, 372-96.

of the Hospitallers, the Duke, and Walter of Brienne, Count of Jaffa, he ratified the truce initiated by Theobald with al-Sâlih Aiyûb, Sultan of Egypt. Amaury de Montfort and the other French prisoners in Palestine were then released, an achievement that was to stand Richard in good stead when he returned to Europe. By this treaty (April 23rd, 1241) the old kingdom of Jerusalem was to some extent restored, consisting now of Jerusalem itself and the coast towns, for on his side Aiyûb ratified the territorial clauses in the Templars' treaty with Damascus. The latest historian of the crusades, M. Grousset,[1] gives high praise to Richard for his discretion in completing the work of Theobald and the Duke of Burgundy, and in taking advantage of the rivalries of the Aiyûbid princes. Richard was acting in this, it appears, as the official delegate of the emperor. By an odd coincidence, on the day the treaty was sealed Henry III was imploring the clergy to be diligent in collecting the money due to Richard from the redemption of crusading vows and legacies to the Holy Land, so that it might be sent out to him at the next opportunity.[2]

The letter in which Richard describes these events can hardly be described as modest.[3] It is reminiscent of the report which he sent home from Gascony as a boy in 1225. But he seems to have been justified in his contempt for Theobald, who agreed to the preliminaries of a truce with the Sultan of Krak and then hastily left the Holy Land with a large part of his army, though he had known for a fortnight before his departure that Richard was on his way. In this treaty, as in the refortification of Ascalon, Richard reaped where others had sown.

On his way home Richard, landing at Trapani (July 1st), spent four months[4] at the court of his brother-in-law, Frederick II, in the Apennines at or near Terni. At this time the emperor had just defeated the city of Faenza, and the Pisan fleet had captured a number of bishops who were proceeding to a general council. Frederick had long wanted to meet Richard, now the continuator of his work in Palestine, so the two met on excellent terms. A vivid picture is given by Matthew Paris of how the emperor looked after Richard

---

[1] *Op. cit.*, iii, 396.   [2] *Cl. R.*, 250.

[3] *Mat. Par.*, iv, 141-3. Cf. Wykes, 86-7. It is addressed to Baldwin de Redvers, whose wardship he had just surrendered (*supra*, p. 40, n. 6), the Abbot of Beaulieu, and Robert [of Asthall], his clerk.

[4] Paris (iv, 148) says 'about two months', but elsewhere 'four months' (iv, 166), which is correct.

on arrival, with blood-letting, hot baths, and fomentations; of the entertainment provided by the Saracen girls who danced on rolling spheres. After a futile but characteristic attempt, at his own instance, to mediate between Frederick II and Gregory IX,[1] Richard made his way back to England through Italy, in company with the liberated French knights.

> He was on the friendliest terms with the emperor, almost like another emperor, and had wealth in abundance; and these French were in a most impoverished state ... Earl Richard, however, liberally provided them with clothes, travelling expenses, and means of conveyance.[2]

At Cremona the triumphant procession was met by the town band and the elephant which Matthew Paris has made famous. He accompanies his detailed description of the beast with a picture, *quia hoc comes plenius enarravit.*[3] From Cremona to Dover, where he was met by the king and queen on January 7th, 1242, his itinerary cannot be traced.[4]

On Richard's arrival in London, which was decorated in his honour, on January 28th, he was allowed no rest. He was immediately forced to associate himself actively in his brother's project for going to Gascony and invading Poitou. The origin of this luckless expedition, which is of considerable importance in the life of Earl Richard, is to be found in Louis VIII's policy of creating large fiefs for his younger sons. In pursuance of the same policy Louis IX at midsummer 1241 invested his younger brother Alphonse with Poitou. This was much resented by Richard of Cornwall, whom Henry had made Count of Poitou in 1225. Secondly, the treacherous Hugh de la Marche and his wife Isabella, who was jealous of Blanche of Castile, proposed a coalition of Aragon, Castile, Navarre, and Toulouse. They invited the help of Henry III, urging that he need bring only money, not troops.

---

[1] *Mat. Par. Hist. Angl.*, ii, 453. Richard's ill-success was natural: he had already opposed the pope over lay patronage, and persisted on going on crusade against Gregory's wishes.

[2] *Mat. Par.*, iv, 166.

[3] *Ibid.*

[4] The date of landing is variously given. I follow Wykes, 89, and *Mat. Par.*, iv, 180. *Ann. Wav.*, 329, says, January 15th, and that he was met at Canterbury by the king and queen and the whole court who gave him presents and came to London with him on January 25th, when he went in procession to St. Paul's and Westminster. The editor, in emending the text, makes the canons of St. Paul's fetch Richard from Canterbury to London, by reading *Postea venerunt [canonici] beati Pauli simul cum eo Londoniam.* The better text is, however, preserved in the Annals of Southwark (Bod. Lib. MS. Rawl. B, 177, fol. 225) which reads *Postea venerunt Lond' in conversione beati Pauli.*

When Richard landed at Dover, Henry had already decided upon this scatterbrained project, and was making active preparations.[1] He had made his decision, as not infrequently, without consulting the barons. He needed money, and had therefore to call a council at Westminster at the end of January. The barons were strongly opposed to the expedition, in spite of the efforts of Earl Richard and others who were sent to state the royal case. The barons advised the king to wait until the truce, renewed comparatively recently by Richard and Roger Bigod, had expired, or until Louis IX broke it. They refused a money-grant point blank. This refusal of taxation was based on grounds that have survived in a famous constitutional document. Henry had not kept the Charters, he had been granted too much money already, and if he had kept his word some must still be in hand, since they had not authorized its expenditure. They urged Henry to remember the crime of the King of Navarre in the Holy Land — apparently alluding to the fact that Theobald had broken a truce with the Sultan of Egypt.

So Henry was reduced to scraping together the money from the monasteries, the Irish Exchequer, and the Jews: only later was he allowed to take a scutage. That he intended to break the truce is clear. Yet before going he made a solemn promise to Richard of Cornwall and Roger Bigod, Earl of Norfolk, that he would not do so, and that they might freely return to England if he did.[2] The day before he made this promise he had granted Richard four good manors.[3] Thus encouraged — he can hardly have been reassured — Richard agreed to sail, and Henry spent a couple of days with him at the Earl's manors of Haughley and Eye (March 19th-20th) before going off to pray at Bromholm (March 23rd).[4] Before the expedition set out, Peter of Savoy and Pierre d'Aigueblanche were sent to advise the Poitevins of Henry's coming. In spite of the departure and death of William the Elect of Valence, Savoyard influence was dominant at court in the person of these two men, particularly the bishop, and in matters of foreign policy. Peter of Savoy was a more moderate man, who never raised any great antagonism in this country. On his arrival in 1241 he had at once been given the lands

---

[1] *Cl. R.*, 1242, pp. 429, 431.   [2] *C.P.R.*, 274 (March 8th).

[3] *Cl. R.*, 404, 406. Cf. *Mat. Par.*, iv, 189-90. The possible significance of this visit to Bromholm will be obvious to readers of Professor Powicke's article concerning another of Henry's visits to that priory in *E.H.R.*, vol. lvi, 529 *f.*

[4] *Cl. R.*, 400 (March 9th, 1242: Newport in Essex, Corsham, Mere in Wilts., and Fordington in Dorset, brought into the marriage settlement in 1243).

of the honour of Richmond, by a remarkable grant that gave him
the right to give, assign, or bequeath them to any of his brothers or
kinsmen (*consanguineis*) — a grant that was widened in a still more
extraordinary fashion in March 1262, when he was given the right
to dispose of the honour by gift, assignment, or bequest, to anyone
whomsoever, whatever the state of his own health.[1] The actual
grant of 1241 seems to have passed without immediate comment,
but when rumours of Richard's return reached the court at Westminster, Peter of Savoy prudently resigned (about January 1st, 1242)
the custody of the 'more eminent and famous castles of which he
had received the custody' and 'ne aliqua perturbacio in regno per
ipsum in adventu ipsius comitis, super hoc quereles forte graves
audituri, oriretur', he received licence to leave the court and go back
to Savoy. He was recalled by Henry III and given the custody of
Dover castle.[2] This story from Matthew Paris is of interest as
showing not only that Richard was still regarded as the natural
leader of the baronage in such matters, but that the barons found
themselves unable or unwilling to make any protest in his absence;
and further, it reveals for the first time that Peter of Savoy, the 'little
Charlemagne', shared with his brothers the family talent for capti-
vating Henry III, and in this case Richard of Cornwall as well, by
their personal charm. For Richard raised no objections to Peter of
Savoy's sudden promotion and the two became friends.

The fleet set sail from Portsmouth in May, with six earls and
about 150 knights, taking with them 20,000 marks' worth of silver
in barrels.[3] The cautious Richard had received his reward in
advance, and reserved to himself a loophole for escape if necessary.
The campaign will show him somewhat after the manner of Hubert
de Burgh, saving the king from the worst results of his folly. But

[1] *Foed.*, i, 417 (May 6th, 1241); *Cal. Ch. R.*, ii, 41 (March 15th, 1262).
[2] *Mat. Par.*, iv, 177-8, and *ibid.*, 42, 44-5, for an exchange of outlying parts of the honour of
Richmond with Edward for the honour of Hastings. Peter of Savoy by his will of 1268
left Richmond to the queen, his niece, so this astonishingly unfeudal transaction lacks what
might easily have been a dramatic sequel (Wurstemberger, iv, 431—*Foed.*, i, 475-6). It is important to note that Peter was not Earl of Richmond. The charter of 1241 did 'not purport to
convey the earldom, or even the honour, of Richmond, but in 1262 the king referred to the
charter as a grant of the honour of Richmond, and no doubt it was intended as such' (G.E.C.,
x, 806, n. (g)). This renders Peter's bequest of the *comitatum Richemundensem* (in his will
of May 7th, 1268) or the *comitatum seu honorem de Richemund* (in the first codicil: *ibid.*, 809,
n. (a)) even more irregular.
[3] *C.P.R.*, 294-7. The fleet was collected by requisitioning all ships capable of carrying
sixteen horses or more from all the ports in England. This procedure, affecting foreign ships
as well as British, must have caused some dislocation of trade, but it was normal. *Mat. Par.*, iv
192, is graphic but inaccurate about the size of the expedition and its departure.

no one could persuade Henry III that he was not a soldier: he could only hope to mitigate the king's irresponsibility in military matters.

When they landed at the mouth of the Gironde they encamped at Pons for three weeks and then moved to Saintes (*c.* June 13th-July 19th), where a pretence was made of negotiating with St. Louis. The stewards of the household, much employed in diplomatic work throughout our period, were sent on this errand. But Henry had already mobilized the Gascon barons. Louis was busy reducing the Lusignan castles in Poitou, and when Henry 'defied' the French king for making war on his stepfather, the latter marched straight down to Taillebourg, a fortified place on the north bank of the Charente, a few miles north of Saintes. Henry and Hugh de Lusignan marched twenty miles downstream (i.e. in a northerly direction), thus passing Taillebourg and neglecting to secure it. By proceeding to Taillebourg, Louis cut off the English from their base. Henry rushed his army back to Taillebourg to prevent the French from crossing the river. Here on Sunday (July 20th, 1242) the two armies were facing each other, separated only by the Charente. At this point Matthew Paris[1] introduces a spirited dialogue between Hugh de Lusignan and Earl Richard, who reminded Hugh that he had advised the English to come with plenty of money but no army, whereupon Hugh replied that he had not done this and that it was all his mother's fault. When he heard this, Richard laid aside his armour and walked across the bridge to the French army, taking with him only a pilgrim's staff. His popularity with the French, some of whom he had liberated in Palestine, was such that he secured a twenty-four hours' truce, thus preventing the capture of Henry III and the loss of his army. Returning to his brother, Richard said, 'Let's get out of here quick'.[2] They did so, fleeing to Saintes, where there was a skirmish outside the city resulting in the capture of six French and twenty English knights.

Such were the 'battles' of Taillebourg and Saintes in the campaign of 1242. Hugh de Lusignan deserted and made a separate peace with Louis. The English retreat became a rout and they had to recross the Gironde to Blaye, near Bordeaux. It was the end of the campaign. There was no further hope of recovering Poitou. Louis fell ill and went home, thus saving the English from further disasters. There was nothing to be done, yet Henry III wasted another whole year in Gascony, arranging futile alliances, with his army gradually

[1] iv, 211.   [2] *Cito, cito transferamus nos hinc. Imminet captio nostra* (Mat. Par., iv, 212).

dwindling away. A five-year truce was arranged in 1243, but Henry remained at Bordeaux in idleness until September, when he came home, defeated and for the time impoverished.[1]

These events throw no fresh light on the character of Henry III, but add something to the picture of Richard of Cornwall derivable from earlier events. In his expedition to Poitou as a boy, in his war with Llewelyn in 1231, in his crusade of 1240, and in Gascony in 1242 he had shown his skill in mediation rather than his qualities as a soldier. There had been some brisk fighting outside Saintes, in which Simon de Montfort and John Mansel distinguished themselves. The court poet, Henry of Avranches, wrote a poem on 'John Mansel's leg', which was crushed by a stone during a minor siege. But there is no word of Earl Richard's part in the fighting. This aspect of his character was perhaps one of the reasons for his refusal to accept the crown of Sicily: he would have had to fight for it, whereas after Frederick II's death in 1250 he hoped to win the empire by diplomacy.

The ostensible reason for Richard's departure from Gascony was a disagreement with the king over the unjust treatment of William de Ros, a north-country knight who found it impossible to remain owing to lack of funds.[2] But there were other and deeper causes.

The fact is that Henry III gave Gascony to Richard at Saintes. This is clearly expressed in Richard's renunciation of all right thereto in 1243.[3] Matthew Paris tries to carry this grant back to 1225, when Richard was made Count of Poitou, but the chronicler is here, unwittingly perhaps, confusing *litterae intendentes* with a charter of enfeoffment.[4] Henry was only at Saintes in June–July 1242, and the

---

[1] Henry's account of the campaign in his letter to the emperor dated September 19th, 1242, from Bordeaux (*Cl. R.*, 530-2) cannot be reconciled with the facts as given by Matthew Paris. He omits to mention the truce made at Taillebourg.

[2] *Mat. Par.*, iv, 228-9.   [3] *Foed.*, 254 (December 1st, 1243).

[4] There is a lucid but indecisive Excursus on this subject by Koch, who allowed himself to be unduly worried by Gebauer's statement (pp. 13, n. *r*, and 76, n. *u*) that Richard received Gascony as a fief in 1225. Gebauer's view was based on the explicit assertion of Matthew Paris (*s.a.* 1252) that Henry III gave Gascony to Richard 'about twenty-seven years earlier' than 1252, i.e. in 1225 or 1226, but there is no reason to believe this. The relevant passages in Matthew Paris are iii, 93 (cf. Wendover, iv, 101) for the order to the Gascons 'to be intendent' to Richard in 1225; iv, 487, which says that Richard claimed Gascony at Bordeaux in 1243, but was prevented from obtaining it by the queen; v, 291, relating the 'grant' of 1225 and the attempted incarceration of Richard in 1243. See also the *Historia Anglorum*, ii, 270, and iii, 251 (the *Abbreviatio*), where the story of a secret charter is again ventilated.

Gebauer shrewdly observed (p. 77) that Richard may have retained great expectations even after his renunciation of 1243 because that document included the phrase 'nisi [rex] ei de novo Wasconiam ex mera liberalitate conferret', and in this connection it may be noted that although Gascony was granted to the young Lord Edward on September 30th, 1249 (*Cal. Ch. R.*, i, 345), he did not receive seisin of it at that time, nor on April 27th-28th, 1252 (*op. cit.*, 386, 389), but only in 1254 (*Rôles Gascons*, ed. C. Bémont, I, ii, xcv-xcvii and cxvi).

most natural interpretation is therefore that the grant was a reward to Richard for saving the king from capture at Taillebourg. Whatever the motive for it, the grant was revoked at the instance, according to Paris, of the queen. The date of the grant would thus be July 20th-29th. Between that time and the end of August the brothers quarrelled. This date too can be fixed fairly narrowly, for on August 22nd Richard received a formal licence to return to England, and on September 2nd he received a second licence to return 'without the king's indignation'.[1] Anyone who has looked at similar licences will agree that this implies a quarrel in the last week of August. It is to these few days that we may assign the story given by Matthew Paris[2] that Henry bribed the men of Bordeaux to imprison Richard. The earl, it is said, took refuge in the church of St. Cross and secretly took ship to England. The account of this episode is circumstantial, but it cannot be controlled. If it is wholly accurate, there must have been more than one quarrel, because something had happened by September 2nd—on September 3rd the brothers were on terms,[3] and Richard remained in Gascony until at least the end of the month,[4] and did not land at Scilly until October 18th.[5] If Matthew Paris is to be believed, King Henry and his brother never afterwards felt the same brotherly affection one to the other. This may well be true, but Richard did, nevertheless, throw in his lot with the court party and did not allow any sense of personal grievance to outweigh his political judgment.

The policy that he was to follow was closely linked with that of his brother through his marriage with Sanchia of Provence. This was to involve Richard for a short time in the politics of Provence, and for the next twenty years in the fate of Western Switzerland. As he and Henry III married sisters their political interests in these regions ran parallel and gave no cause for friction between them. They had quarrelled over Gascony, which Richard wanted, and were going to quarrel over Sicily, which he did not, but over Provence and Savoy their ideas were completely in harmony. The only difference was that when the Savoyards turned to England for money, Henry gave them presents, Richard only loans. He had

---

[1] *C.P.R.*, 318, 320. The words of Matthew Paris (*Hist. Angl.*, ii, 466), *petita sed non obtenta a rege licentia*, and the *Flores* (ii, 259), *non clare licentiatus*, also point unmistakably to a quarrel.

[2] v, 291-3.

[3] *C.P.R.*, 320. Bond to Richard in £1,000.

[4] He attests (I give the evidence for what it is worth) a royal charter on September 30th (*ibid.*, 328).

[5] *Mat. Par.*, iv, 229; *Theok.*, 128.

barely been married a year before his wife's uncle, Boniface, Arch-
bishop-elect of Canterbury, had 'touched' him for a thousand
marks.[1]

The lady of Richard's second choice was described as of incom-
parable beauty.[2] Richard may have met her at her home in Tarascon
as he passed through on his way to the Holy Land, but the arrangements were not of long standing. Sanchia, the third daughter of
Raymond Berengar V of Provence and Beatrice, daughter of
Thomas I of Savoy, had already been betrothed to the Dauphin,
and only the year before her marriage to Richard had been sought
by Raymond VII of Toulouse.[3] There is no reason to postulate any
political motive for the alliance, since Henry III was already firmly
attached to Provence and Savoy, and the bride brought no marriage-
portion with her.

At Pons on May 26th, 1242, Richard empowered Peter of Savoy
to make the necessary contract for him. This was completed on
July 17th at Tarascon, with the help of Pierre d'Aigueblanche, the
Savoyard Bishop of Hereford and keeper of Henry's wardrobe.[4]
Richard had intended to go to Provence to see his betrothed, but it
is not known if he did so.[5] One writer says that he set out, but
being warned of an ambush he returned to England.[6] There seems
no reason to reject this story, though it might be merely another
version of Henry III's plot to imprison him at Bordeaux.

On his way home Richard narrowly escaped shipwreck, and
consequently vowed to build an abbey, a pledge which he redeemed
magnificently a few years later at Hailes.[7] When he reached England the king's anger against him had cooled, and royal houses and
castles were put at his disposal.[8] But Sanchia's arrival in this country
was delayed by English relations with France. On January 21st,
1243, her father, Raymond, was asked not to send his daughter under
safe-conduct of the King of France, as the truce had not yet begun to
run.[9] Richard had therefore a full year in which to prepare for
Sanchia's arrival. How he occupied his time, except that he had

---

[1] *C.P.R.*, 446 (December 8th, 1244).   [2] Wykes, 117.
[3] Fournier, *Le Royaume d'Arles*, 156, 164.   [4] Wurstemberger, iv, 86, 87.
[5] *C.P.R.*, 328 (September 28th, 1242). Promise to pay his expenses if he has to go to
Provence via Aragon.
[6] *Theok.*, 128.
[7] *Infra*, 76. Richard came home with Walter Marshal and Richard de Clare, landing at
Scilly on October 18th (*Mat. Par.*, iv, 229).
[8] *Cl. R.*, 81. On the other hand, there are no gifts to Richard on the Liberate Rolls
1230-1240.
[9] *C.P.R.*, 399.

Berkhampstead castle repaired, is a mystery.[1] On November 14th, Sanchia landed with her mother Beatrice, and the marriage took place at Westminster on the 23rd.[2] The king held his Christmas court with them at Wallingford, and was at great pains to be affable to the bride.[3] Beatrice, whose visit Matthew Paris regarded as *nimis fastigiosa*, left England shortly afterwards, well provided for, but with the knowledge that her husband was dying.[4]

For the marriage Richard received two thousand pounds in cash and a thousand marks a year or the equivalent in lands.[5] Sanchia was dowered by Richard at the church door at Westminster with a third of his lands, Berkhampstead castle and manor being the capital messuage. As part of the marriage settlement Sanchia was granted the custody of the heirs if she should survive Richard, and Richard received licence, as was not unusual with magnates in the thirteenth century, to make his will.[6] Sanchia bore Richard two, if not three, children, of whom Edmund survived to become Earl of Cornwall. Little is heard of her until her coronation with Richard in 1257, and her lonely death in 1261, save a letter from Adam Marsh thanking her for many acts of kindness,[7] and a gift at her instance of a hermitage by the church at the Tower to one John of Apulia.[8]

As a sequel to the marriage Richard renounced, on December 1st, 1243, all his rights in Ireland or Gascony, with explicit mention of the grant at Saintes, in return for confirmation of his right to the county of Cornwall and the honours of Wallingford and Eye.[9] From about this time he drops the style Count of Poitou, though it is occasionally found at a later date.[10]

Provence became of interest to him through the sudden death on August 19th, 1245, of Sanchia's father, Raymond Berengar V. In the hope of preserving the independence of his dominions Raymond

[1] *Ann. Dunst.*, 161; *Cl. R.*, 111.

[2] *Mat. Par.*, iv, 263; *C.P.R.*, 414. Wykes, 91, puts the marriage at Wallingford, and *Ann. Dunst.*, 161, at Canterbury, but the Patent Roll is decisive.

[3] 'Cui rex cum summo conamine totum se exhibuit serenum et jocundum' (*Mat. Par.*, iv, 283, cf. *Theok.*, 132).

[4] *Mat. Par.*, iv, 505. Paris exaggerates her pension, which was £400 a year for six years, to 4,000 marks a year for five years.

[5] £1,000 was paid on September 3rd, 1242 (*Cal. Lib. R.*, ii, 155, cf. ii, 230, 299; iii, 42, 84, 144, 171).

[6] *Mat. Par.*, iv, 283-4; *C.P.R.*, 414, 416, 418.

[7] *Mon. Franc.*, p. 292.

[8] *Hist. MSS. Comm. 8th Rep.*, App. 87b, dated January 27th, 1256.

[9] *C.P.R.*, 437 = *Foed.*, i, 253.

[10] E.g. *Foed.*, i, 257 (August 13th, 1244) and *Cl. R.* (1247), 498.

had left them all to his unmarried youngest daughter, Beatrice, and
her heirs, carefully excluding the Queens of England and France, and
the Countess of Cornwall, but admitting the more distant claims of
Aragon. Through the persistence of Blanche of Castile and the
acquiescence of the widowed Countess Beatrice, the heiress, in spite
of the efforts of Raymond VII of Toulouse to wed her himself,
married Charles of Anjou, the handsome nineteen-year-old brother
of Louis IX, on January 31st, 1246. Charles had received a papal
dispensation for this a month earlier, as he and Beatrice were related
through their great-grandparents, Sancho and Sanchia, children of
Alfonso VII of Castile. He at once marched troops into Provence,
even before the marriage.[1]

In the face of this *fait accompli* Henry and Richard turned to the
pope, but too late for protection. Richard's proctor at Rome,
brother Ralph, a Trinitarian, and Henry III's proctors begged the
pope to send a legate to Charles of Anjou to prohibit him from
continuing to occupy the towns and castles of Provence until the
case had been tried before the pope, and implored him to put no
faith in Raymond's will, which they said he had revoked. Innocent,
however, refused point blank to interfere directly, though he said
that he would induce King Louis and Charles of Anjou to give their
sisters-in-law their rights in Provence and that he would not believe
the will further than was just.[2] Thus the efforts of Richard and
Henry to dispute a will which Charles of Anjou proceeded to
administer for himself were quite unavailing. From this time,
either as husband of Sanchia or as King of the Romans and nominal
overlord, Richard has no further dealings with Provence.

It was otherwise with Savoy. Richard was brought much into
contact with his wife's uncle, Peter of Savoy, who already owed
him a considerable sum in 1246. The amount is not stated, but the
loan was backed by the king, and if Peter died before it was repaid,
it was to be a first charge on the issues of his lands.[3] In this year
England was bound even more closely to Savoy by a little-noticed
transaction.[4] In spite of Frederick II's deposition on July 17th, 1245,

---

[1] R. Sternfeld, *Karl von Anjou*, kap. 1, *passim*. There is a vivid and very inaccurate story
in *Mat. Par.*, v, 403-5.

[2] Berger, *Reg. Inn. IV*, no. 1967.

[3] *C.P.R.*, 479.

[4] This transaction gains its interest from Pierre d'Aiguebanche's letter to Henry III with a
definite offer of Savoy's homage which he says he has already proposed in council. He
urges that it be accepted and mentions that William Bonivard is coming on the count's
behalf. Shirley in *R. L.*, ii, 200-1, dated the letter '? 1261' with reference to what he took to be

Count Amadeus IV of Savoy did homage to him in that month, and in practice remained his faithful and even zealous supporter.[1] This did not prevent him from offering to hold the Alpine passes from Henry III. The matter was initiated by Pierre d'Aigueblanche, the Savoyard Bishop of Hereford, and carried through on January 16th, 1246, by William Bonivardi, the count's wicked minister.[2] In return for £1,000 a year and the promise of an earl for his daughter, Amadeus did homage for Susa, Angliana, St. Maurice in Chablais, and Fort de Bard.[3] The story put about in England, and related by Matthew Paris, was that Amadeus could do this without disloyalty to the emperor because he only held *aquas et transitus* from him. But, as Pierre d'Aigueblanche's letter to Henry III explicitly states, it is precisely the *districta passagia*, essential to Frederick II's campaigns in Italy, that he offers to Henry III. A better example of successful and unscrupulous Savoyard diplomacy would be hard to find. The count's bait in offering his homage was that he would be able to fight against Henry's enemies, for he made his offer at the very moment when Charles of Anjou's marriage was being arranged. The treaty with Amadeus can thus be regarded as the answer of Savoy to the appearance of the French monarchy in force on the left bank of the Rhône, and a step in the equally futile attempts of Henry III and Richard of Cornwall to stem this advance. Richard, at any rate, remained consistent for many years in his support of Savoy and all its doings.

In 1249 Peter of Savoy acknowledged another loan, this time of

Henry III's change of style, as the word 'Normannie' has been dropped before 'Aquitanie'. But the style 'Dux Hibernie Comes Andegavie' cannot be technically correct at any period, as Anjou was given up with Normandy. The following probabilities suggest themselves: (i) There would be no point in addressing Henry III after Richard of Cornwall had become King of the Romans in 1257. (ii) Any date after 1246 forces us to make an unreal distinction between the towns for which homage was actually done and the *districta passagia* to which they were the key. (iii) The offer to fight the king's enemies might naturally refer to Charles of Anjou. (iv) A possible alternative might seem to date the letter after October 14th, 1254, when Pierre d'Aigueblanche is going to Rome to receive seisin of the Kingdom of Sicily for Edmund (*C.P.R.*, 344). He would thus be offering the services of Thomas of Savoy, Count of Flanders and Regent of Savoy (he attests as Count of Savoy in B.F. 13926) who had been made nominal Prince of Capua by Edmund on October 12th (*ibid.*) and who next year was empowered to retain knights to the king's use and take them abroad (*C.P.R.*, 413, dated June 20th, 1255). Thomas did in fact go abroad, but was captured by his neighbours of Turin whence he was rescued by Peter of Savoy (see p. 54). But this alternative conflicts with (ii) above, so the more likely date is late 1245.

[1] Fournier, *Le Royaume d'Arles*, 176.

[2] William Bonivardi (whose ill deeds and those of his master caused an avalanche killing 9,000 people at Maurienne: Fournier, 180, n. 1, and *Mat. Par.*, v, 31) was to have received a pension of £20 a year from Henry III, but the grant, dated January 10th, 1246, was cancelled (*C.P.R.*, 469).

[3] *Mat. Par.*, iv, 550; *Foed.*, i, 264.

five hundred marks.[1] It is fair to Richard to say that we have no means of knowing whether these loans were free of interest or not. In 1256, when Peter was preparing an expedition to set free his brother Thomas, who was held a prisoner in Turin, Richard lent him £1,000[2] and made himself responsible for Peter's property while the latter was away.[3]

As King of the Romans Richard intervened with greater effect in the affairs of Savoy. When Thomas of Savoy was about to renew his struggle with Turin, Richard freed him (April 14th, 1258) from all engagements he had made as a prisoner[4] and on December 11th, 1259, gave him the strategically important castle and town of Gumminen, to strengthen his hand against the House of Kybourg.[5] Finally, on the death of Hartmann the younger of Kybourg his imperial fiefs were granted to Peter of Savoy (by a deed dated at Berkhampstead, October 17th, 1263). This Richard did on the eve of a war between the House of Savoy and the House of Habsburg, for the domination of Western Switzerland between Lausanne and Berne. His action threw Rudolph into the arms of Conradin and thus appreciably weakened his position as King of the Romans. Personal friendship for Peter of Savoy, who had arranged his marriage for him, seems to have influenced his political judgment, but the move could be defended.

The years 1244-1257 show a gradually mounting opposition to Henry III's bureaucratic government, but the barons, continually demanding the appointment of a responsible justiciar and chancellor (later treasurer as well), were to some extent frustrated by the skill of the royalist party in making contact with their opponents, by the alliance of Richard of Cornwall and Henry III with the papacy, and by the financial expedients which saved the king from bankruptcy and enriched his brother.

From 1244 onwards the faith that Henry placed in Richard's soundness of judgment is fully evident. It is he who, with the Archbishop of York, negotiates the treaty with Alexander II of Scotland at Newcastle in August 1244.[6] The settlement was not particularly advantageous, but it avoided an unnecessary war. In the same year,

---

[1] *C.P.R.*, 54.   [2] *Ibid.*, 469.   [3] *Mat. Par.*, v, 564.   [4] Fournier, 201.
[5] *Infra*, 202. A second grant of the same date investing him with Savoy, Chablais, and Aosta is mythical (Prévité-Orton, *Early History of the House of Savoy*, 381-2). The genuine deed is printed in Wurstemberger, iv, as no. 627.
[6] *C.P.R.*, 434; *Foed.*, i, 257; *Mat. Par.*, iv, 380.

probably in November,[1] Richard was elected one of the committee of twelve appointed by parliament to report upon the reform of the realm. On this committee the royalists were represented by Boniface of Savoy, Richard of Cornwall, the Earl of Norfolk, Simon de Montfort, and perhaps others. Apart from Grossetête the baronage may be considered leaderless, both at this time and for many years to come. It therefore seems doubtful whether the committee ever achieved anything.[2] But something may be added to the well-known story of the constitutional crisis which had provoked the barons to refuse supply until their grievances had been redressed. The king had returned from Gascony about Michaelmas 1243 defeated and hard up, but by the spring (especially late March to late April) of 1244 there is evidence of a strong royal council in action.[3] A possible hypothesis would be that this was the immediate result of the appointment in this year of Paul Pevre, Sir John Laxton, John Mansel, and Lawrence of St. Martin to the council, but this must remain a hypothesis as the date of appointment is not given. It is, however, striking that John Mansel should join the council and that the strong hand of the administrator should appear in the same year. Whatever may be thought of this, it is at least certain that the constitutional crisis of 1244 was closely connected in time with an outburst of administrative zeal, and in this the events of 1244 are to some extent parallel with those of 1236-1238.

When the crisis of 1244 had subsided the Earl of Cornwall found himself stronger than ever. He was already lending money to the government, and in 1245 had enough to spare to send £1,000 to the Holy Land after the fall of Jerusalem,[4] and also to finance Henry III's Welsh campaign to the amount of £2,000. The campaign was doubly unfortunate for Richard, since four of his household were killed, and he lost much popularity through a very widely-spread rumour (which Matthew Paris did not believe) that he favoured his nephew, David of Wales, too much because Henry at the instance of the queen had refused him Chester and Gascony.[5] In November of the same year the king refused to admit the Mayor of London to

---

[1] The chronology of this year is confused. See *E.H.R.*, lviii, 405, n. 2.

[2] An attempt has been made elsewhere (*E.H.R.*, *loc. cit.*) to show that the Twelve were not responsible for the 'Paper Constitution' attributed to this year.

[3] *Cl. R.*, 239-44, concern (i) a general inquest into *Terrae Normannorum*, (ii) prohibition of wool-sales without licence, (iii) distraint of knighthood, (iv) prohibition on money-lending by merchants, (v) a *quo warranto* inquiry, (vi) a forest eyre.

[4] *Mat. Par.*, iv, 415-16. Perhaps in answer to Frederick II's appeal to him (*ibid.*, 300-5).

[5] *Ibid.*, 482-3, 487. The four killed were Alan Buscel, Adam de Moia, Sir Geoffrey Sturmy, and Raymond, a Gascon crossbowman 'of whom the king used often to make sport'.

office in the absence of the earl.[1] A few months earlier he had been appointed to a committee set up to deal with those who had tourneyed against the royal prohibition.[2] Richard and Sanchia spent Christmas (1245) with the king and queen at London.[3]

For the moment, the royal brothers appeared to be completely in accord, particularly over the burning question of the time — opposition to papal exactions from the English clergy. On August 10th, 1244, Henry III had written to Mr. Martin, the papal agent, in the strongest possible terms,[4] and this attitude he endeavoured to maintain throughout 1245, but he was probably half-hearted, for in July of that year the barons had to expel Mr. Martin from the country on their own initiative, after coming to a decision at a tournament at Dunstable.[5] But at that very moment Innocent IV had deposed Frederick II at the Council of Lyons and flushed with triumph, refused to moderate his demands upon the English clergy to any considerable extent. Henry continued to stand for the freedom of church and state in the March parliament of 1246, when he and the whole *communitas* wrote in protest to the pope.[6] But at the next parliament, at Winchester on July 7th, 1246, specially summoned to hear the pope's reply, Richard of Cornwall changed sides and forced the king to give way to the pope. The reasons, according to Matthew Paris, were hidden,[7] but in another place he gives the obvious cause, that Richard was bribed by the pope. The earl had in 1238 received a grant of the *pecuniam de redemptione votorum*, to help towards the expenses of his crusade. This privilege seems to have been without any mention of a term of years, but the collection of the money did not cease.[8] An exact computation is impossible,

[1] *Lib. de Ant. Leg.*, 11.

[2] *Cl. R.*, 363, cf. 466, where he is named as a possible arbiter in the matter of the Justiciar of Ireland's salary.

[3] *Mat. Par.*, iv, 503-4.

[4] *Cl. R.*, 259; cf. 357, which is an undated and unfinished letter perhaps rendered unnecessary by baronial action.

[5] One of the few concrete pieces of evidence to show that, as has so often been remarked, tournaments offered an excuse for political conspiracies.

[6] *Mat. Par.*, iv, 526, 536. The letter *Sic mater ecclesia* from the *communitas* is on p. 533.

[7] 'Et cum constanter pararetur dominus rex stare pro regni et ecclesie liberatione, comminationibus comitis Ricardi fratris sui qui ob occultas causas domino pape specialissimus, factus est et papalibus negotiis propitius . . .' Certain bishops, notably Cantilupe of Worcester, were also concerned (*Mat. Par.*, iv, 561).

[8] The grant also applied to legacies *in terre sancte subsidium*. An interesting receipt by Richard is printed in *Hist. MSS. Comm. Rep., Var. Coll.*, i, 360. It is for £59 10s. paid to William Blundel, his clerk, in respect of such legacies, from the dignities and prebends of the See of Salisbury in accordance with the mandate of Cardinal O[tho] formerly legate, enforced by a rescript of Innocent IV (June 3rd, 1244) here recited, and by a mandate of Archbishop Boniface of Canterbury; dated at Salisbury, December 21st, 1244.

but it is probable that the amount received was of the order of £1,000 a year.[1] On March 13th, 1246, Innocent IV regranted this privilege,[2] and this was apparently the signal for a new drive to collect the money, under the supervision of Mr. Berard de Nympha. Considerable scandal was caused, as the Franciscans and Dominicans were called in to persuade people of either sex, old or young, no matter what the state of their health, to take the Cross, and then allowed them to buy themselves out next day, or even on the spot.[3] An unpleasant case of trickery is reported whereby Mr. Berard obtained twenty-six marks from the executors of one Robert de Haya by falsely insisting that he had taken the Cross.[4] Even the emperor wrote accusingly in 1246, because Richard 'appeared to be coalescing with the papal party to the ruin of the English kingdom and the detriment of the Empire, and because he had collected money with papal permission from the crusaders'.[5] To Matthew Paris the two topics — the *pecunia de redemptione votorum* and Richard's change of policy are closely connected, and the evidence of the documents bears out this view, for Richard was violently anti-papal at the March parliament of 1246 and vigorously pro-papal in July. Between the two dates Innocent's grant to him arrived. The facility with which Henry III yielded is a measure of his increasing dependence on his brother's advice.

Thus Richard of Cornwall had in 1244 blocked (we may suppose) the baronial scheme of reform and made a treaty with the Scots; in 1245 he had financed the Welsh expedition; in 1246 he secured a reorientation of English foreign policy; and now in 1247 he was to acquire control over the whole currency of the realm.

[1] Notes in the *Additamenta* to *Mat. Par.* (vi, 135, 635) show that in 1247 Richard thus received £25 from St. Albans and £600 from an unnamed archdeaconry.
[2] *Mat. Par.*, vi, 117, cf. 135. See also Berger, *Reg. Inn. IV*, no. 3523, for a confirmation of December 31st, 1247. Richard's envoy at Rome at this time was brother Ralph, a Trinitarian (Berger, *op. cit.*, no. 1967—Bliss, i, 227).
[3] *Mat. Par.*, v, 73-4 (1249), 146 (1250).
[4] *Ann. Dunst.*, 172 (1247).
[5] *Mat. Par.*, iv, 577-8, cf. 630, 636. Richard was not alone in making money out of would-be or pseudo-crusaders. William Longespee collected 1,000 marks, and another noble, not named, employed the same method (*ibid.*, 630). The relation in which their privileges stood to those of Richard is not at all clear.

CHAPTER FOUR

FINANCE, RECOINAGE, AND THE JEWS

BY 1247 Richard of Cornwall had made himself indispensable to Henry III, both politically and financially. He had already rescued his brother from more than one predicament, and in spite of their periodical disagreements, had obtained the reputation of a man without whom any really important business could not be transacted. He was in addition a man of reputedly boundless wealth, now powerful enough to acquire control of the currency. This he did by providing the necessary capital, and by undertaking to farm the Mint for twelve years, at the same time reforming the coinage — a step which had not been taken since Henry II's day. The scale on which the recoinage took place was only matched, in later centuries, by the reforms of Henry VIII, Elizabeth, and William III. Like Elizabeth and William (or rather Sir Isaac Newton, the then Master of the Mint), Richard made a profit. But if the available figures are even approximately reliable, his profit vastly exceeded theirs. He not only provided the cash to start this financial operation, the greatest of its kind in this century, but he made all the rules and regulations for the Mint, and was present at the first recorded trial of the pyx in March 1248. He was not only allowed half the profits, but before any profits were declared he was to receive back new coins for all the old ones he had provided. A quarter of a century earlier the Mint had been farmed for 500 marks a year:[1] Richard showed how it could be made to yield, at any rate for a good many years, far more than this. The recoinage of 1247-1248 is therefore worthy of considerable attention.

By 1247 the coinage of England had been seriously debased by clipping. This was ascribed to the Jews, the Flemings, and the 'Caorsins'. Even the legend around the coin was clipped, so that when men came to change old money for new they received barely twenty shillings for thirty which they had brought.[2] The idea of

---

[1] *Pat. Rolls* (1216-1225), index *s.v.* Mint.

[2] *Mat. Par.*, iv, 632; v, 15-18; *Lib. de Ant. Leg.*, 13. Neither Matthew's *Exschambium enim paucis civitatibus exercebatur*, nor Wykes's (pp. 96-7) *Non solum in maioribus civitatibus ut assolet sed et in universis oppidis per regnum*, is quite accurate. The list of mints given in the *Red Book of the Exchequer*, App. B., for 1248, with the names of the officials in each case, is as follows:

calling in the old money and starting afresh was a measure of out-standing importance, not attempted since 1180. That it could be carried through so smoothly was due in part to the fact that the pound sterling, the mark, and even the shilling were still only units of account: the only English coins were the silver penny and half-penny.[1]

The agreement between Richard and the king is dated June 13th, 1247, but the matter had been decided upon at a general parliament held at Oxford on April 15th. This agreement was varied in detail from time to time, but fundamentally it remained the same. Richard was to share the profits of the farm of the Mint (*moneta*) and ex-change of money (*cambitio*) equally with the king, and to cause new money to be made in the king's name. He was to receive one new mark for every old mark of silver supplied by him — he made an initial loan of 10,000 marks — before the profits were calculated. He was also to have complete control of the operations: all 'com-pacts, rules, or covenants' which he saw fit to make touching the Mint were to be observed by the king.[2] On July 27th the original contract was amplified to cover England, Ireland, and Wales for seven years from November 1st, 1247, and again by a patent of the same date extended to twelve years.[3]

From about 1180 there had been a tendency to concentrate the work of the Mint at London. The coin was manufactured under the superintendence of a Master, who was under contract to the king, and a Warden, whose most important function was to collect the seigniorage or farm due to the king. The other chief officers were the Assay Master, responsible to the king for the fineness of the coin, and the *Cuneator*, who superintended the engravers of the dies, which were made in London and thence circulated to other mints. Under the Master were the Moneyers whose names appear

---

Canterbury, London, St. Edmundsbury, Bristol, Carlisle, York, Gloucester, Hereford, Ilchester, Lincoln, Newcastle, Northampton, Norwich, Oxford, Shrewsbury, Wilton, Winchester, Exeter, and Wallingford. To these nineteen Ruding, *Annals of the Coinage* (1819), ii, 68, adds Bideford, Taunton, Durham, and perhaps Hadley. Matthew also gives the charge for exchanging silver as 13d. in the pound, but it was 16d. or 10d. according to whether the king's farm (which he does not mention) was included or not. He is incomplete about the term of the contract and assigns to the king, who took half the profits, only a third.

[1] In 1222 it had been ordered that only round halfpennies and farthings should circulate (*R.Lit.Cl.*, i, 516).

[2] *C.P.R.*, 503.

[3] *Ibid.*, 505, 511. Repayment of the 10,000 marks was to be made at the rate of 2,000 marks at Easter and 2,000 at Michaelmas, and so on, being a first charge on Exchequer receipts with no cavilling (e.g. by papal indulgences) on the part of the king. The Irish patent was re-granted for twelve years on May 8th, 1251 (*C.P.R.*, 94).

on the coins. The ordinance of March 11th, 1248, is quite explicit in granting 10d. in the pound to them and claiming 6d. in the pound as the king's farm.

The rules inspired by Richard of Cornwall set into operation seventeen local mints each with four moneyers, four keepers of the dies, two goldsmiths (assayers), and a clerk. They were supplied from London with dies and a sufficiency of new coin to start business with.[1] In spite of the magnitude of the task the work proceeded rapidly. The recoinage was not delayed by Richard's mission to France.[2] He was sent to negotiate with Louis IX for the surrender of Normandy, and he returned on October 28th, 1247, with his son Henry, after a long and friendly conference with Louis, but having obtained no satisfaction at all over Normandy. After his interview he had visited the shrine of St. Edmund at Pontigny, where he presented a collar encrusted with jewels of great value. As he had been unable to be present at the actual translation on June 7th he made up for his absence by paying for a fourth part of the shrine. His subsequent devotion to the saint cured him of a mysterious illness that had brought him to the point of death.[3]

A few days after his return the new coinage was being made according to plan, and by the end of the year another warning was issued concerning the limited validity of clipped money.[4]

The right to coin ran from November 1247 to November 1259. London and Bedford were getting their new pennies in November 1247 and Winchester about the New Year.[5] There was naturally a lag in the north. It was not until July 1248 that the citizens of York were told to elect a moneyer, keeper of the assay, and keeper of the dies. They were officials of the archbishop (who took his profit), appointed by the city, and sworn to the king.[6] On March 11th,

[1] These officials were elected by a jury of twenty-four citizens. The writs to Norwich, Exeter, Winchester, Lincoln, and Northampton are in *Cl. R.*, 107, dated February 26th, 1248.

[2] *Cal. Lib. R.*, 141 (September 20th, 1247), the Sheriff of Kent to find transport for Richard, the Bishop of Hereford, and Ralph Fitz-Nicholas. Pierre d'Aigueblanche was full of these silly schemes. Ralph Fitz-Nicholas, a Steward of the household, was the professional diplomat of the party.

[3] *Mat. Par.*, iv, 632, 645-6, cf. v, 94.

[4] *Cl. R.*, 102, cf. *Mat. Par. Addit.*, 150-1, for another writ dated November 17th, 1248.

[5] *Ann. Wint.*, 91, states that the new coinage was made at Winchester after January 13th, 1248; *Ann. Dunst.*, 175, says it became current about November 11th, 1247; *Lib. de Ant. Leg.* says it began to be current immediately after All Saints, 1247. We do not know what arrangements were made for exchanging it until the ordinance of March 1248. An order for a new die to be delivered to St. Edmund's is dated December 6th, 1247 (*Cl. R.*, 12, 101, 102).

[6] *C.P.R.*, 22.

1248, the first recorded trial of the pyx was made,[1] to test by assay the fineness of the new coin. The procedure was thus: twelve citizens of London, headed by the mayor and sheriffs, together with twelve goldsmiths, in the presence of the king, Earl Richard, the Treasurer, William Hardel (Warden of the Exchange of London and Canterbury),[2] and Ralph of Ely (Baron of the Exchequer), made an assay of the new money and the old, and as the new money fell short of the pound by 6d. only and the old money by 10d., they agreed that of every pound of the old received 6d. should be taken by the king and the earl as the farm (or seigniorage), and 10d. should go to the moneyers. Thus the vendor of old money would lose 16d. in the pound. But if the vendor thought his old money was worth more than this, he could have an assay at his own cost and peril, and pay according to the result. If he brought pure silver, he paid only the farm: if impure, he paid his 6d. plus what was lost at the fire, or he could have it purged at his own risk. In all cases the farm was the same.

The royal profit did not vary with the purity or impurity of the silver brought to the Mint, but the public lost heavily on the old coinage, as many coins had been so clipped that the legend had vanished.[3] There was no alteration in the weight or fineness of the coins. The most material difference was the extension of the 'short cross' to the edge of the coin. It was, and is, commonly said that this was done to eliminate the likelihood of clipping, but if a man would not hesitate to clip off the inscription, it seems unlikely that he would be deterred by a lengthened cross. The other new feature was the use of the word TERCI to distinguish Henry III from his predecessors.

Immediately after the trial of the pyx the officials of the mints of Norwich, Exeter, Winchester, Lincoln, and Northampton were summoned to the Exchequer in a body to be instructed in their work, and to receive £1,000 from Richard of Cornwall with which each mint was to set up business on a large scale.[4] Then in May, William Hardel was sent round the local mints with his experts to see that the work was up to the required standard, as was lately provided before the king at Windsor in Richard's presence.[5] The whole

---

[1] Described in *Oxenedes*, 291-300. A wrongly-dated transcript is in the *Red Book of the Exchequer*, iii, 1072. This is summarized and the contract recited in *C.P.R.* (1247-1258), pp. 12-13, dated April 27th, 1248.

[2] Appointed April 28th, 1248 (*C.P.R.*, 13). He was also Controller of the Wardrobe, 1244-1249.

[3] *Mat. Par.*, v, 15.   [4] *Cl. R.*, 107, Summons for March 16th, 1248.   [5] *Ibid.*, 45.

country was searched for unlicensed changers and there were some prosecutions for coining and clipping.[1] As bad money drives out good, it was found necessary to prohibit the circulation of Scottish money (or any other money except the king's) throughout England.[2]

The accounts of the successive Wardens, William Hardel (to 1249),[3] John Silvestre (1248-1252),[4] John de Somercotes (1252-1257),[5] and William of Gloucester (1257-1261)[6] among the 'foreign accounts of the Pipe Rolls, show Earl Richard's (latterly King Richard's) representative accounting side by side with them. The wardens change, but Richard's clerk, Henry de Wroxhall, is there for the whole period 1248-1261. It is a little surprising that a man in this responsible position should be completely ignored in every other context where his master is found. He is not a known member of Richard's *familia* and does not seem to have had any record of other public service.

At the first division of profits in 1252 some £5,513 from Mint and Exchange went to Richard of Cornwall.

The whole extent of Richard's profit out of this twelve-year contract as shown on the Pipe Rolls was £11,000 odd plus the profits on his original loans of 10,000 marks or more. Thus Matthew Paris's estimate of £20,000 is of the right order of magnitude. A simple calculation shows the actual amount of money minted, for £20,000 represents 6d. in the pound or $2\frac{1}{2}$ per cent of the silver minted namely £800,000. This can be checked by the figures for 1222, when the king's declared profit on an issue of £3,890 0s. 4d. was £97 9s. 2d.[7] Thus about a million pounds' worth of pennies were minted in England between 1247 and 1261.[8]

It may now be asked, how had Richard become rich enough to put down 10,000 marks in cash, with which to finance the initial exchanges and the setting-up of local mints? One answer would be that all his life he lived largely at other people's expense. Until 1227

[1] *Cl. R.*, index, *s.v.* Mint, Money.
[2] *Ibid.*, 549, dated July 8th, 1251.
[3] Hardel died before December 16th, 1249 (*Cal. Lib. R.*, 268).
[4] Appointed warden, 'of the mint throughout England', January 18th, 1249 (*C.P.R.*, 36).
[5] Appointed warden 'of the whole change of England', May 9th, 1252 (*C.P.R.*, 138).
[6] Formerly the king's goldsmith. Appointed warden of the changes throughout England on October 1st, 1257 (*C.P.R.*, 580).
[7] Ruding, *Annals of the Coinage* (ed. 1819), i, 179.
[8] To expedite the work foreign workmen 'cunning in any kind of minting and exchange of silver, were imported by Reyner of Brussels in 1247 and Jordan of Brunswick in 1248 (*C.P.R.*, 1232-1247, p. 508; 1247-1258, p. 21; *Cal. Lib. R.*, 194).

he was subsidized and had no independent household. Thereafter his income from estates[1] was continually being supplemented by special grants of one kind or another. His Crusade was financed by a papal grant of sums paid by those who took the Cross but for one reason or another could not or would not go. The later grant to him of these sums was a scandal, because he neither went, nor had, so far as is known, any intention of going to the East, and further the money was collected in an extortionate way. The friars, authorized by the pope to preach the Crusade in England, persuaded men to take the Cross, and then — for a fee — absolved them from going.[2] The profits were collected for Richard by Mr. Berard de Nympha, an Italian clerk in his pay.[3] It appears to have been in this way that the earl's financial operations of 1247-1248 were made possible.

The recoinage was apparently meant to be complete. That is, all the old coins were called in. It was the greatest measure so far undertaken for the improvement of the currency, and it was the last in which the weight and fineness of the penny suffered no appreciable diminution. Even Edward I in 1279 set 243 instead of 240 pennies to the pound. Edward, indeed, coined about as much as Richard, making about £35,000 profit in five years.[4] In this, as perhaps in other matters, Edward may have learned more from his uncle Richard than from Simon de Montfort.

Richard of Cornwall's reforms may have caused, as Matthew Paris laments, great personal hardship, but their effect upon trade, particularly foreign trade, is likely to have been good. The recoinage was a sensible, conservative, and efficient step, typical of the man who had planned it.

As the need for new coin decreased some of the local mints ceased to function. It was probably for this reason that the die was taken away from Bristol in 1250.[5] The Irish mint was ordered to cease and the dies to be sent to England in 1254, when Richard was regent.[6] He continued to keep in close touch with the work while he was in England,[7] but in May 1257 he went to Germany and stayed there for eighteen months. He had only been gone a few weeks

[1] See Appendix, p. 162.   [2] *Supra*, p. 57.
[3] *Qui clericus extiterat Ricardi* (Mat. Par., v, 707, relating Mr. Berard's death in 1258 and the discovery of a chestful of blank, sealed parchments).
[4] Devon, *Issue Rolls*, 327.   [5] *Cl. R.*, 297 (June 24th).
[6] Ibid., 13 (January 8th, 1254).
[7] When St. Edmund's claimed quittance of amercements *pro escambio monete* within the banlieue in June 1255 the case was postponed until the king had the counsel of Richard of Cornwall and the barons of the Exchequer (*Cl. R.*, 103).

when Henry III decided to try his own hand at the business of coining. As might have been expected the result was very beautiful and quite useless.

The gold penny of 1257 was struck in pursuance of a writ dated at Chester on August 16th, where Henry III was preparing the last of his ineffectual campaigns against the Welsh. This was the first gold coin since the Conquest, an imitation — though not in design — of the new Italian florin.[1] It was a remarkable advance in beauty of design and skill of execution over the silver penny, to which it stood in the ratio of twenty to one, raised in 1265 to twenty-four to one. But it was never popular, partly because it was overvalued in relation to silver, partly because — as the Londoner chronicler was aware — few people at that date had much use for a coin of so high a denomination. The mayor and aldermen of London objected to it in the king's presence at the Exchequer on these grounds, and also because it would bring down the price of gold. The king, however, was adamant.[2] After the withdrawal of this coin from circulation about 1270 there was no further issue of gold until 1344.[3] It is not unlikely that this beautiful piece of folly was struck at Henry's own instigation. An imprudence of this nature, committed as soon as Richard's back was turned, would be entirely in keeping with Henry's character. If Richard of Cornwall had anything to do with it, which is not probable, it would be his only known lapse into shaky finance.

Richard's profits from the coinage were swelled by fines for breaches of the currency regulations. Such crimes were normally a subject of inquiry at the general eyre (e.g. 1244 and 1251), but there was no eyre in or near 1248,[4] so it is unlikely that the amercements amounted to much until 1251, when special commissioners went round the whole country to investigate the conduct of the mints and exchanges and to amerce offenders.[5] The scale of these fines is shown by London's payment of 600 marks in 1254 to be quit of all

[1] A writ of October 2nd, 1251, for eighteen marks to be 'put into gold money, such as bezants or obols of Muz or other gold money' is indexed in the *Close Rolls, s.v.* Money, as if it meant that gold money was to be made. The phrase is *poni in*, which I take to mean 'to be laid out in' not 'coined into'. Obols of Muz or Musca were used for offerings at shrines and suchlike.

[2] *Lib. de Ant. Leg.*, 30.

[3] In consequence of its short life it is exceedingly rare: only a dozen or so examples are known to be extant. Possibly the foreigners liked them for export. On August 30th, 1257, William of Gloucester, the king's goldsmith, was ordered to let William de Valence have twenty-two marks of the king's new gold money in his keeping, for 220 marks 6s. 8d., that is 1,760 gold pence (*C.P.R.*, 576).

[4] H. Cam, *Oxf. Soc. and Legal Studies*, vi, 93.

[5] A formidable set of special *capitula* is in *C.P.R.* (1247-1258), pp. 114-15, cf. 141, 159.

Mr. Anthony Thompson has very kindly supplied the following description of these coins

(1) **Gold Penny or Bezant** (= 20 Silver Pennies, 1257). Weight, 45 grains. Brooke: page 112, plate XXII, note 25. *London Mint. Obverse:* King enthroned. **HENRICUS REX III.** *Reverse:* Long cross voided. Rose between 3 pellets in each angle. **WILLEM ON LUNDE.** (William, the king's goldsmith, appointed 1255).

(2) **Long Cross Penny.** Group III (1248-1250). *Bristol. Obverse:* **HENRICUS REX' III** Star ✶ at beginning of legend (before **Ib**). Facing head without sceptre (later coins sometimes have it). *Reverse:* **+ IEC OBO HISIR VST** (letters run together). Moneyer Jacob. Long voided cross with pellets in quarters.

(3) **Short Cross Penny.** Group VII (1223-1242). *Obverse:* **HENRICUS REX.** Facing head bearded, cut off at chin. Curls: 2 on each side formed of 'amulets' (O). *Reverse:* **+OSMUND ON CAN.** (Osmond, moneyer at Canterbury). Short voided cross with 4 pellets in each quarter. G. C. Brooke, *English Coins*, page 111.

such amercements.[1] It may be significant that this took place when
Richard was regent. On the occasion of another general commission
to inquire into the working of the exchange and transgressors of the
rules thereof, it is explicitly stated that half is to go to the earl.[2]
This is the background for the complaint by Matthew Paris that

> if anyone who was about to undertake a journey, or to do any
> piece of business however trifling, exchanged any money with a
> neighbour or friend, however small the sum . . . he was accused
> of having kept an exchange, to the prejudice of the king; and
> thus he was severely punished, as if he had opened a money-
> changer's shop; and Earl Richard, by this means, to the im-
> poverishment of many, amassed many thousand marks in his
> treasury.[3]

The main outlines of Richard's financial relations with his brother
during the years 1240-1272 are easily visible, far more so indeed
than his relations with the Jews. The loans to the king, though easy
enough to tabulate, are less easy to interpret, as it is not known how
far the mandates for repayment were executed, or how far raising a
new loan overlapped the repayment of an old one.[4] These loans
first became considerable in 1244 with 1,500 marks, rising to 3,000
marks in 1245, 10,000 marks in 1247, and £10,000 in 1254. The
year after this Richard refused to give any financial support either
to king or pope, and in 1256 he spent a total of 28,000 marks in
securing the votes of three of the German electors. He had clearly
built up a large cash reserve, but his wealth cannot have been anything like so great as Matthew Paris reports. The chronicler would
have us believe that Richard could have spent a hundred marks a
day for ten years out of capital, which implies a capital of 365,000
marks, and he states that Richard took a similar sum with him in
cash to Germany in 1257.[5]

Richard always insisted on first-class security. He lent on the
Mint, the Jewry, or solid gold pledges. He refused to lend to the
pope in 1255 and refused the crown of Sicily on this principle of no
advance without security.[6] When he lent to the Lord Edward or

---

[1] *Lib. de Ant. Leg.*, 21.   [2] *Cl. R.*, 481-2, dated June 28th, 1253.
[3] *Mat. Par.*, v, 629.
[4] See Appendix, p. 157. It is to be kept in mind that the silver mark, worth 13s. 4d., is
a unit of account, not a coin. The mark of gold was worth nine or ten times this.
[5] *Mat. Par.*, v, 607.   [6] *Ibid.*, 361.

F

Peter of Savoy he got the king to guarantee that the repayment of
the loan should be a first charge upon the debtor's lands if he died.
Further, the evidence as tabulated shows that except where gold is
pledged over a long period, or where fines are to be imposed for
Jewish default, there is nothing that even resembles the payment of
interest. This is very important. It would alter our whole concep-
tion of Richard's character if we found him acting as a usurer. There
was no concealment of interest in contemporary royal borrowings
from merchants, but Richard was not a merchant.[1] Thirdly, he
did not squander all his wealth in trying to conquer Germany, for
in the last years of his life he was again lending considerable sums to
Henry III, he bequeathed 8,000 marks to the Holy Land, and he
handed down his estates unimpaired to his son.

It has sometimes been assumed that Richard of Cornwall derived
his great wealth from the stannaries, but this is only part of the
truth. Richard, unlike his son, did not farm the stannaries in Devon,
and this, too, has been a source of confusion.[2] Still, the profits from
the Cornish stannaries represented the bulk of the mining royalties
behind the pewter industry, and should have meant to Richard a
sum between 1,000 and 3,000 marks a year, the equivalent of the
annual surplus in money from an earldom. This can easily be
demonstrated. The most valuable right in connection with the
stannaries was the earl's right of pre-emption.[3] The accounts printed
by Miss Midgley for 1296-1297 show a yield of at least 850 thousand-
weights. This is described as being left over from last year, and only
a small fraction of it was sold. This yield is of the same order of
magnitude as the annual yield in John's reign,[4] so it is safe to assume
that the 850 thousand-weights is not a freak, but represents the bulk
of one year's output, which for some reason or other had not been

[1] Ramsay, *Dawn of the Constitution*, 151, is very misleading in stating that Richard received
8,000 marks in return for 5,000 lent in 1255. The extra 3,000 are explicitly stated to be in part
repayment of an earlier loan.
[2] Pauli, cited by Bappert, p. 61, stated that Richard's financial position was strengthened
[about 1262] by the discovery of new mines in Devon. This appears to be a misunderstanding
of a patent committing to Adam de Grenville and John Silvestre 'all the king's mines of gold,
silver, copper, lead and all kinds of metals in the county of Devon, lately found . . .' (*C.P.R.*,
256, April 25th, 1263). So far from improving Richard's position, this, like the discovery of
'pure and abundant tin' in Germany in 1241, could only weaken it. Matthew Paris (iv, 151)
says that this latter discovery reduced the price of tin, which had hitherto been found only in
Cornwall. This is not quite accurate, as Henry of Huntingdon (*c.* 1150) says that it was
imported from Germany, and it is mentioned as an import in Ælfric's *Colloquies* (see Cunning-
ham, *Econ. Hist.*, i, 126, 184).
[3] Midgley, vol. i, pp. xxiv-xxix, 249.
[4] H. C. Darby, *An Historical Geography of England before 1800*, pp. 227-8.

sold. Now in 1296-1297 Edmund of Cornwall was buying tin at three marks and selling it at seven marks. At that time he bought and sold so little that the profit of four marks a thousand-weight amounted only to £200-£300, but from this the potential profit on an annual output of 1,000 thousand-weights is thus of the order of £2,000. This fits reasonably well with the fact that the Cornish stanneries were in 1220 farmed for 1,000 marks a year.[1]

From considering Richard of Cornwall's abnormal sources of income it is natural to turn to his relations with the merchants. The merchants concerned come from the Rhineland and Northern Germany, never farther south, and they are not known to have been a source of profit to Richard. Except for one or two small matters his relations with them arose out of his position as King of the Romans and have therefore a political importance.

This political interest is immediately apparent in 1257. A week before Richard's coronation the burgesses of Lübeck received protection at his instigation. This patent for seven years was duplicated for Brunswick and Denmark, and was made conditional upon their loyalty to Richard.[2] In 1260 he procured a confirmation of privileges for the merchants who had the house in London 'commonly called the Gildhall of the Teutons'.[3] On May 16th, 1258, the citizens of Groningen received freedom from arrest in England, except in certain cases, at Richard's request,[4] and on April 26th, 1261, the merchants of Brabant received protection for three years, again at Richard's request.[5]

The merchants, too, were politically minded enough to worship the rising sun. When the merchants of Hamburg and Lübeck were allowed to have a Hanse throughout England in 1266, it was no longer to Richard that they turned. Their privileges were granted at the request of Albert, Duke of Brunswick, and in 1267 confirmed for as long as they should be in the dominion and power of the said duke.[6] Albert had held the Archbishop of Mainz in prison at the time of Richard's election, but he recognized Richard as king, and he married the queen's niece, the Marquis of Montferrat's daughter, with a marriage-portion of £1,000 provided by Henry III. However, in 1271 Richard's position in Germany was much better than it had been in 1266-1267, and in the licences to export wool from England at that time he is one of the three kings whose merchants receive

[1] G. R. Lewis, *The Stannaries*, 136.
[2] *C.P.R.*, 553, dated May 11th, 1257; cf. Hakluyt's *Voyages* (Everyman ed.), i, 111.
[3] *C.P.R.*, 77=*Foed.*, 398.   [4] BF., 11,811, citing *Hans. Urkb.*, i, 178.
[5] *C.P.R.*, 149.   [6] *Ibid.*, 5, 10, 23.

protection — England, France, and Germany. The total number of sacks to be exported by merchants described as 'his' is then 4,892, or perhaps a quarter of the total. There are on the Patent Roll three lists of English and foreign merchants licensed to export wool in 1271,[1] which may be analysed as (i) licences till May 24th, issued March–May, for [resident] merchants who have found resident pledges that they will not export wool to Flanders, (ii) licences till November 1st, issued July–October, for [resident] merchants, the sanction being forfeiture of their goods, (iii) licences for [non-resident] merchants, the sanction being the loss of the right to import. Most of Richard's merchants are of course in the third category. They come chiefly from Cambrai, Malines, Louvain, Soëst, Lübeck, and Cologne, but Dortmund, Liége, Antwerp, Brussels, Aachen, Dinant, Littelseth, Nymwegen, and Middleburg are also mentioned.

The question arises what is meant by 'his' merchants. In the above instances 'his' merchants are merely his lawful subjects. He had also merchants, some of the above no doubt, who were 'his' because he patronized them — court merchants 'by appointment'. It was customary for important people to procure protection and privileges for 'their' merchants.[2] Some great men, such as the Count of Aumale about 1220 and the Earl of Chester in 1230, went further and granted their own passports to their merchants.[3] Richard had also 'his' merchants, in a more intimate sense, who stood in some contractual relation to him, dealers in corn and other merchandise. Two of them from Hamburg brought a corn-ship to England and had it stolen by the men of Dunwich.[4] Before he became King of the Romans he had as Earl of Poitou and Cornwall in 1243 'his' merchant Bartholomew de Chaumund who brought corn to Cornwall in the earl's ship.[5]

From a general review of the evidence it seems legitimate to deduce that Richard of Cornwall was a conservative financier. He had come to maturity at a time when the Jews, in spite of the competition of the Caorsins and the Italians, were still the most important moneylenders and bankers in the country, and from at least 1231 he showed them favour, and at certain crises upheld their cause. It is remarkable that a man of Richard's financial capacity should

---

[1] *C.P.R.*, 553, 558, 593 in the order (ii), (iii), (i).
[2] e.g., the Duke of Brunswick, *supra*; Waleran Teutonicus in 1225, *Pat. R.*, 40, 46; Margaret, Queen of Scotland, had her merchant of Douai, *C.P.R.* (1266–1272), p. 548.
[3] L. F. Salzman, *English Trade in the Middle Ages*, 92–3.
[4] *C.P.R.* (1258–1266), p. 103.   [5] *Ibid.*, 720.

not have employed, so far as we know, the Italian merchants in any of his affairs, for they were destined, even in his lifetime, to supplant the Jews as the bankers of the king and everyone else of any standing. Richard, however, clung to the Jews. His picturesque and manifold relations with them became a source of profit to him, and this he achieved without losing their goodwill.

In 1235 it was granted to Richard that the Jews at Berkhampstead, who had apparently settled there without permission, might remain with their chirographer's chest.[1] This was probably a recognition of Richard's already close acquaintance with Abraham of Berkhampstead, one of the richest Jews in the country, who had been specially favoured by him since 1231. In 1242 the earl was permitted to transfer the Jews and their chest to Wallingford,[2] perhaps because he had spent great sums on the castle and it would therefore be a safer place in the event, then looming on the horizon, of civil disturbance.[3] Before the transfer, the whole Jewry of England had in 1237 granted him 3,000 marks towards the expenses of his crusade.[4]

Abraham of Berkhampstead was not Richard's personal Jew during these years, but in 1249 when he was in trouble with the crown, the Justices of the Jews were ordered to let him alone until the king had conferred with Richard.[5] His chattels were confiscated in 1250, but in 1251 he was allowed to keep 'the residue' at Richard's instance.[6] In 1254 he played into the earl's hands in some way. The story given by Matthew Paris is that he bought a picture of the Virgin and Child and so placed it in his house that it would, as nature took its way, be desecrated from time to time. When his wife Floria refused to imitate him and cleaned the picture, he suffocated her. He was therefore imprisoned in the Tower. At his offer to betray all the other Jews in England to Richard, the community of Jews offered the earl 1,000 marks to have him kept in prison. Richard continued to support him and he was allowed to make his peace with the king for a fine of 700 marks.[7] In the same year, 1255, Richard intervened to stop the execution of Jews following upon the ritual murder of St. Hugh of Lincoln. Eighteen were put to

---

[1] *Cl. R.*, 46.

[2] It is likely that from this time until 1272 Wallingford was the administrative centre, rather than Berkhampstead, of Richard's estates.

[3] *Ibid.*, 393.　　　[4] *Ibid.*, 410; *C.P.R.*, 173 (January 17th, 1237).　　　[5] *Ibid.*, 235.

[6] *Ibid.*, 284, 556.

[7] *Mat. Par.*, v, 114-15. Paris, insinuating a scandal, says that Abraham was at Wallingford and Berkhampstead as one of Richard's household more than he should have been, and that his wife was an attractive lady.

death at Christmas 1255, but twenty-one others were released at Richard's instance in May 1256.[1]

Concurrently with these sordid happenings, or perhaps to some extent as a sequel, Abraham of Berkhampstead, now described as Richard's Jew, was granted to him bodily, and at the same time a chirographer's chest at Wallingford, its keys kept by two Christians and two Jews of Oxford, was granted to him. A list of the debts due to Abraham, amounting to about £1,800, was compiled, and these were to be collected to Richard's use.[2] It was in this year that Richard lent the government 5,000 marks on the security of the whole Jewry. The Jews realized their position so keenly — they were being bled to death — that, if Matthew Paris is right, Elias le Eveske, their *pontifex*, asked permission for them to leave the country. This was refused.[3] Two years later this Elias, who had been arch-presbyter since 1243, committed a great trespass against Richard, now King of Almain, by delivering debts to him and afterwards receiving the money to his own use.[4] He was deposed and Cresse and Hagin his brother on behalf of the community of Jews paid a fine of three marks of gold so that he should never recover the priest-hood and that the Jews should in future elect their own priest and present him to the king for approbation.[5]

Before he left for Germany, Richard settled with the government (December 7th, 1256) for the Jewry committed to him.[6] He then appointed Cresse and Hagin as his attorneys in charge of his Jewish interests.[7] They may have done him 'good service in furthering his candidature' in Germany: this is an intriguing possibility, but the evidence is lacking.[8]

[1] *Ann. Burt.*, 340-8, 371; *Mat. Par.*, v, 552.

[2] *C.P.R.*, 393, 396, 403; *Cl. R.*, 170-2, cf. 203-4 for Abraham's son Deudon' who tried to escape with some of the money.

[3] *Foed.*, 315, 316; *Mat. Par.*, v, 488; *Hist. Angl.*, iii, 334. The history of the loan is in *C.P.R.*, 439-40, 464, and Abraham's subsequent activities are noted by C. Roth, *A History of the Jews in England*, 272 and refs. Dr. Roth points out that Elias le Eveske is not identical, though often confused, with the subject of his paper on 'Elijah of London, the most illustrious English Jew of the Middle Ages' in *Trans. Jewish Hist. Soc.*, vol. xv.

[4] *C.P.R.*, 564 (June 28th, 1257).

[5] Madox, *History of the Exchequer* (ed. 1711), 177. The confusion mentioned in note 3 above was possibly started by Madox who took *Cresse et Haginus frater ejusdem Judaei* to mean 'Cresse and Hagin brother of the same Jew [Elias]' but it is an ambiguous way of saying 'Cresse and Hagin his brother, Jews'. Cresse and Hagin were brothers of the 'good' Elias, and Hagin became the next archpresbyter.

[6] *Cl. R.*, 14.

[7] *Cl. R.*, 70-1 = *Foed.*, i, 365.

[8] The quotation is from *D.N.B.*, *s.v.* Richard of Cornwall, p. 170, but the references there given are not relevant to the problem. The first is to Cresse and Hagin (as note 3), the second has nothing to do with the Jews.

By 1256 Richard had attained a position of unexampled importance in English financial and political matters. Partly through the redemption of crusading vows, partly through the recoinage, and partly through his dealings with the Jews, he had amassed a large fortune. Politically his advice was almost always sought in matters of importance. He was at the peak of his power and reputation, ready to turn his attention to the acquisition of a foreign crown.

CHAPTER FIVE

POLITICS AND THE REGENCY
(1247-1256)

WHILE Richard of Cornwall was busy with the recoinage of 1247-1248 little is heard of his political activity. Even his whereabouts are for the most part unknown, though he was much at court. In 1247 he was at London on January 19th,[1] at Oxford in April,[2] and spent the autumn on the futile embassy to France.[3] Though present at the February parliament in 1248, when the demand for three responsible ministers was first put forward, he is not known to have been at all active. But he had enabled Henry to laugh at such demands for the moment by providing him with a small fortune from the profits of the Mint. At the beginning of May he was with the court at Windsor, arranging for an ordinance concerning the Mint which was made in his presence there,[4] and at the end of July Henry III stayed with him at Risborough.[5] On October 13th, connected with the Translation of St. Edward, he was at Westminster for the usual celebrations, but left the court to spend Christmas at Wallingford, returning to London for his birthday and the other feast, the deposition of St. Edward, on January 5th, 1249.[6] To these celebrations of St. Edward, of which Henry III was passionately fond, the magnates were specially summoned. Their importance had been increased in 1247 by a phial of our Lord's blood sent to Henry from the Holy Land. That year the king carried it himself with the utmost devotion, on foot and in humble dress, in procession from St. Paul's to Westminster, the first Corpus Christi procession in England, and ordered Matthew Paris to write the account which has come down to us.[7]

The next gleam of light upon Richard's behaviour issues from his refusal to attend the Easter parliament of 1249. He retired, says Matthew Paris, to a distant part of Cornwall *as if on business*, and the

---

[1] *Cal. Ch. R.*, ii, 378.   [2] Wykes, 96-7.   [3] *Supra*, p. 60.
[4] *Cl. R.*, 45, dated May 5th and citing the ordinance lately made at Windsor. Henry III had been there since April 20th.
[5] *Ibid.*, 71.
[6] *Mat. Par.*, v, 5 ff., 28-9, 47-8.
[7] *Ibid.*, iv, 641. See further *infra*, p. 174, for the cult and the Blood of Hailes.

whole work of the parliament was nullified by his absence.[1] The reason for Richard's absence and the truth of his side of the story can happily be verified. He wrote a letter, rather mysterious because now mutilated, appearing to say that Henry was urging him to behave dishonourably by breaking his private engagements. The letter is dated April 10th at Risborough.[2] Henry's attitude seems a little ungenerous, as Richard had very recently lent him 5,000 marks,[3] and the substantial truth of Richard's excuse is shown by the survival of a deed executed in his presence at Launceston during the Easter Term, 1249.[4] It is possible that this coolness had arisen out of a renewed sense of grievance on Richard's part over his loss of Gascony, which was formally granted to Edward, now ten years old in September of this year.[5]

Henry's annoyance with Richard did not last. There was important work to be done abroad and Richard was obviously the man to undertake it. Early in March 1250 he led an embassy to France, nominally to renew the truce. On March 3rd, Philip of Eye received letters of protection as one who had gone to France with Earl Richard.[6] On March 5th Richard and Peter of Savoy were given power to renew the truce with France.[7] On March 8th the French government was notified that they were accredited agents.[8] When he did set out, on an unknown date, Richard went with a retinue of unusual magnificence. With him went Gloucester, Leicester, Hastings, Thurkilby, Grossetête, the Bishops of London and Worcester, Sanchia, and Richard's son Henry, accompanied by forty knights.[9] Meanwhile on March 6th Henry III took the Cross with great ceremony and quite obviously with no intention of going abroad. Richard reached Lyons, where Innocent IV was holding his court, on April 6th. The whole Curia came forth to meet him and on the same day he dined with the pope. The long and secret conferences which they are reported to have had are explained by the issue on April 11th of the bull granting to Henry III a Crusading Tenth of

[1] *Mat. Par.*, v, 73.

[2] *R. L.*, ii, 106-7, where it is wrongly dated '?1255'. *D.N.B.*, *s.v.* Richard of Cornwall, has 1247, but this is also impossible.

[3] March 12th. See Appendix, p. 157.

[4] *Hist. MSS. Comm. Rep.*, *Var. Coll.*, iv, 60. Settlement of a dispute between the city of Exeter and the dean and chapter before the itinerant justices.

[5] *Supra*, p. 48, n. 4. To retain, or regain, his goodwill Richard was given more presents than usual this year, including judicial amercements in five counties in settlement of his loans (*Cl. R.*, 164, 174, 254, 285).

[6] *C.P.R.*, 1247-1258, p. 61.   [7] *Ibid.*, 62=*Foed.*, i, 272.   [8] *R. L.*, ii, 59.

[9] *Mat. Par.*, v, 96-7, 117-18.

clerical revenues for three years. This did not prevent rumours that
the pope, knowing Richard to be adroit and rich, wanted to use him
against the Greeks, or that he had a design of taking up residence in
England, or that he had offered Richard the Sicilian throne.[1]
Richard returned to England on April 26th, and next day there was
a gathering of crusaders at Bermondsey, equipped and ready to
start at midsummer, but Henry III with papal support forbade them,
and had the coasts guarded to prevent them from sailing.[2] The
momentous bull of 1250 marks an epoch in the reign of Henry III,
for it was to involve a much more complete subservience to the
papacy than John had ever contemplated. It set the seal on that close
and almost fatal alliance to which Henry III was by upbringing and
temperament inclined.

As Richard grows older and shrewder his political attitude becomes more and more difficult to define. He grew more magnificent — he could afford it — and never cast aside his ambition to
become an independent potentate. He was entitled to hope, until
the birth of the Lord Edward in 1239, for the succession to a crown
to which he was heir presumptive; he probably continued to toy with
the idea of a principality in southern France until 1243, and the
failure of this project rankled for years.[3] It has been said that his
political attitude was still in doubt in 1250,[4] and this is a natural
conclusion from the evidence of his administrative activity. For in
spite of his betrayal of baronial hopes in 1238, and his doubtful behaviour in 1249, he was, almost to the day of his death, repeatedly
called in to arbitrate between bitterly opposed factions, of which
the crown was not infrequently one. He appears, indeed, to have
had at all times an unbounded confidence in his powers as a mediator.
He was prepared to reconcile the pope with the emperor, or to persuade the French to give up Normandy.

When he came home from France in April 1250 Richard occupied
himself similarly in matters of domestic interest. Five important cases
(1250-1252) are recorded, including that already mentioned of
Abraham of Berkhampstead. In 1250 the earl, with Simon de

---

[1] *Mat. Par.*, v, 347.

[2] *Ibid.*, 102, 110, 134. On his way home Richard made a second pilgrimage to the shrine
of St. Edmund at Pontigny and then returned by St. Denis, where he concluded the purchase
of Deerhurst Priory in Gloucestershire. The monks, says *Mat. Par.* (v, 112), were expelled
because Richard proposed to build a castle on the site to guard the passage of the Severn. This
remarkable transaction never took full effect: the priory was not dissolved until 1540 (*V.C.H.
Gloucs.*, i, 103).

[3] *Mat. Par.*, v, 366.   [4] *D.N.B.*, *s.v.* Richard of Cornwall.

Montfort, mediated between the Londoners and the Abbot of Westminster on behalf of the citizens, who were angered at the unheard-of
privileges granted to the abbey by Henry III. The Londoners had a
real grievance because the king had granted the abbey a new fair,
during which not only all shops and stalls in London were to be
closed, but all other fairs throughout England, thus causing considerable dislocation of trade. But the matter seems to have been
fought out on other, purely legal, grounds, and a settlement was not
reached until the king had taken the city into his hands.[1] Some time
in 1251 Richard acted as arbiter with John Mansel between the
abbot and the convent of Westminster, because the abbot would not
agree to the division of lands made between his predecessor and the
convent. By the award of August 15th, 1252, the abbot lost three
manors, and this probably pleased the king, who loved the abbey
even better than he did the abbot.[2]

In February 1251 Henry of Bath, the chief judge, was accused of
bribery and corruption. Earl Richard intervened on his behalf and
he was let off with a fine of 2,000 marks.[3] He was formally forgiven
on July 8th, but not fully restored to favour until 1253, when Richard
was regent.[4] One reason for this was perhaps that Henry of Bath's
wife was a Basset. Philip Basset, with whom Richard was always
friendly, also helped in this case, and in 1257, when Richard became
King of the Romans, it was Fulk Basset, Bishop of London, whom
he left in charge of his estates.

The next occasion on which Richard is known to have intervened
in politics was perhaps the last time that he publicly supported Simon
de Montfort. The two men, although so utterly dissimilar in character, worked together in harmony — in spite of Richard's short-lived
anger at Simon's marriage with his sister — until Simon finally took
his stand against the king. On January 4th, 1252, Richard was
appointed an arbiter, with others, to determine the amount due to
Simon for his expenses as the king's Lieutenant in Gascony since 1248.[5]
It may have been Richard's support of Simon on this occasion that
led to the reiteration of the Lord Edward's right to Gascony on
April 28th.[6] This so irritated Richard that he left the court, and

[1] *Mat. Par.*, v, 28-9, 128; *Lib. de Ant. Leg.*, 16-17; *C.P.R.*, 65; *V.C.H. London*, i, 440.
[2] *Mat. Par.*, v, 239, 303-4.
[3] *Ibid.*, 213-15, 224, 240.
[4] Foss, *Judges*, ii, 223-7.
[5] *R. L.*, ii, 68.
[6] *Cal. Ch. R.*, i, 386, 389; *C.P.R.*, 141; *Mat. Par.*, v, 113-14.

had to be loaded with gifts throughout the summer.[1] Unconnected with these territorial privileges, there came in Lent, from another quarter, a present of the first buffaloes seen in England.[2]

At this time Richard must have had his Cistercian foundation of Hailes, a daughter house of Beaulieu, much in mind. The site had been granted to him by the king in 1245,[3] to enable him to fulfil a vow made when he was in peril of the sea on his way home from Gascony in 1243. The work had proceeded far enough by 1246 for the monks to enter their church (August 15th), which with the other buildings had cost the earl 8,000 to 10,000 marks. On November 9th, 1251, the church was dedicated by Walter de Cantilupe, Bishop of Worcester, assisted by thirteen other bishops, in the presence of the whole court. Richard said to Matthew Paris afterwards: 'Would to God that all I have spent on Wallingford castle had been spent as wisely.'[4] After its partial destruction by fire in 1271 it was rebuilt by Edmund of Cornwall, who inherited all his father's zeal for religious foundations. The family attachment to this house is shown by the fact that Richard, Sanchia, Henry, and later Edmund of Cornwall were all buried there.

By now the baronage, though usually prepared to accept Richard as an arbiter, can hardly have retained any hope that he would throw himself wholeheartedly into their cause. They still awaited a leader. The hopes aroused by Richard Marshal in 1233 and Richard of Cornwall in 1238 may momentarily have flickered round Roger Bigod in 1245, when he led the English deputation to the council of Lyons, but they were soon extinguished. In 1253 the death of Grossetête, who in spite of his immense learning and great gifts had no known political programme, left the clergy as leaderless as the baronage. By a strict attention to business and a reasonable amount

---

[1] The gifts were: Oakham, co. Rutl. (May 16th, *Cl. R.*, 92), with weekly market and yearly fair (June 5th, *Cal. Ch. R.*, i, 392); Lechlade, co. Gloucs. (May 22, *Cl. R.*, 95). The two together were worth over £160 a year, but were to be part of Sanchia's marriage settlement, and thus only payment of what was already due. He also received free warren throughout his demesne in England and a weekly market at Watlington, co. Oxon. (June 20th, *Cal. Ch. R.*, i, 393), the right of tallaging all his 'ancient demesne' manors (June 20th, *Cl. R.*, 110), a herd of deer from Wychwood Forest (June 1st, 5th, *Cl. R.*, 99, 101), and 33 oaks for building his houses at Showell, near Swerford, co. Oxon (August 11th, *C.P.R.*, 138, 139).

[2] *Mat. Par.*: v, 275. 'Est autem bubulus genus jumenti bovi consimile, ad onera portanda vel trahenda aptissimum cocodrillo inimicissimum.'

[3] *Cal. Ch. R.*, i. 288. See *Cl. R.*, 286, 329, 404 for gifts towards the construction of the abbey.

[4] Wykes, 102–3; *Mat. Par.*, v, 262; *Theok.*, 146; *V.C.H. Gloucs.*, ii, 96. *Mat. Par.* gives two accounts of the dedication of Beaulieu, under 1246 (iv, 562, 569) and 1249 (v, 86). The former, which is the correct date (*Ann. Wav.*, 337; Wykes and Oseney, 34), says that Richard took thirteen monks for Hailes: under 1249 he says 20 monks and 30 lay brethren.

of support for Simon de Montfort in Gascony Henry might yet have saved himself from the worst effects of his folly. He chose, however, to listen to his foreign advisers and to quarrel with de Montfort. By 1252 the breach between the two had become almost irreconcilable and Henry had decided to replace Simon in Gascony by going there in person.

In preparation for a regency during the king's absence, a number of grants were made to Richard, including the right to build a stone castle at Mere in Dorset.[1] These grants may be regarded as reasonable compensation for the 2,000 marks which Richard lent to Henry on the security of the crown jewels. But the earl was not specifically appointed regent. On June 22nd the Great Seal was demised to the queen, under the king's privy seal, with the seals of Richard, and certain others of the council.[2] On July 7th Queen Eleanor was formally appointed to keep and govern the realm of England, with the lands of Wales and Ireland, with the counsel of Richard.[3] They had power to remove sheriffs and bailiffs, but not castellans. There was uncertainty about their right to appoint to benefices.[4] As the Queen was pregnant (she had a daughter, Katharine, in November) the burden of the regency fell upon Richard.[5] There was not much formal correspondence between the two halves of the Council in Gascony and England, at any rate under the Great Seal. The mention of warrants for the use of the Seal is very marked in the documents emanating from England, as it was under the baronial councils of 1258 and 1264-1265. The regency council was, however, not entirely independent of the king. It is on record that he revoked at least one of their judgments.[6]

Henry III had not been many months in Gascony before he found it necessary to send home for reinforcements, thus from one point of view justifying Simon de Montfort's recriminations. In December 1253 he asked for two hundred sergeants to be sent immediately,

[1] *C.P.R.*, 208; *Cl. R.*, 386. Richard was allowed to take an aid for knighting his eldest son of 40s. on the fee (*C.P.R.*, 204), and Sanchia was given wardships to the amount of £80 a year (*ibid.*, 208).

[2] *C.P.R.*, 200.

[3] *Ibid.*, 209. Richard was at Wallingford, August 1st, 1253, with Roger Thurkilby, Henry of Bath, and other friends (charter to Okebourne Priory, co. Wilts., in *Mon. Ang.*, old ed., i, 583).

[4] *C.P.R.*, 214, cf. 206. Subsequent letters are made *coram consilio ipsius regis in Anglia* and are tested by the queen or *per reginam et comitem*. See *Cl. R.*, 408 *ff*. Letters by Richard and the queen together run till the end of May 1254, thereafter they are by Richard alone. See *Excerpta e Rot. Fin.*, ii, 170-200.

[5] *R. L.*, ii, 99; *Mat. Par.*, v, 415.

[6] *Mat. Par.*, v, 443, a case between an itinerant justice and St. Albans.

and he also asked for financial support.[1] This led the regency to summon (on December 27th) a parliament of magnates, lay and ecclesiastical, for January 27th, 1254,[2] at which Roger Bigod and Gilbert Segrave put the king's case — that he was in imminent danger of attack from Castile. Richard of Cornwall took the lead by promising three hundred knights *per annum*, but shrewdly added *si vera sunt que dicuntur*.[3] At a time when the 'quota' system of knight-service was in vogue, this may well sound preposterous. If he had been able to find his knights and had paid them an average wage of 3s. a day — it might have been as low as 2s. or as much as 4s. — this venture would have cost him £15,750 a year. The bishops answered for themselves that they would make a grant if the king was attacked by the King of Castile, and the earls and barons adopted the same attitude. The bishops had said that they could not speak for the lower clergy: the barons that they could not answer for their tenantry. So no money was forthcoming from this source, partly because it had become common knowledge from Simon de Montfort's first-hand account of what was happening in Gascony that the menace from Castile was a pure fable, and that Henry III was at that moment negotiating a marriage alliance for his son Edward with Alfonso's daughter. Richard, however, went forward with his preparations for going to Gascony himself. On January 31st he sent for ships to convey him thither after Easter.[4] He tried, apparently with little success, to obtain money from the Jews.[5] On February 5th the magnates were summoned to assemble at London three weeks after Easter, ready to go to Gascony.[6] On February 11th, taking up the line suggested by the answers received in Parliament, the regency summoned two knights from each shire to be present a week before the magnates assembled.[7] They were to be elected in

---

[1] *Cl. R.*, 294. [2] *Ibid.*, 107, 108.

[3] *Mat. Par.*, v, 423-5, 440. At some point in these deliberations Richard kept parliament waiting for three weeks, according to Matthew. The negotiations were faithfully reported to Henry in a letter from Richard and the queen dated February 14th, 1254, in which they urge that the laity (apart from the earls and barons) will not grant an aid unless the charters are published in the shires (*R. L.*, ii, 101-2).

[4] *Cl. R.*, 110. [5] *Mat. Par.*, v, 441. [6] *Cl. R.*, 111-12.

[7] Stubbs, *Select Charters*, 9th ed., pp. 365-6 = *Cl. R.*, 114. The writ itself is undated, but letters immediately preceding are either *ut supra* (= February 5th) or February 9th or 11th and the next letter after the Beds. and Bucks. writ is dated February 11th. The policy of the regency council may have been developed piecemeal — for Earl Richard was no opportunist — in this way: (1) February 5th (*Cl. R.*, 111), summons of magnates to London for three weeks after Easter, prepared to go, according to their promise, to Gascony, with 'distraint of knight-hood' on the £20 level; (2) February 11th (almost certainly (*Cl. R.*, 114)), summons of two knights from each shire for a fortnight after Easter; (3) February 25th (*Cl. R.*, 119), writ to all sheriffs for a general military summons of knights and sergeants for three weeks after Easter.

the shire court and to come *vice omnium et singulorum*. They were not explicitly given *plena potestas*,[1] so it remains uncertain whether they were delegates or representatives. Since this was the first time that the government had summoned elected members from the shires to grant a national tax, the occasion is an 'important landmark' in our constitutional history. There is a tendency nowadays to minimize the importance of any parliamentary models, but it is worth suggesting that this manœuvre was inspired by the calculating and orderly mind of Richard of Cornwall. It failed, but the underlying idea of summoning county members to Westminster had so far progressed that the precedent was in little danger of being lost. Richard had, as when he tried on his own initiative to make peace between pope and emperor, perhaps overestimated his powers of persuasion.

If Richard of Cornwall had summoned the boroughs with the knights to the Easter assembly of 1254 modern writers would have paid more attention to his action. But he was too conservative, and preferred to deal with the Jews. The publication of the Close Rolls has shown up this parliament as 'but one incident in a great national rally' arranged to coincide, in part, with the meeting of the magnates and clerical assemblies in each diocese. It was to be followed by 'a great gathering in arms',[2] but if this gathering ever took place it was a failure, for when the queen eventually went to Gascony at the end of May, only forty knights went with her. There was no longer any shadow of excuse for a large expedition after the publication of Henry's treaty with the pope accepting the Kingdom of Sicily for his son Edmund.

When the queen joined Henry III in Gascony, Richard was left as sole regent.[3] That he was not acceptable to everyone is shown by the nomination of Walter de Grey, Archbishop of York, who refused the office.[4] It seems possible that Richard was not above using the council of regency for his own ends. The case of Henry of Bath, the corrupt judge, had been settled in August 1253,[5] when Richard was not yet formally sole regent. But a clearer instance

---

[1] See J. G. Edwards, 'The *Plena potestas* of English Parliamentary Representatives', in *Essays in Medieval History presented to H. E. Salter*, p. 141. On this parliament see also Pasquet, *Origins of the House of Commons*, pp. 32-4, and Bémont, *Simon de Montfort* (trans. by E. F. Jacob), p. 121, n. 5.

[2] See Professor Powicke's review of the *Close Rolls* (1254-1256) in *E.H.R.*, xlvi, 469.

[3] Until this time he is merely one of the queen's council. See *Ann. Dunst.*, 189, and for some other points touching the regency Maxwell Lyte, *The Great Seal*, p. 168.

[4] *Mat. Par.*, v, 447.   [5] Cf. p. 75.

occurs when the city of London had obtained for 500 marks the right of presenting their Mayor to the Barons of the Exchequer. This privilege was not exercised in 1253: they presented their candidate to the queen. In 1254 the barons would not receive the city's candidate, and sent the applicants to Richard. This was unwelcome to them as they were already quarrelling with the earl over the coinage. At length they made fine with Richard for 600 marks, to be released from *omnes occasiones excambii*, and the mayor and sheriffs were confirmed.[1]

On June 18th, 1254, Richard, as sole regent, ordered 200 marks to be levied from each firm (*societas*) of those, including Caversins and Ultramontanists, who had broken the rules of the Mint.[2] These, however, are matters in which public and private interest coincide. In public matters where he had nothing but reputation to win or lose he behaved with magnificence, as in the offer of three hundred knights, and his celebration of Henry's favourite feast of St. Edward with unsurpassed magnificence. And when he allowed Sanchia to go to meet her sisters in France in 1254 great trouble was taken to provide her with a retinue not inferior to the queen's and fit to create admiration in the French.[3] There was something of the same spirit, with a touch of magnanimity, in his destruction of the 'kidels' on his estates, in accordance with the precept of Magna Carta. He was the first to do this, we are told, and he did it as regent to encourage the others,[4] because in spite of the famous confirmation of the Charters in May 1253, they were only ordered to be published in the county courts, at Richard's instigation, on March 24th, 1254.[5]

During the Gascon expedition Richard had served his brother well, and he soon received his reward. Since Henry was quite unable to pay his debts he sold all the Jews in England to Richard.[6] But when parliament was in session at Westminster, October 13th, 1255, Henry asked for a further loan, and this Richard refused. He was annoyed with Henry and reproached Pierre d'Aigueblanche, the Savoyard Bishop of Hereford, and Robert Walerand, a prominent

---

[1] *Lib. de Ant. Leg.*, p. 21.   [2] *Cl. R.*, 76.   [3] *Mat. Par.*, v, 395, 467-8.
[4] *Barth. Cott.*, 131: 'Eodem anno comes Ricardus fecit comburare primo retia sua, que kidellos vulgariter appellamus, de quibus mentio fit in magna carta de communis libertatibus, ut sic et aliorum retia liberius concremaret.' The same entry, word for word, is in John of Wallingford's chron. in *M.G.H.*, xxviii, 509. The kidells of Magna Carta were weirs with openings covered by stake-nets to trap fish. Henry III had taken similar action on the Severn in 1251 (*Cl. R.*, 509), but seems to have got no credit for it.
[5] *C.P.R.*, 281.   [6] *Infra*, p. 159.

civil servant who had been with the king in Gascony, with having infatuated the king, by encouraging him to accept Sicily for Edmund. At about the same time Richard refused to lend 5,000 marks to the pope, on the ground that no security was offered.[1] *Nolo thesaurum superiori commodare quem non possum distringere.*[1] This was a blow for Henry. He was forced to adopt numerous degrading expedients to raise money, and he found it more expensive to borrow from Italian merchants than from Richard, for they charged him five per cent per month.[2] It was the more humiliating because Richard was by no means short of ready money at the time;[3] he probably never had more; but he felt great resentment at not being consulted over the Sicilian treaty. He must have been fully acquainted with the facts, for the pope had been soliciting his aid either as Emperor or as King of Sicily since 1247, and on two occasions at least he had given the matter serious thought. On the Emperor Frederick II's deposition in 1245 Innocent IV had lost little time in finding his own candidate for the empire. In 1247[4] and again after Frederick's death in 1250[5] he turned to Richard of Cornwall. On a third occasion, late in 1252, he sent Mr. Albert, a papal notary, to offer the crown of Sicily, for he knew that Richard had 'an unquenchable thirst for power and worldly dignity'. This explains, says Matthew Paris, why the pope had done him so much honour at Lyons.[6] Most people thought he had refused because he was not physically strong, nor brave or skilful in war, and because it might appear dishonourable to supplant his nephew Henry. Some such account of the matter he gave to Matthew Paris himself, but the true reason was that the pope would not give money, or the frontier castles, or hostages. So Richard, realizing that he was being

[1] *Mat. Par.*, v, 520-1, 524, 538-9. Richard was at Canterbury on December 24th, 1254, and Dover on Christmas Day (*Cl. R.*, 17, 151). At some time in 1255 he was at Lincoln on pilgrimage to St. Robert, and there intervened on behalf of some Jews accused of a ritual murder (*Ann. Burt.*, 344, 348). Other instances of the importance attached by the government to his counsel in 1255 are on *Cl. R.*, 158-60 (January); *C.P.R.*, 431, 435 (April); *Cl. R.*, 113 (June); *Cl. R.*, 373 (November).

[2] Mitchell, *Studies in Taxation*, chap. viii; *C.P.R.* (1248-1257), pp. 562, 629.

[3] About this time Richard lent £1,000 to Peter of Savoy and 4,000 marks to his nephew, the Lord Edward. This last item came to the chronicler from Philip of Eye, Richard's treasurer, who was at St. Albans in January 1257 (*Mat. Par.*, v, 548, 593, 608; *C.P.R.*, 469, 532).

[4] *Mat. Par.*, v, 201, puts this, by implication, between February and October 1247, so possibly when Richard was at Potigny in the autumn.

[5] *Ibid.*, v, 111, 118.

[6] *Supra*, p. 56. 'Noverat enim Papa, quod comes hydropisi pecuniali insatiabiliter laborabat et dignitate temporali' (*Mat. Par.*, v, 347). The formal offer of Sicily to Richard was made in Innocent's letter to Henry III of August 3rd, 1252 (*Foed.*, i, 284).

G

offered the moon, refused again in 1254,[1] and wrote a polite letter of thanks to the pope. It is evident that Innocent was much in earnest over his offer. In August 1252 he had written to Henry asking him to press Richard to accept, and Henry replied in January 1253 thanking the pope for choosing Richard as King of Sicily.[2] But by June, Richard's refusal was regarded as definite. Innocent realized that 'in vain the net is spread in the sight of any bird', and offered the crown, though with no success, to Charles of Anjou. He then turned to Henry III.[3] The king, to whom foreign policy was almost a domestic matter, not to be interfered with by baronial caprice, was determined to put his ideas into practice. An excellent opportunity presented itself when he was in Gascony in 1254. He shared with Richard a taste for magnificence and vain show, but unlike his brother he did not always count the cost. Whoever wanted Sicily now would have to fight hard for it.

Frederick II had left two sons, Conrad and Manfred, and on the former's death in 1254 Manfred, though not the direct heir, conquered Naples and Sicily for himself. Till his death in 1266 he ruled Sicily well, in spite of the efforts of three successive popes to turn him out. By his treaty with the pope, Henry III had committed himself to paying the expenses of the war against Manfred up to date, that is 134,000 marks — two or three times the annual revenue of England. Henry contrived to stave off disaster for another four years, in the face of baronial refusal to make any grant until responsible ministers had been appointed, by continuing to tax the clergy. The war being a failure and future liabilities unlimited, this over-ambitious foreign policy was extremely irritating to Richard of Cornwall. He had seen Henry's troubles mounting up year by year, and had helped to alleviate them from time to time, but Henry clung to his Sicilian project with amazing tenacity, and though Richard persistently refused the Sicilian crown over a period of years, he could not wean his brother from that fatal project. His own candidature for the empire was based on very different grounds. Neither he nor his rival Alfonso X of Castile (whose alliance of 1254 with Henry did not extend to this matter) had any lands in Germany, nor any support that they did not buy. But Richard was prepared to buy a working majority and spend some years in building up his position. That he did not achieve as much as he had hoped was not

[1] *Mat. Par.*, v, 346-7, 361, 457; *Ann. Burt.*, 339; BF., 5286[W].   [2] *Foed.*, 284; *Cl. R.*, 449.
[3] *Mat. Par.*, v, 680-2.

due to any personal folly. He might reasonably have supposed that Germany offered wonderful scope for his talents as a mediator. The size of the country, where, so far as is known, he had never set foot, and the degree of disintegration it had already reached, must have been seriously underestimated by him, and for this he cannot be acquitted of responsibility, though the whole matter was arranged by the brothers working for once in full co-operation. When the intrigues started Richard was being treated almost as an oracle in matters of English foreign policy.[1] But there remains a question how far Henry and Richard were influenced in this policy by the men whose task it was to execute it — John Mansel and Pierre d'Aigueblanche.

John Mansel was at this time at the height of his power. Officially he was from 1244 a member of the king's council: he was Provost of Beverley and Treasurer of York, and in addition becoming one of the greatest pluralists of the century. He seems to have been educated at court, and by 1234 occupied a subordinate position in the Exchequer. Though a clerk, he was also, like Peter des Roches, a distinguished soldier, who had made a name in Henry de Trubleville's Italian campaign of 1238, and in the Gascon expedition of 1242-1243. His military career was cut short at the siege of the monastery of Vérines in 1243, where his leg was crushed by a great stone hurled from above.[2] After this he is repeatedly spoken of by the chroniclers as chief counsellor, and as one who was all-powerful at court. Twice at least he held the Great Seal for a period (in 1246-1247 and 1248-1249) though he was never styled Chancellor. But his real importance was in the execution and, to an extent which still remains unknown, the direction of foreign policy. Of his numerous missions, most of them successful, three are important in the life of Richard of Cornwall. These three, outstanding in the history of the century, resulted in the treaty with Innocent IV over Sicily, the Castilian treaty, and the nomination of Richard of Cornwall as King of the Romans. These were all put through without reference to the baronage, but as the first two inevitably raised questions of taxation and foreign service it was widely felt that the *universitas*

---

[1] See the letter (dated January 30th/February 1st) from Henry III to John Mansel, giving a long account of Richard's advice on what the ambassadors to Castile should be prepared to say. It is full of liberal promises *and* the necessity of taking securities (*Cl. R.*, 389-91 = *R. L.*, ii, 110-14).

[2] This perhaps explains why so warlike a person took refuge in the Tower of London when the Barons' Wars broke out in 1263.

regni should have been consulted. Mansel may well have looked upon the Castilian treaty by which Edward married Eleanor of Castile and Alfonso gave up all claims on Gascony, as his master-stroke, because it had been feared that the Gascons, already market-ing their wines in Cordova, Seville, and Valencia, would transfer their allegiance to Spain. It marked the end of that period during which it seemed that the south of France and the north of Spain might coalesce.[1]

The treaty with the pope was undoubtedly carried through by Pierre d'Aigueblanche and John Mansel, and it is therefore interesting that the Castilian treaty was ascribed by Richard of Cornwall to the infatuation of Henry III by Pierre d'Aigueblanche and Robert Walerand. For Robert Walerand was in some measure the successor of John Mansel. He reached the peak of his career about the time of the *Dictum de Kenilworth*, and in 1254 was certainly far less impor-tant than Mansel. He is not even named — Mansel naturally is — among the counsellors who agreed *de facto Appullie*.[2]

At the time, then, that the kingship of Germany became vacant, Richard of Cornwall had good reason to be exasperated with his brother. Matthew Paris under 1255, just before the investiture of Edmund with Sicily, dilates upon the wretched condition of the kingdom of England, but states that Gloucester, Warenne, Lincoln, and Devon were still on the king's side. 'Earl Richard,' he adds, 'who was reckoned to be the chief of all the nobles, was neutral, as also were many others.'[3] Under 1256, when relating Henry's reac-tion to complaints made by Gascon merchants against the Lord Edward's purveyors in Gascony, Matthew reports Henry as saying: 'My own flesh and blood attack me; already my brother Earl Richard has been excited against me, as also is my first-born son.'[4] Yet though there was probably a mutual antipathy, it was not in the interests of either to quarrel. Matthew has even a story that after Richard had lent his nephew Edward 4,000 marks the king gave orders that no chancery writ was to be issued which could be pro-ductive of injury or loss to Richard his brother, Richard Earl of Gloucester, Peter of Savoy, or any of his brothers (i.e. the Lusignans).[5] In everyday matters Richard's advice was taken as a matter of course. On April 5th, 1255, the road through the forest of Dean was ordered

---

[1] *Mat. Par.*, v, 277-8.   [2] *Cl. R.*, 240=*Foed.*, 322 (November 21st, 1255).
[3] *Mat. Par.*, v, 514.   [4] *Ibid.*, v, 539.
[5] *Ibid.*, v. 594.   I cannot control this story, which is alluded to again in the description of the parliament of May 5th, 1258 (*ibid.*, 689).

to be widened by his counsel in the form advised by Henry of Bath, namely by a cutting six perches wide on either side of the road.[1] An itinerant judge might well be as solicitous as his unwarlike protector for the safety of the roads. Richard was similarly concerned over the road through Windsor forest in 1262, and for the protection of the roads in Germany in 1259-1260.

[1] *C.P.R.*, 435.

CHAPTER SIX

RICHARD, KING OF THE ROMANS
(1257)

THE intrigues by which Richard of Cornwall became King of the Romans came to light shortly after the death of the papal nominee William of Holland, on January 28th, 1256. We first suspect them on February 5th, so that Richard must have taken action immediately. On that day John d'Avesnes, Count of Hainault and son of the Countess Margaret of Flanders, was granted a fee of £200 a year at the English exchequer 'by counsel of Richard, earl, etc.'[1] It was this John who brought the formal offer of the crown to Richard eleven months later. Richard was a man of great deliberation and it is safe to assume that this was no sudden whim. There seems no reason to reject the obvious implication that this is his first step towards acquiring the crown, and that the initiative came from Richard himself. This move was followed by sending to Rome on February 20th, 1256, a marshal of the king's household, Sir William Bonquer. On or about March 27th he was instructed 'ut talis in regem Alemannie eligatur, qui ecclesie Romane devotus et nobis dilectus existat'.[2] To have a friendly German king was indeed vital for the success of Henry III's Sicilian plans, an integral part of the far-reaching diplomacy of John Mansel. Richard had an international reputation of many years' standing, and he was very rich. He had, too, the additional qualification that he could speak English. This may be regarded as an accomplishment still unusual amongst the earls and barons of England. Jocelin of Brakelond tells us that the Abbot of Bury could speak Latin and French in a plain way and read English well, though with a Norfolk brogue. Archbishop Pecham in 1285 advised the Abbot of Cluny to choose a Prior of Lewes who could speak English. Between these dates it would be difficult to prove that many of the secular nobles, apart from Richard

---

[1] *C.P.R.*, 461. Baldwin d'Avesnes received 100 marks a year on April 17th (*C.P.R.*, 468). The question who first suggested Richard's candidature has been much discussed by German writers. The very significant piece of information given above was not known to Koch, Bappert, or Lemcke, and appears to clinch the old view of Busson against them. See Koch, 111 and refs., and Lemcke, especially p. 11.

[2] *Cl. R.* (1254-1256), p. 408 = *Foed.*, 337 = R. L., ii, 114-16. More could be said of Bonquer as a professional diplomat, expert on Spanish affairs (*C.P.R.*, 463, 583; *Mat. Par.*, v, 555, 576). Two other of his missions are mentioned in 1259 (R. L., ii, 143) and 1260 (*ibid.*, ii, 152).

of Cornwall and his nephew the Lord Edward, were familiar with the language that was rapidly becoming a second vernacular for educated people, though it was not yet their mother tongue. The significance of this to contemporaries, according to Matthew Paris, was that English sounded like German.[1]

In the eyes of the electors and the towns these were all desirable attributes. It was also much in their interests to have as king a man who could so influence the course of trade. Not the prosperity of Cologne alone was affected. The whole of the lower Rhineland was to a large extent dependent upon England for its wool. With hardly an exception the five hundred wool-importers who styled themselves 'merchants of the king of Almain' came from that part of Germany that acknowledged Richard as king.[2] His political influence hardly extended beyond the sphere of Anglo-German economic interests. But there is no evidence that in seeking to attain the German crown Richard was influenced by economic motives. He could make a fortune out of papal grants or the regalian right of minting money, but, as he said himself, he was not a merchant, and the direct acquisition of money by controlling trade was a matter which may never have occurred to him as possible for one in his position.

The attitude of Alexander IV in 1256 is obscure.[3] His primary aim must have been to keep Germany and Sicily apart and when events forced him to make a choice between two candidates he at first favoured Alfonso, who had been chosen by the city of Pisa on March 18th.[4]

The next move came from England. Richard was at Cippenham on March 18th[5] and at Windsor on May 9th with Henry,[6] perhaps planning with John Mansel the embassy of Richard de Clare, Earl of Gloucester, and Robert Walerand who were accredited to the princes of Germany on June 12th.[7] For it is remarkable that this is not merely a private enterprise on Richard's part. The ambassadors

---

[1] *Mat. Par.*, v, 601 *ff.* For other aspects of this question of language see V. H. Galbraith in *T.R.H.S.*, IV, xxiii, 124, 'Nationality and Language in the Middle Ages', and R. W. Chambers on 'Continuity in English Prose' in the introduction to his edition of the *Life of Sir Thomas More* (E.E.T.S.).

[2] *Supra*, p. 67.

[3] Alexander's letter of June 11th, 1256, which mentions the embassy of William Bonquer and de Solario, concerns Sicily and carefully omits all reference to the problem of Germany.

[4] BF. 5484-7.   [5] Magd. Coll. Oxon. MS. deeds, Berks., iii, 12.   [6] *Cl. R.*, 415.

[7] *C.P.R.*, 481 = *Foed.*, 342. The letters of credence are 'warranted' by Gloucester, Mansel, and Walerand. This has caused confusion to many writers, who relying also on the testimony of Paris and Wykes (p. 111) have added Mansel to the embassy. The chroniclers have probably confused this embassy with the second one of 1257.

to Germany and to the pope are the king's ambassadors. Henry and Richard are completely at one in the matter and Richard receives the full support of the English government. John Mansel, almost the Wolsey of his age, was as deeply involved in this as over the Spanish treaty and the Sicilian affair. He does not, however, bear the whole responsibility, for it was Robert Walerand not Mansel whom Richard accused of infatuating the king over Sicily, and it is Walerand not Mansel who goes on this crucial embassy to Germany. At the beginning of November 1256 Richard had 25,000 marks out on loan, of which he called in on November 4th gold pledged to him by the crown for more than 10,000 marks. This was almost enough for the three votes he was now to buy.

After eleven months of negotiating, about which hardly anything is known, the Count Palatine agreed on November 25th-26th at Bacherach to support Richard of Cornwall. Count Ludwig was to marry a daughter of Henry III, Richard to renounce Sicily, and the bride was to receive 12,000 marks. It is not said whether Richard or Henry was to be financially responsible. The treaty was carried through apparently by John d'Avesnes and his brother Nicholas, Bishop of Cambrai, but after his initial support of Richard Ludwig withdrew from his court because of the hostile relations existing between himself and Ottocar of Bohemia.[1] The next step was to secure the support of Conrad of Hochstaden, Archbishop of Cologne, at Zünsdorf, on December 15th, for 8,000 marks.[2] Long-standing English trade relations with Cologne may have helped to induce Conrad to vote for Richard, though it must be borne in mind that he was usually at war with his flock. Conrad had spent part of the summer on a visit to Ottocar of Bohemia, whose attitude remained in doubt up to the last minute. The Archbishop of Mainz received a similar sum, and it was said that Arnold of Isenburg, Archbishop of Trèves, could have had even more, but he refused to be bought. It was useless to approach Saxony and Brandenburg.

At London on December 26th the crown was solemnly offered by the Archbishop of Cologne, who pretended that the electors were unanimous. Richard accepted with a fine show of humility and John d'Avesnes was empowered to act on Richard's behalf.[3] With

---

[1] Lemcke, *Beiträge*, cap. iii.

[2] The detailed contract is printed in Lacomblet, *Urkundenbuch*, nos. 429, 430.

[3] This important document was at Düsseldorf when Koch wrote in 1887 (p. 122 n.). See also B.F. 5289. The highly imaginative account in Matthew Paris (v, 601-3) professes to be the truth as told to the chronicler by Richard, Bishop of Bangor, a man of some diplomatic experience.

two archbishops and the Count Palatine in his favour Richard
needed only Ottocar of Bohemia, who later voted for Alfonso but
repented, to give him a majority of the seven electors who now for
the first time 'definitely exercise the right of choice'. He was elected
on January 13th, 1257, by his three supporters, Cologne, voting also
by proxy for Mainz, and the Count Palatine. On the day of the
electoral diet Richard's opponents held Frankfurt, so he was pro-
claimed outside the city.[1] In this election there was one candidate
only, and he was duly elected, at a cost of 28,000 marks. Ottocar of
Bohemia and the Archbishop of Trèves nominated Alfonso of
Castile, the grandson of Philip of Hohenstaufen, two months later.
Alfonso was also supported by the electors of Saxony and Brandenburg, but with the exception of Arnold of Trèves no one ever
raised a finger to help him. His candidature remained a purely
diplomatic nuisance and a stumbling-block to indecisive popes.

Richard was at Wallingford on January 31st when the news
reached him after dinner that Ottocar of Bohemia had decided to
support him.[2] Four days later Henry III wrote to the Bishop of
Hereford that he had heard for certain that his brother had been
elected and that he proposed to accompany him to Germany.[3]
Richard can hardly have allowed him to entertain so foolish an idea
for long. Matthew Paris does not allude to it in his account of the
famous visit of Henry to St. Albans in March, when the king recited
the list of two hundred and fifty baronies, the electors of Germany,
and the sainted kings of England, and *direxit scribentis calamum satis
diligenter et amicabiliter.*[4]

Richard made his final arrangements at the Easter parliament at
London, where the Archbishop of Cologne, Florence, Count of
Holland, and other German magnates came to do him homage.
Characteristically, Richard added to his tally of mediations by
writing about this time to Llewelyn to intervene between him and
the Lord Edward.[5] On April 10th he left London, granting a

---

[1] See the letter of Conrad and Ludwig announcing their unanimous choice of Richard
(January 14th: *Mat. Par. Addit.*, 341-2); Wykes, 112-14. The embassy of Gloucester and (this
time) John Mansel mentioned by Paris (v, 603) was probably in February 1257. They reported at the mid-Lent parliament (*ibid.*, 620).

[2] The date is from Richard's letter to the Archbishop of Messina (*Foed.*, i, 353; *Ann. Burt.*,
392). Ottocar cast a second vote for Alfonso (B.F. 5291). On February 3rd the Archbishop
of Cambrai's *vallettus* was given a robe for announcing to the king the first rumours of
Richard's election (*Cl. R.*, 36), and on February 16th, Richard's yeoman, Thomas de Mara,
received the same (*ibid.*, 37).

[3] *Cl. R.*, 119. This letter is wrongly dated January 17th in *Foed.*, i, 353.

[4] *Mat. Par.*, v, 617.   [5] *Ibid..* 613-14. See further, J. E. Lloyd, *History of Wales*, 720.

charter to the Trinitarian friars at Knaresborough before he went,[1] and the honour itself to his son Henry.[2] On April 15th letters patent of Richard, now a foreign power, and Henry were delivered into the wardrobe concerning a 'confederacy' between them. Fulk Basset, Bishop of London, and Philip Basset were left as *capitales custodes* of his lands in England.[3] In view of the political situation this was a very shrewd choice. It is typical of the state of government at this time that on the point of departure he had to cut down thirty-six oaks in the royal forests, on his own authority, because those ordered for him by the king were not ready.[4] The wind being unfavourable they did not sail until April 29th, when Richard and Sanchia with their sons Henry and Edmund left Yarmouth with a large retinue, including the German magnates, in forty-eight large ships and two little ones.[5]

The retinue led by Richard to Germany was not organized for war or prolonged service abroad, but was merely decorative and detachable. In the list of 'protections'[6] thirty-two are valid only until Michaelmas 1257. They are going to make a brave show at the coronation. A detailed analysis would be difficult to give, as they form a very miscellaneous party, headed by a bishop-elect, an earl to be, and five other barons. These are:

Richard, Bishop-elect of Coventry,
John de Warenne, Earl of Surrey, 1258-1304,
William de Muncheney of Norfolk, Northants, and Essex,
Hugh le Despenser,
Thomas le Blund of Suffolk,
James de Audeley, the marcher,
William de Stuteville and John his son.

Of these only John de Stuteville occurs as a witness (once) to a charter of Richard. Six others appear in the attestations:

Thomas de Warblinton (who also went in 1262),
Roger de Aumary,
Herbert de Neville,
Hugh de Hoyville,
Walter de la Grave,
Stephen de Chenduit.

---

[1] *Cal. Ch. R.*, ii, 240. See further, *V.C.H. Yorks.*, iii, 296.
[2] John of Wallingford's chron. in *M.G.H.*, xxviii, 511.
[3] *Cl. R.*, 65 (June 12th); *Mat. Par.*, 622, 629.   [4] *C.P.R.*, 554.
[5] *Foed.*, 355; Wykes, 116; *Gerv. Cant.*, 206.   [6] *C.P.R.*, 589-90 = *Foed.*, i, 355.

The remaining eighteen, most if not all being knights, are:

Walter de Baskerville (who went to France with Richard in 1250),
Andrew de Baskerville,
Robert de Turberville,
John de Turberville,
Baldwin de Akynny,
Guy Galyun,
Adam de Dotton,
Richard de Coleworth,
*Gilbert de Elsefield,
Roger Crawe,
Richard de Amundevill,
Nicholas de Meuling,
Roger de Somerton,
Thomas de Hereford,
*Joyce Fitz Robert,
*Thomas de Pavely,
*John de Sancto Walerico,
Hamo de Gatton.

No one of these occurs in any one of twenty charters of Richard of Cornwall. Four (*) are Oxfordshire tenants. The Baskerville family held of the Lacy honour of Weobley in Herefordshire and the honour of Cormailes in Gloucestershire. The Turbervilles held of the honour of Clifford in Herefordshire, and the Ferrers honour of Tutbury in Berkshire. Culworth held of the Pinkeney fee in Northamptonshire and Berkshire, and with Amandevill in Trop by Banbury. Gatton held in Kent and Surrey of the honour of Peverel of Dover. The other seven have not been traced; no doubt they could be, but sufficient has been said to show that no tenurial principle underlay this collection of barons and knights. We are in no better case with the three men who received protection for two years, Robert de Ostgod, Alan le Waleys, and Giles FitzWilliam; or Hamo le Gros for three years. But the length of the term suggests a contract with the king-elect, and this is even more likely with William Blundel, the only man to receive protection for four years, for Blundel is identifiable as an official already in Richard's service. Finally there are nine, five of them known to be officials, who receive protection 'for as long as they shall be in the service of the said king-elect in Germany', namely Robert de Molineux, a yeoman, Philip of Eye, who became Treasurer of England, Michael of Northampton, one of Richard's executors, Roger de la Launde, Hugh le Sauser, Reginald Folyet of Oxfordshire, Thomas de la Pulle, a yeoman of his household, William Talbot, who had been with him in Gascony in 1227, and Peter de Anesy of Herefordshire and Hampshire.

The value of the alliance with Holland was at once shown, for Richard was able to land on May 1st at Dortrecht, at the mouth of the Rhine. On May 11th they reached Aachen, where the ceremonious reception betrayed much preparation by all concerned. On Ascension Day, May 17th, Richard and Sanchia were crowned with the proper insignia by the Archbishop of Cologne, and next day, *secundum morem patrie*, Richard's eldest son Henry was knighted. The coronation feast was one of unexampled magnificence, that astonished the Germans and was long remembered even in England. Richard had probably always wanted to be king since as a child he had arrived at Corfe with his trumpeters. He promptly wrote home as *Dei gratia Rex Romanorum semper Augustus*, to the Lord Edward, the Earl of Gloucester, and, less intimately, to the mayor and citizens of London, and to his 'chief steward',[1] that after a bad two-day crossing all had gone well, and that the Archbishop of Trèves, the leader of the opposition, had been thoroughly defeated at Boppard on the Rhine the previous week. It was commonly said, he reports, that none of his predecessors for the last two hundred years had entered Aachen without opposition. He added proudly (to his steward) that 3,000 knights, 30 dukes and counts, 2 archbishops and 10 bishops were present. He now proposed to devote his energies to crushing Arnold of Trèves, and so moved slowly up the Rhine to Cologne. Before they left Sanchia wrote much more briefly to the Prior of Wallingford.[2]

In taking over William of Holland's position, Richard took over also his prothonotary, Mr. Arnold of Holland.[3] He showed his common sense and independence, however, by breaking at once, in one small point, with the German tradition (at least since Barbarossa's time) of dating by the Roman calendar. From May 18th

---

[1] This letter (beg. *Libenter votivos*), the primary authority for the coronation, was probably widely circularized. See *Ann. Burt.*, 392-5 (to the Lord Edward), *N.A.*, xiii, 219 (to Gloucester), *Lib. de Ant. Leg.*, 26-9 (to London), *Mat. Par. Addit.*, 369 (to his steward). See also Wykes, 117, *Mat. Par.*, v, 640 f.

[2] *Mat. Par., Addit.*, 366 = *M.G.H.*, xxviii, 373.

[3] In English documents Mr. Arnold is often called Arnulf and sometimes styled chancellor.

Richard's formal documents, which are rhythmical, are dated by the place, the day of the month, the year of our Lord, the indiction and the regnal year, which was reckoned from his coronation. This little reform did not outlast the reign: Rudolf of Habsburg and his successors reverted to the ancient style. Even a casual inspection of Richard's *acta* as King of the Romans reveals that from the administrative point of view, there is no connection between Richard as king and Richard as earl, except in the person of Mr. Arnold, and whatever staff he may have had as prothonotary. Nicholas of Cambrai was his chancellor, Philip of Falkenstein his chamberlain, Waleran of Jülich his marshal, and Werner of Boland his steward.[1] Richard's English tenants and followers find no place in his German *acta*. This trend in German history was in the mind of Paris when he contrasted the results of Frederick II's English marriage with those of Henry III's French connections.

At Aachen, Richard's welcome had been surprisingly warm: at Cologne the citizens were less enthusiastic than might have been expected from their longstanding commercial intercourse with England. Richard was able to proceed upstream, confirming charters on the way, almost without opposition. At Mainz he stayed for some time, holding his first Diet here on September 8th. Ten days later he reached Oppenheim, and on September 30th Weissenberg. About this time, probably according to plan, he sent home his son Henry, Hugh Despenser, James de Audeley, Stephen Chenduit, and very many others[2] — no doubt most or all of those who had received 'protection' until Michaelmas. Richard himself returned to the lower Rhineland, where his supporters were most numerous, for the winter. In October he wrote to Henry of Lexington, Bishop of Lincoln, one of his characteristically boastful letters claiming that all who mattered in Alsace, Swabia, Franconia, Saxony, and Upper Burgundy had done him homage, except the towns of Worms and Speier.[3] Next year he repeated this performance, spending April-May at Aachen, where he loaded the citizens with privileges, and built them a town hall — King Richard's *curia*,[4] and on July 25th

[1] For these appointments, antedated in *Ann. Dunst.*, 203, see B.F. 5304 (May) and 5314 (July). John of Avesnes was not, as Matthew Paris thought, a steward.

[2] *Mat. Par.*, v, 653; *Ann. Dunst.*, 203.

[3] *N.A.*, xiii, 220. In this letter (beg. *Quia ex innata vobis bonitate*) Richard claims to have reached the Alps, but as Bappert (p. 20, n. 2) points out, his journey to Bâle, assigned by D.N.B. and others to this year, is best put, with B.F., in 1263. The crux is a later comment in *M.G.H.*, xvii, 122, cf. 111, 113.

[4] *D.N.B.*, citing Miranda, 1.

received the submission of Worms. It was about this time that John, Bishop of Lübeck, to secure his city's allegiance to Richard, wrote home that the new king was 'orthodox, prudent, strenuous, wealthy, well-connected, energetic, and moderate' and summed up his achievements by saying that he was king 'from Berne to the sea'.[1] On October 19th Richard was again at Worms. A month later he was back in Flanders at Cambrai, where he had arranged to meet Louis IX and Henry III.

In the brief space of sixteen months Richard had obtained recognition in Germany to a degree never afterwards, in his three subsequent visits, surpassed by him. During the fifteen years of his reign he spent only three years and nine months in Germany, and it was only in the first and last of his four visits that he achieved anything of note.[2] He was King of Aachen and the Rhineland rather than of Germany. The towns of the centre and of the south acquired new privileges (unlike the Rhenish towns which for the most part had to be content with confirmations) and made their submission dependent upon Richard's recognition by the pope. The nobles to the east of the Rhine largely ignored him, and apart from the annalists of Worms and Hamburg the chroniclers were uninterested in his doings.

Yet at the end of 1258 he was widely recognized as the lawful and anointed king. His competitor had not appeared. There was no one in the field against him. The importance that contemporaries would attach to the fact that his itinerary was limited in scope is perhaps not very great. Henry III wandered up and down the valleys of the Thames and Severn, occasionally digressing into East Anglia, Hampshire or the south-west, but in a reign of fifty-six years was only some three times north of Trent.

The chroniclers tell us that Richard poured forth money like water and had to return to England when his resources came to an end.[3] But the truth seems to be that Richard had not entered upon this venture without counting the cost. He paid a total of 28,000 marks for his three votes, and he had been prepared to pay much more,[4] but there is no evidence that after election he continued to

---

[1] *Urkundenbuch der Stadt Lübeck*, i, 233-5. See Lemcke, 68, for the date.

[2] The four visits to Germany were: April 1257 to January 1259, June to October 1260, June 1262 to February 1263, and August 1268 to August 1269.

[3] 'Hic effudit pecuniam ante pedes principum sicut aquam' (Hamburg annals, *M.G.H.*, xvi, 384). 'De eius pecunia multa incredibilia sonuerunt' (*ibid.*).

[4] 'Quindecim enim milia marcarum sterlingorum oblata eidem Arnoldo archiepiscopo Treverensi' (*Gesta Trever.*, *M.G.H.*, xxiv, 412).

lavish money on his new subjects. It would be much more in
keeping with the rest of his life if he had decided what he could
afford to spend in Germany and came home when he had reached
his self-imposed limit. Any pecuniary embarrassment he felt was
never more than temporary.

Richard did as much as any man could have done at that time
without a territorial basis in Germany. As there was no real capital,
no royal system of administration upon which to build, and as he
was not prepared to fight, the reality of power outside the Rhineland was bound to elude him. The task was not made easier by the
election of a Hohenstaufen candidate, Alfonso X of Castile, two
months after Richard's election. Alfonso had important advantages
— the support of Louis IX of France, friend of Pope Alexander IV,
and of the Duke of Brabant. Because the family of Avesnes rode
with Richard, Guy de Dampierre, Count of Flanders, was naturally
in the opposite camp. Alfonso had, too, the active assistance of
Arnold, Archbishop of Trèves, the leader of his party in Germany,
the Bishop of Worms, and the towns of Worms and Speier. On the
other hand, he like Richard had no lands in Germany, he shot his
bolt too late, and he never set foot in what he described as his kingdom. His assets wasted rapidly before the fact of Richard's presence
as a crowned monarch in the traditional home of German kingship,
and the loss of French support after the treaty of Paris. He could
best have ruined Richard's prospects by winning over the Count of
Holland and cutting communications with England. His intention
to launch an attack on Italy was met by Matthew Paris in an
apocryphal boast that Richard would fight outside Germany,[1] and
in fact frustrated by threats to his position in Spain by the Moors.

It was in vain, and much too late that Alfonso complained to
Henry III that he had been wronged by Richard and sought English
help according to the terms of the treaty of 1254. Henry replied, on
December 14th, 1257, that he had known nothing whatever of
Alfonso's plans in the matter, nor had he been able to learn anything
whatever about the electors or the princes of Germany that might
concern him. The princes of Germany had sent ambassadors to
Henry and Richard before Christmas more than a year ago to learn
their will, and Richard had been duly elected and crowned in the
traditional place and by the proper persons. Henry promises to send
messengers to Germany to discover the truth of the matter and then

[1] *Mat. Par.*, v, 694.

proceed to do what is right by all parties.[1] This did not prevent
Alfonso from returning to the charge in 1258, and Henry replied on
June 25th, just before the barons had taken over the Great Seal, to
much the same effect, adding that if he can do anything that will
redound to the honour of Alfonso and Richard he will certainly do
it, and that he will send to his brother to see if they can find a formula.[2] Matthew Paris has been much blamed by German writers
for his account of the events leading up to Richard's coronation and
election,[3] but it is clear from these letters that he is only following,
almost summarizing, the official view of what happened.

Matthew Paris seems to have believed that Alfonso's election, and
even the fact that Richard's election was not the work of seven
electors, was skilfully concealed from the public in England. This is
difficult to believe, and he certainly goes too far in saying that a
knowledge of it was kept from Gloucester and John Mansel, but it
would be of a piece with the secrecy in which the ten months of
intrigue after William of Holland's death seem to have been involved. This may have prevented trouble with the English baronage, but it did not prevent Alfonso from making mischief at Rome.
Alexander would have to decide between the two elected kings, and
the embassy sent by Henry III to Rome in June–July 1258 was
partly no doubt to help him in his choice,[4] but Alfonso at once
agreed to accept papal arbitration. This made it difficult for the
pope to crown Richard as emperor without the fullest inquiry, but
Richard, partly through pride, kept putting off the appointment of a

[1] *Cl. R.*, 284-5 (December 14th, 1257) '. . . dum de fratris nostri vocacione ad regnum
agaretur supradictum, nichil penitus ut de vestra voluntate seu proposito novimus; nichil
omnino de electoribus vel principibus regni supradicti, quod vos modo quolibet tangere
videretur, audire, vel ullis prorsus judiciis intelligere poteramus'. Cf. *Mat. Par.*, 657-8.

[2] *Cl. R.*, 314-15 (June 25th, 1258). This important letter begins with the return from Spain
of the Abbot of Shrewsbury and John de Castello, and touches on the affairs of Gascony and
a proposed marriage between Henry's daughter and Emanuel, son of Alfonso. It announces
Henry's willingness to make an expedition to Africa with Alfonso if the pope would give his
permission, which was unlikely because of Henry's commitments in Apulia. It continues: 'De
subsidio vobis faciendo contra fratrem nostrum, satis, ut credimus, regie providencie exposuer-
unt nuncii nostri predicti qualiter nec nos nec frater noster predictus, eciam cum jam esset
electus et in possessione dominii gentiam et terrarum Alemannie pro magna parte et demum
coronatus in regem, de voto aut proposito vestro in parte illa nichil prorsus scivimus aut
probabiliter scire potuimus. Verum si a principio scivissemus illud nobis preceteris placuisset
et ad hoc, sicuti et ad omnem exaltacionem et honorem vestrum, patrocinium dedissemus.
Unde, si postmodum aliqui forsan de principibus Alemannie in vos vota direxerint, vestra non
debet circumspeccio in facto hujusmodi dicti fratris aliquid nobis injuriosum et prejudiciale
notare . . . Si formam aliquam in premissis vobis et vestro convenientem honori invenire
possimus.' Cf. *Mat. Par.*, 694-5. For a fabulous letter of Richard to the pope against Alfonso
see *Ann. Burt.*, 466.

[3] Lemcke, *Beiträge, passim.*

[4] *Foed.*, i, 359; cf. Bémont ed. Jacob, *Simon de Montfort*, 133.

representative to plead his case, though he agreed in principle to papal arbitration. We know from Richard's letter to the senate and people of Rome and a letter of Gregory da Montelongo, the patriarch of Aquileia, that in 1257 Richard was eager to be crowned,[1] but to gain papal support he had first to be sure of the friendship of France, and it was therefore much in his interest to push forward the treaty of Paris.

Negotiations for this had been going forward actively since the Bishop of Worcester had been sent to France in June 1257, with orders to proceed thence to Germany and seek Richard's advice.[2] On his part Richard sent his prothonotary, Mr. Arnold, papal chaplain and Provost of Wetzlar, to France with full powers to make a complete renunciation of what he or his successors could claim in France, and to confirm the treaty of Paris.[3] Mr. Arnold sealed it on June 8th, 1258, reserving Richard's claim on the Angoumois against the Counts of La Marche by reason of Isabella of Angoulême, his mother.[4] On June 22nd Richard ratified this.[5] The treaty was to be kept secret until November 25th, when there was to be a conference between Louis IX, Henry III, and the King of the Romans, at Cambrai. Henry notified the pope and asked for a legate to be sent, but his request was refused by Alexander.[6] As the English barons refused to let Henry leave the country, sending an embassy under Simon de Montfort instead, and because Louis would treat only with principals, there was no conference.[7]

Richard had already decided to come to England and had been urged by the government to take the oath to the Provisions of Oxford, for the barons were afraid of him.[8] He had made a promising beginning in Germany, but he could not hope to maintain his position if by the success of a baronial revolution in England he permanently lost his English estates. He may also have been worried by his dwindling capital,[9] but he was an extremely astute financier and it would be naive to suppose that he came to England to fill his treasure chests in a literal sense, or that his resources would be materially increased by his presence. It has been pointed out that he could afford to gather a 'large army' at St. Omer with which to force his way, if necessary, into England.[10]

---

[1] *N.A.*, xiii, 685; B.F., 11, 800.   [2] *C.P.R.*, 594.
[3] *Layettes du Trésor des Chartes*, iii, no. 4413 (May 22nd, 1258, at Oppenheim).
[4] *Ibid.*, no. 4423.   [5] *Ibid.*, no. 4426.
[6] *Foed.*, i, 376; Gavrilovitch, *Étude sur le Traité de Paris*, p. 27, n. 1.
[7] *Mat. Par.*, v, 720-1.   [8] *Cl. R.*, 460=R. L., ii, 132 (November 4th, 1258).
[9] *Ann. Dunst.*, 206, stating that he wrote from Germany in 1257 to sell his woods *propter defectum pecunie inopinatum.*
[10] Bappert, 33, 36.

H

CHAPTER SEVEN

ENGLAND (1259–1263)

SECOND AND THIRD VISITS TO GERMANY

RICHARD'S departure for Germany in 1257 had been a momentous event, a prime factor in letting loose the biggest political storm since Magna Carta. For twenty years and more he had prevented the baronial movement from achieving its objects, sometimes by active opposition, latterly by the force of his counsel or his mere presence. 'While he was in England he had managed the king and the affairs of state, and on his nod hung all the business of the realm.'[1] Through his absence he had lost the whole of his political influence in England, but the strength of the baronial opposition to his landing shows how quickly he was expected to regain it.

On January 14th, 1259, after the failure of Louis and Henry to appear at Cambrai, Richard was at Arras.[2] When he had reached St. Omer a baronial embassy came to forbid him to land until he had sworn to observe the Provisions of Oxford.[3] Richard replied that he could not be compelled to do this outside the kingdom, adding that as soon as he landed he would take the oath if his brother told him so to do. The barons would not agree, and said further that anyone who ferried him over would be executed. After discussions lasting eleven days, during which he is said to have claimed that he had no peer in England,[4] King Richard agreed to swear that he would, in the presence of his peers, take the required oath, if the king enjoined him to do so. The 'king' (i.e. the baronial council) did so enjoin him on January 23rd, and warned him at the same time against admitting the king's brothers to the realm.[5] On these terms he was allowed to cross the Channel and landed at Dover, where he was met by Henry III and Archbishop Boniface on January 28th. The barons would not allow them to enter Dover Castle, so they proceeded straight to Canterbury, where the oath

[1] Wykes, 118: 'Qui dum esset in Anglia regem et regni moderamina gubernaverat, ad cujus nutum universi regni negotia dependebant.'
[2] B.F., *Acta Imperii Selecta*, pp. 310–11 (charter interpreting the criminal law of Cambrai).
[3] The best account of this is in Wykes, 121–2.
[4] *Mat. Par.*, v, 729–30, 735–6. [5] *C.P.R.*, 10.

was administered to him not as King of Almain but as Earl of Cornwall. He had come with only two German barons, each with three knights, and eight knights for himself.[1]

On February 2nd he reached London, which was cleaned and decorated for the occasion. At Westminster, on February 10th, he and Henry of Almain ratified the epoch-making treaty of Paris,[2] important to Richard in that it prepared the way for that other treaty of alliance with France which Mr. Arnold had secured for him in the preceding summer. This treaty, ruining the hopes of the pro-Spanish faction in the Rhineland, was now confirmed with the treaty of Paris.[3]

Little is known of Richard's life during this year. He attended the consecration of Henry de Wengham as Bishop of London on February 15th,[4] and is next found at his own Cistercian foundation of Hailes in Gloucestershire on April 6th.[5] He is then lost sight of for six months, not reappearing until October, a few days before Henry III's eventful visit to France. Richard's absence in Germany had prevented him from taking any part in English politics during the seven months after the Mad Parliament and the 'Provisions of Oxford'. This subsequent blank of six months makes it likely that he played no active, certainly no open, part in the events leading up to the publication of the 'Provisions of Westminster' in October 1259. He had been regarded as neutral in 1255 and was no doubt still striving to maintain this attitude of aloofness that was to be the strength of his position during the next few years. Although his first object in leaving Germany — friendship with France — had been achieved, it was still difficult for him to go to Rome, without exposing himself to the possibility of a humiliating rebuff, until the pope had made up his mind. This was an added reason for keeping out of English politics, for the baronial opposition to Henry III was thoroughly distrusted at the papal curia, and it was extremely difficult to do much good there while the baronial council was still rejoicing in its strength, and the Bachelors were roaring after their prey. But the treaties with France had an immediate effect. In March 1259 the first-fruits of Mr. Arnold's work at Rome appeared.

[1] *Lib. de Ant. Leg.*, 41; *Flores*, ii, 421; *Gerv. Cant.*, ii, 207.   [2] *Layettes*, iii, nos. 4462–3.
[3] *Ibid.*, 4461. Henry III and Edmund his son ratified the treaty of Paris on February 20th and 24th (*C.P.R.*, 14). It was issued in another five *expéditions* before the final sealing in Paris in December 1259.
[4] *Flores*, ii, 443.
[5] Bappert (p. 36) gives this without reference, which should be to *M.G.H.*, xvi, 483, where it is wrongly entered under 1258.

Alexander IV, who had once favoured Alfonso, now turned to Richard.

On March 14th the pope wrote to the Count of Burgundy enjoining him to give every help to Richard 'in Romanorum regem electus et coronatus, in imperatorem auctore domino promovendo' and accrediting to him the Franciscan Walter de Rogate.[1] But Alexander still hesitated and not till April 30th did he finally make up his mind. He then wrote that he had received Richard's envoys, Mr. Arnold and brother William the Trinitarian, and also heard what the Bishop of Rochester and Robert de Baro had to tell him, both publicly and secretly, on Henry III's part. He apologizes for the delay, and accredits brother William de Rogate, his familiar and plenipotentiary, whom he is also sending to Germany. Embedded in all this is an assurance that he is taking thought for Richard's promotion.[2] This invitation would be received by Richard about the end of May. He agreed to go to Rome, and sent on the papal messengers to Germany with their letters to the princes. Richard's answer seems to have been evasive, but opinion at St. Albans was clearly that this time the pope was in earnest, and that Richard was only biding his time, living quietly and saving up money for the occasion.[3] Alexander had been moved to summon him because now that the Sicilian affair had gone so badly the danger to Rome was no longer from a union of Germany and Sicily, but from the increasing power of Manfred, both north and south of Rome. Alfonso had his hands full in Castile, and Richard would be a useful counterpoise to Manfred. Richard, however, was in no hurry to respond, preferring to build up his reserves. It was not until the Provisions of Westminster were being published that Richard sent the Abbot of Abingdon, William of Newbury, 'beyond seas' on his service (October 18th)[4] and received licence to tallage his ancient demesne because he is 'very shortly going to the court of Rome' (October 29th).[5]

At this time Richard was still 'lying low',[6] perhaps in the west. He was at Mere on December 11th[7] and at Launceston castle for Christmas and his fifty-first birthday.[8] He had been in London on

[1] *Layettes*, iii, no. 4472. *Dum magnifica.*

[2] *Ann. Burt.*, i, 469 = *Foed.*, i, 384 (wrongly dated April 21st).   [3] *Flores*, ii, 425, 428.

[4] *C.P.R.*, 45.

[5] *Ibid.*, 57. These two patents are printed in *Foed.*, i, 377 under 1258. This had misled Lemcke, 62-4.

[6] *Flores*, ii, 425, 'latitavit secretius', cf. *Mat. Par.*, v, 746.

[7] B.F. 5364: grant of Contamina to Peter of Savoy.   [8] Wykes, 123; *Cal. Ch. R.*, iv, 387.

December 7th,[1] proposing to go to France with Henry III to meet
St. Louis at Abbeville,[2] but he changed his mind. Henry went to
France without him and by a masterly stroke of policy stayed there
far longer than was necessary to seal the treaty. He took half the
council with him, thus weakening the reformers who, now at the
height of their power, were striving to implement the promises
contained in the Provisions of Westminster. The Provisions of 1258
had been directed largely against the king, in the interests of the
magnates: the Provisions of 1259 hit at the privileges of the latter in
favour of the country gentry and freemen. In attempting to enforce
these later Provisions the reforming party naturally alienated some
of their own members, beginning with those who had most to lose,
e.g. the Earl of Gloucester. There is no evidence that Hugh Bigod's
extraordinary eyre of 1258 ever invaded the franchises, but this is
precisely what the reformers now set out to do. On January 26th,
1260, Richard of Cornwall was warned that, unless he amended the
transgressions of his bailiffs of the honour of Wallingford, the king's
court would do it for him.[3] Richard won this point on October
20th, 1260, when he was empowered

> in pursuance of an ordinance (*condictum*) made by the whole
> council that every magnate of the realm shall have the power of
> correcting the excesses of his bailiffs and serjeants when com-
> plaint is made to him of their trespasses — to compel certain
> free men in the vicinage of his lands and manors to be sworn
> (*ad sacramentum prestandum*) so that he may do justice, etc.[4]

It had been provided in the instructions for the eyre of 1259–1260
that, after security taken for prosecuting, full justice should immediately be done to the complainant, not only in the case of royal
officials, but 'in the case of magnates and of their bailiffs, *if their
lords, when requested to do so, do not do justice to whosoever complains
about them*'.[5] The complaints of 1260–1261 were in fact 'directed
against the officers of great magnates more generally than against
royal officials'.[6] There are plenty of complaints against the officials
of great men, such as Peter of Savoy or the Earl of Gloucester, but
none of them seems to have taken advantage of the clause in question
except Richard of Cornwall. This is remarkable, because though in
its negative form in the instructions to the Justices, as an explicit

---

[1] *Cal. Ch. R.*, ii, 25 (Richard's charter to Exeter).   [2] *Flores*, ii, 429.   [3] *Cl. R.*, 26.
[4] *C.P.R.*, 97.   [5] Jacob, *Studies*, 97.   [6] *Ibid.*, 107 *ff.*

and even emphatic general ordinance, it tore a large hole in the Provisions of Westminster. Richard played for time in this matter. He won a second (January 1261) and a third (April 1261) round but received a set-back in a fourth (January 1262), when he received a similar power but only *pro hoc vice*, and on condition that the parties be brought before three persons named.[1] The local government of Richard's estates does not appear to have aroused any very harsh criticisms, and it may be that he was better placed than some other magnates to take advantage of regulations made by the barons themselves.

The first warning to him to see to his bailiffs, in January 1260, had come at the end of the council's period of unchallenged supremacy. Henry III was writing bland letters from France, postponing his return, and postponing also the parliament which according to the Oxford settlement should have been held in February.[2] The barons, however, were determined to have a parliament, and one was summoned to London for April 25th. The writer of the *Flores* brings this into connection with the prohibition of a tournament for which the barons had assembled at Blyth. He seems to telescope events, for the only known tournament arranged for Blyth about this time was June 10th-12th, 1259. His argument nevertheless is that the barons being prevented from settling their quarrels at Blyth, were summoned — he does not say by whom — to come armed to London. The most important of the disputes in progress was that between the Lord Edward and Gloucester, the immediate causes of which are obscure, though conflicting rights over Bristol castle played their part. The fundamental difference between them was that Gloucester was at best half-hearted in his support of the Provisions which Edward and the *Bacheleria* had sponsored. The story runs, and it is well documented, that the two earls rode to London with their retainers proposing to lodge within the city, a design calculated to provoke civil war. On being warned of this by Henry III, the King of the Romans came to London and after

---

[1] *C.P.R.*, 196. He had written on January 21st, 1261, that he would amend the transgressions of his bailiffs of which complaint had been made before Hugh le Despenser, before the quinzaine of Easter, and the justiciar and justices in eyre were therefore ordered not to hear any complaints against his bailiffs, but to send them to Richard for trial (*Cl. R.* 335). In Cornwall in June 1261 his Steward was commissioned with the coroners to attach malefactors touching tin, parks, stews, fisheries, drying-grounds, larcenies, and the like, and have them before the next eyre (*C.P.R.*, 186). On April 26th, 1261, as he had still done nothing, the matter was postponed till Michaelmas and the pledges of those bailiffs who had been distrained to face a charge were released (*Cl. R.*, 471).

[2] *R. L.*, ii, 148-50.

conference with the mayor and aldermen, the justiciar, and Philip Basset, persuaded them to exclude the two earls and set a watch upon the gates by night and day.[1] The peacemakers, instead, were lodged within the city. When the king, who made considerable political capital out of these events, returned to England (April 23rd, 1260) he admitted Gloucester to London, but kept Simon de Montfort and the Lord Edward outside. The King of the Romans, no longer needed in the city, retired to his house at Westminster, to finish off his good work methodically by writing up another couple of Awards.

By the end of April Richard had reconciled Edward with his father, who believed or professed to believe that he had been plotting with Simon de Montfort for the king's downfall.[2] The award between Edward and Gloucester was probably made easier by this reconciliation, as Gloucester had been won over to Henry's side while they were in France. It was only pronounced by Richard immediately before his departure for Germany, and published by Henry on June 22nd, so that it had to be sent after King Richard to the Continent for sealing. It looks as if one or both of the parties had been extremely obstinate, though it could equally well be that Richard knew that they would not cause trouble while waiting for his decision, and so purposely left it until the last minute. The pronouncement, made jointly with the king, was to the effect that all contentions before June 17th — the day on which Richard left London — were to be dropped, and all covenants made before that date to be kept.[3]

Having thus contributed very materially to the resurgence of a royalist party in the first-half of 1260, Richard left England on June 18th-19th,[4] followed by the lamentations of the St. Albans chronicler, who in this period is not infrequently wise after the event in his rather nebulous manner.[5]

[1] *Lib. de Ant. Leg.*, 44–5; *Cl. R.*, 282–3. Henry also wrote to Richard to prevent his Poitevin kinsfolk landing in Cornwall. This is not sense as it stands, but is perhaps to be interpreted by Henry's complaint in July 1260 that Simon had made peace with his half-brothers without the consent of king or council (Treharne, 240). *D.N.B.* states in error that Richard summoned the April parliament.

[2] Treharne, 232–3. [3] *C.P.R.*, 79.

[4] *Lib. de Ant. Leg.*, 45, states that he left London on June 17th and embarked at Dover on June 19th; Wykes, 124, gives June 18th; *Flores*, ii, 452, gives June 17th, from Gravesend, where his queen met him.

[5] *Quo absente quamplures fluctuabant sub ambiguo, quippe cum ejus nuper presentia imminentem guerram prepedisset, formidabant quod pax prelocuta, absente illo, nullius stabilitatis existeret* (*Flores*, ii, 453).

Richard's preparations for this second visit to Germany were deliberate and comprehensive. He had received a further visit from the Franciscan, Walter de Rogate, who received his safe conduct as papal nuncio on April 13th.[1] We do not know what message he brought, but we may assume that Richard would not have set out for Rome without the clearest assurance that the pope was going to be as good as his word. As King of Almain, Richard had sought new support in North Italy, soliciting, though to little purpose, the aid of Azzo of Este and Palavicini,[2] and by one of his rare alienations of imperial lands he granted Gumminen to his friend Peter of Savoy, whose lands lay astride the Great St. Bernard Pass, the classic road to Rome.[3] He had also, it seems, issued an order for the protection of the roads in Germany,[4] and busied himself with the promulgation of a land-peace in the lower Rhineland.[5] To secure immediate supplies of cash Richard began to call in some of his loans. By April 15th Henry III had sufficiently recovered his power to be able to order that Richard must at all cost be satisfied out of the Jewry of his loans to the crown,[6] and on May 30th to ask Louis IX to pay out of the money due under the treaty of Paris 5,000 marks which Richard had lent to the government.[7]

Richard was still in London on May 19th, when he issued a charter to the town of Bisanz, that it should never be separated from the empire,[8] and probably on June 15th, when Henry confirmed the privileges of the German merchants.[9] His *familia* was small. Some of his permanent officials had protections that were still valid. It is fortunate that the one recorded addition — for Philip of Oye, his steward — is stated to be for two years.[10]

For the object of this journey was to pass rapidly across Europe and proceed straight to Rome for coronation as emperor. Even thus he found it necessary to stay ten days at Cambrai, where on June 27th he enfeoffed Margaret, Countess of Flanders, and her son Guy with the imperial county.[11] In spite of all his preparations he was not to be hurried. Having reached Worms by August 12th, remained there until September 17th and then turned back, travelling rapidly by way of Mainz and Boppard to England, where he

---

[1] *C.P.R.*, 120.   [2] Bappert, 41.   [3] *Supra*, p. 100, n. 7; Wurstemberger, iv, 267.
[4] The extract in Goldest, *Constit.*, i, 308, is of doubtful authenticity.   [5] Bappert, 41.
[6] *Cl. R.*, 255.   [7] *C.P.R.*, 74.   [8] B.F. 5367.
[9] *Supra*, p. 67, for the *Gildhalla Teutonicorum*.
[10] *C.P.R.*, 73. Philip of Oye and Philip of Eye attest side by side in *Cal. Ch. R.*, ii, 25.
[11] B.F. 5369.

arrived on October 24th.[1] It was almost a flight and, as he had met
with no opposition, at first sight difficult to explain. It was certainly
the turning-point in his career as King of the Romans, for after this
he made no real effort to obtain the imperial crown.

It is clear that Richard came to his decision at Worms. It was here
that he learned the futility of proceeding. Though he had started
his journey well by winning over Flanders, Trèves, the new Archbishop of Mainz and the Bishop of Strassburg, by the time he had
reached Worms his supporters were growing cool.[2] He himself
was making strong efforts to enlist the support of the Guelfs of
North Italy. An ambassador, William Beroardi, came to him from
the citizens of Florence, but proposed to go on to negotiate with
Conradin.[3] Richard wrote to Bologna announcing his intention of
coming to Italy and asked the citizens, with a great air of condes-
cension, to prepare the way for him, recommending to them Sir
John de Castello, Mr. Matthew de Celis, his notary, and Peter
Ricardi, his familiar.[4]

If Richard had started a couple of months earlier he might have
reached Rome in time, for his decision to turn back seems largely to
have been caused by two events. In the first half of September
Alfonso X had got wind of Richard's intentions — if indeed he had
not heard sooner — and had sent to Rome his brother Manuel, who
persuaded the pope to become neutral again.[5] Perhaps even worse
than this for Richard was the crushing defeat of the Guelfs at
Montaperto on September 4th. These two facts are likely to have
decided Richard's policy. He determined to return to England and
for the rest of his reign was content to do what he should as King of
Germany without going farther afield. That he did not intend to
revisit his kingdom in the near future is possibly to be seen in the
creation of vicars to rule the Wetterau and Alsace in his stead.[6]

The speed of Richard's return and the manner of it caused much
surprise and speculation in England. He was said to have been so
hard up on landing that he had to borrow horses from the Prior of
Dover.[7] The numerous rumours that circulated are summarized by

---

[1] Wykes, 124. For the itinerary see B.F. 5370-82.   [2] Bappert, 45-8.

[3] B.F. 5373[a].

[4] Gebauer, 377. This undated letter is assigned by B.F. 5382 to late August 1260. It is possible
that *R. L.*, ii, 157 should be taken with it, but see *infra*, p. 172.

[5] B.F. 9140 and, for the date, Bappert, 49, n. 3.

[6] *C. Med. Hist.*, 125, n. 2, correcting Bappert, 51.

[7] *Gerv. Cant.*, 211. Borrowing horses in these circumstances is not of course an indication
of poverty. What annoyed the Dover chronicler was that he kept them for a week.

the St. Albans' writer as follows:[1] that Manfred's followers had
robbed Richard, that the Germans could not undertake the journey
with winter so near at hand, that Richard had returned to look
after his property, and that the pope asked him to return. The first
and most far-fetched of these theories shows the alarm aroused by
the name of Manfred in England. Even Gebauer in 1744 could
comment on the credulity that believed in Manfred's followers, who
had plenty to do in Italy, hastening from a distance to terrify
strangers in Worms. Yet Richard himself wrote home, it was said,
to Edward reporting that Manfred was sending assassins to deal
with him and his brother Edmund.[2] There was thus little idea in
England, even at St. Albans, of the real reasons for Richard's return.
He was quick enough to boast about his successes, but had little to
say when he had no achievements to magnify.

While Richard was away his brother's position *vis-à-vis* the barons
and his prospects of regaining complete control over the central
government had considerably improved. Simon de Montfort's trial
by his peers on charges preferred by the king in the July parliament
had resulted in an acquittal, but the effect was sufficiently damaging
to cause his disappearance from politics for the rest of the year. The
appointment in October of a treasurer, chancellor, and justiciar who
were men politically colourless at the time does not necessarily
imply any clear set-back to the royalist party.[3] The baronial council
was disintegrating. The ordinance of October 20th, 1260, made 'by
the whole Council' that all magnates should have power to amend
the transgressions of their own bailiffs, was a confession of weakness.
This edict was passed in the absence of Richard, yet he seems to
have been the only baron who took advantage of it.

A few days after his return from Germany, Richard was with
Alexander III of Scotland and Henry III in London (October 29th).[4]
Thence he probably went off to supervise the management of his
English estates at Wallingford.[5] He is found at his manor of Beckley,
near Wheatley, in Oxfordshire, on December 8th, helping Oseney
Abbey and Roger Damory, his tenants, to come to an agreement,
which was sealed in his presence, over the manor of Weston.[6]

[1] *Flores*, ii, 457.   [2] Gebauer, 162; *Ann. Burt.*, 395.
[3] For another view see Treharne, *op. cit.*, 238-44.   [4] *Lib. de Ant. Leg.*, 45; *Flores*, 459.
[5] Edmund of Cornwall is known to have had his administrative centre at Berkhampstead
(Midgley, p. xix), but there are some indications that Wallingford was more important to
Richard. See Appendix.
[6] *Oseney Chartulary*, ed. H. E. Salter, vi, 3; cf. *Ann. Osen.*, 208-10. B.F. 5390 puts this
in error under December 9th, 1261.

Christmas he spent at Windsor with Henry, but Sanchia, presumably already ill, stayed alone at Berkhampstead.[1] Early in 1261 Richard betook himself to Wallingford, where he transacted some formal German business,[2] and at the same time took thought for his own affairs. By January 28th he had been granted leave to munition his castles, beginning with 15,000 cross-bow bolts.[3] Henry retreated to the Tower for ten weeks, but emerged on February 12th, when he had the support of Richard's presence, to receive an oath of fealty from every Londoner over twelve.[4] The King of Almain improved the occasion — perhaps he had been dragged away from the country to provide moral support and felt it should not be unrewarded — by procuring an Exchequer pension of twenty marks a year for his Chancellor, Mr. Arnold of Holland.[5]

From February until he appears again in London in October to play a decisive and public part in the affairs of the realm, Richard's movements are not known. That he was not idle is clear. What is in doubt is the extent to which he shaped or helped to shape Henry III's policy. Of his importance there can be no doubt, and it is tempting for the biographer to magnify the part he played. The records are silent, but the chroniclers agree, and when at length some months later we can intercept his private correspondence we learn enough to justify the view that Richard was supporting Henry's efforts to throw off the baronial yoke with all his power. The continuator of Gervase of Canterbury, a good authority for this period, assures us that Henry was relying on his brother's counsel.[6] It would be strange indeed if he were not, in view of their friendly relations at this period, and Richard's far more comprehensive knowledge of European affairs. The testimony of the *Annals of Bermondsey*, a much later compilation, is to the same effect, though of little worth.[7] More important is the reiterated comment of the chronicle of Battle that the barons did what they liked *usque ad plenum reditum Ricardi regis Alemannie in Angliam*, and when he came the king was released from his oath to the Provisions by the pope.[8] It seems that Richard was keeping in the background as much as possible, and that he must have deceived the barons utterly as to the real strength of his sympathies with the king, for they continued to accept his arbitration and, for some time, to abide by it.

[1] *Flores*, 461. [2] B.F. 5385-6 (January 7-8th, 1261). [3] *Cl. R.*, 339. [4] *Lib. de Ant. Leg.*, 46.
[5] *C.P.R.*, 141 (February 13th, 1261), cf. 177, grant of a benefice worth 50 marks (October).
[6] *Gerv. Cant*, ii, 211. [7] *Ann. Berm.*, 462.
[8] *Chron. de Bello* in Bémont, *Simon de Montfort*, pp. 373-4.

In the spring and summer of 1261 both parties were very active. The king had sent John Mansel to Rome to procure his absolution from the Provisions, and Mansel was back with his precious burden by May 25th. Henry fortified the Tower, plucked up enough courage to slip down to Dover and seize the castle from Hugh Bigod, and arrange for mercenaries from Flanders and Gascony. The biggest contingent came under the Count of St. Pol, who brought with him two friends of John Mansel, namely Gerard de Rodes and Alenard de Seningham.[1] When Philip Basset and Walter de Merton were put into office as Justiciar and Chancellor (May-July), the barons, now both angry and alarmed, urged each other to come armed to Winchester, where Henry was. So Henry fled back to the Tower, perhaps fearing for his personal safety, but in no way dismayed at the progress of his plans. For on July 9th he precipitated the crisis that finally led to the crystallization of both parties and quite rapidly to a more than passive resistance, by appointing a new set of sheriffs for the whole of England, to keep the castles as well as the counties.

Each side knew full well what was happening, for Simon de Montfort as well as Henry was raising troops.[2] The King of Almain called in all the debts from the Jews that he could, and his personal Jew, Abraham of Berkhampstead, was given similar facilities.[3] Thus the king, having first split the council and then edged it out of business, having replaced the special eyre by one of the old-fashioned kind, superseded three lukewarm officers of state by royalist partisans, and now joined issue with his opponents on the vital question of the appointment of the sheriffs, through whom either side could control the whole local administration of the country. The reaction to this wholesale change of local officials must have been rapid. Whether it was organized, or blazed over the land from county to county like a forest fire, no one can yet tell. Henry had certainly asked for trouble. His action of July 9th was far more provocative than his appointment of Peter des Riveaux to thirty-two shrievalties nearly thirty years ago, and in the eyes not only of the barons but the *Bacheleria* — indeed, all the country gentlemen — it must have seemed the blackest treachery that the sheriffs appointed under the Provisions of Oxford should be thus dispossessed.

Baronial anti-sheriffs were appointed, and were active in at least

---

[1] For whom see *infra*, p. 172.   [2] *C.P.R.*, 185.
[3] *Ibid.*, 150 (April 9th), 165 (July 12th).

twenty-two counties in the summer and autumn of 1261.[1] Emboldened by the success of this movement, Simon de Montfort, Gloucester, and the Bishop of Worcester summoned three knights from each shire to meet at St. Albans on September 21st.[2] Since they had control of so many of the county courts they could give this manœuvre something of the appearance of an organized parliament, though from the constitutional point of view it had no sanction. In more normal times they would have held it under cover of a tournament or round table. Henry III countered by summoning the knights to Windsor, where, he said, he would be on that day (September 21st) meeting the said *proceres*, i.e. Simon, Gloucester, and the Bishop of Worcester, discussing peace with them.[3] In the resultant confusion it is thought that there was probably no meeting at all. In spite of the local disorganization the king felt strong enough to summon 150 tenants-in-chief to come to London on October 29th, and busied himself with preparations (October 21st) for the arrival of Flemish and Gascon mercenaries in considerable numbers.

It was at this point that King Richard intervened with decisive effect. He had been staying at St. Martin-le-Grand while Henry was at St. Paul's (September 26th–October 12th), where they probably laid their plans. We know that the two kings were working hand in glove together, from Richard's letter to Henry dated October 23rd at Berkhampstead.[4] It is couched in a formal style with a full salutation, and dated with the day of the month, the indiction, and the regnal year. It is brief and to the point, saying that before the foreign mercenaries are summoned, it ought certainly to be ascertained if they will be allowed to land. He does not doubt that if they are denied entry by the Cinque Ports, he himself can easily arrange for them to be brought in by another route. Richard was happily placed to implement this promise, for he could land the mercenaries in Cornwall, and he was on good terms with the Countess of Flanders.[5] As events turned out there was no need for

[1] Henry's letter of protest of October 18th is addressed to fourteen counties where certain persons (unspecified) assume the custody of the counties (*R. L.*, ii, 192 from the Patent Roll); nine others are involved by Professor Treharne's list (*op. cit.*, 267–8) of the sixteen counties in which the baronial keepers were in 1262 and 1263 asked for repayment of their receipts.

[2] *R. L.*, ii, 179 = *Cl. R.*, 490.

[3] *R. L.*, ii, 179.

[4] *Ibid.*, ii, 193. Shirley is wrong in thinking that this and other letters are misdated. Richard calculated his regnal years from his coronation (May 17th, 1257) and this is correctly dated *anno quinto*.

[5] *Supra*, p. 104.

this foreign aid. Richard, it is clear, was quite prepared to make use of it, but he preferred, as usual, more peaceful methods. The way to a settlement was opened by another quarrel between Simon and Gloucester, which made it possible for Richard to negotiate on behalf of the king with Gloucester, who represented the barons.[1] This was such a blow to Simon's prestige that he withdrew to France.[2] The barons had had safe-conducts to come unarmed to Kingston on October 29th, to treat for peace. It seems unlikely that they came on the appointed day, as even a provisional peace was not sealed until December 5th.[3] Even then there were recalcitrants.[4]

The terms of this peace have not been fully preserved. The Oseney annalist has it that there were to be six arbiters, whom he names, three royalist and three baronial. If they could not agree they were to call in the King of Germany, as a seventh, and if he could not bring them to agreement, Louis IX as an eighth. They are to come to terms on the Provisions of Oxford and other matters of state, and they are to publish their award by Whitsuntide. This is a committee with very wide terms of reference. There is no mention of sheriffs, for this question had been settled provisionally, possibly — because it is such a reasonable compromise which might save the face of each party — by Richard and Gloucester. The arrangement made was that each county that wished to might elect four knights and present them at the Exchequer on January 7th, where Henry was to choose one of them. This is known from Richard's letter to Henry dated [November] 28th, 1261, at Wallingford.[5] The King of the Romans is sorry that he cannot be at the Exchequer to receive them himself, but will send one of his knights. As there would be no point in solemnly explaining this to Henry if it were not fresh news, the date is likely to be November rather than December. Otherwise there would be no time for the counties to be informed.

Thus far we are on reasonably safe ground. We may now dismiss the imposing Committee which was to have dealt with the whole question of the king, the barons, and the Provisions. It is not known whether it achieved anything or even whether it met.

Richard's next intervention was at the request of a wholly distinct

[1] *Gerv. Cant.*, ii, 213.

[2] The date is uncertain; I follow Professor Treharne (*op. cit.*, 271) on this point.

[3] *Ann. Osen.*, 128-9, which also says that the terms were made on November 21st. That peace has been made is stated on December 7th (*C.P.R.*, 195).

[4] On December 16th Henry had to write to fourteen barons individually requiring them to seal the peace (*R. L.*, ii, 196).

[5] *R. L.*, ii, 198.

committee, set up very likely by the peace sealed on December 5th.[1] The royalist nominees were now Philip Basset, Robert Walerand, and Walter de Merton. The issue now was whether the king or his barons should control the local administration. At that time it was hardly possible for the royalists to give up their claim that the king should have complete liberty of choice, as the *Bacheleria* when not at Westminster were the very men who controlled the county courts. To allow them to appoint their own sheriffs would have admitted the whole baronial programme by the back door. This could not be done until the ultimate question of the prerogative had been decided by the test of battle. When that had been settled a large part of the baronial programme could become law in the statute of Marlborough, and though their demands as to sheriffs were not immediately conceded, they received even more than they claimed of the king's gift in 1300 when the counties were allowed to elect their own sheriffs. By that time the matter, with the decline of the discretionary powers of the sheriff, had (according to the text-books) ceased to be of much interest. The baronial three in 1262 did not claim quite so much. They said that the king should appoint *per consilium suum*, that the sheriffs must come from the counties to which they were appointed, and that this method should be tried for ten years. This was the method decided upon in 1258, by which four good men were to be selected in the county court and one of them appointed by the barons of the exchequer.[2] This, oddly enough, was precisely the manner in which the sheriffs of the south-west were chosen in the reign of John. It began in Cornwall, when the county made fine (6 John) and had a charter (10 John) for choosing suitable men of their own county for presentation to the king, who was to choose one, if one was suitable.[3] The men of Cornwall very properly complained in 1274 that under Earl Richard they had lost this right, but there is no indication that they suffered by it.[4] Similar privileges were bought by Dorset and Somerset and Devon

[1] This body has no member in common with the first committee. It is known from Richard's own account of what happened, in his undated award, and by their report that they are totally unable to agree (January 29th, 1262) and have submitted themselves to his decision. Both the report and the award are in *Foed.*, i, 415, and the latter is also printed in Gebauer, 379.

[2] Treharne, 95-7 and *passim*; Jacob, *Studies*, 74-5, 140 and *passim*.

[3] Madox, *Hist. of the Exchequer* (ed. 1711), i, 279 n. (*t*), 283 n. (*l*).

[4] *Infra*, p. 164. The scanty indications of Richard's policy in Cornwall show that he pursued an enlightened policy, e.g. with regard to chartering boroughs, and the amicable settlement of boundary disputes, and in small ways as in his grant (1259-1261) 'for the common advantage of the land of Cornwall, allowing all the inhabitants to take sea sand without payment and to heap the sand on their lands' (*Cal. Ch. R.*, ii, 36).

on occasion. The whole question, from the point of view of the shire, turned upon the sheriff being a local vavasour and not a foreigner from another county or even Poitou. Richard's sheriffs in Cornwall were probably local men. It is just possible that Richard's award was so long delayed because he was troubled by the apparent reasonableness of the baronial claim, but he was bound to come down on the side of prerogative. This he did in his award of February–April 1262. He explains in this award that by a *forma pacis* king and barons submitted themselves to the *mise* of six arbiters, and since these could in no way agree it now pertained to him, according to the form of the *mise*, to say that Henry could appoint whom he liked as sheriffs. This award seems to have been accepted.

While Richard was occupied in putting Henry III's affairs in order for him he found time to consider a proposed marriage between Edmund of Lancaster and the daughter of Guy, Count of Flanders. Henry had naturally consulted him on this point, but though Richard gave the matter precedence over the mere question of sheriffs, which seemed to give him little trouble, he replied somewhat coldly that, as he did not know what the Count of Flanders had to offer, or under what form Henry wished the marriage to be contracted, he could offer no advice.[1] Possibly Richard was in no mood to talk about marriages, as his own wife had died a few weeks earlier. She had borne him two sons, of whom Edmund, his sixth child, was now a boy of eleven.[2] Richard and Sanchia had been married nearly twenty years, but, though Richard did not marry again for seven years, it would be unwise to assume any great degree of affection between them. He had left her alone at Berkhampstead the preceding Christmas, and then on Saturday, November 5th, she grew weaker[3] and on Wednesday the 9th she died at Berkhampstead.[4] But Richard on the 8th and 9th was transacting German business in London,[5] and when Sanchia's body was translated to Hailes on the

[1] R. L., ii, 197-8. In the end Edmund married Blanche, daughter of the Count of Artois (1275).

[2] The eldest was born in July 1246 and died on August 15th (*Mat. Par.*, iv, 568-9). Edmund was born about January 1st, 1250. The notes to Hemingburgh, ii, 98, describe as a younger son of Sanchia, without authority, the Richard, brother of the Earl of Cornwall, who was killed at the storm of Berwick in 1296. *Flores*, ii, 471, mentions Richard, nephew of Henry III, who died August 5th, 1261, at Winchelsea, *cognominatus de Paris, eo quod Parisius natus est et sepultus est apud Boloniam.* The editor states 'this was a son of Richard of Cornwall', without authority. Henry III and Richard could have had a number of *nepotes*, sons or daughters of John's numerous progeny. Earl Richard had for example besides his brother Eudo (*supra*, p. 41) a brother Ivo who attests his charter to Launceston (Oliver, *Mon. Dioc. Exon.*, p. 23).

[3] *M.G.H.*, xvi, 483.   [4] *Ann. Osen.*, and *Wykes*, 128.

[5] B.F. 5388-9 (correspondence with Engelbert of Cologne, about the regalia).

15th by Archbishop Boniface, two bishops, Peter of Savoy and other magnates, it was done in the absence of Richard.[1] Her death was even anticipated, it seems, with indecent haste by her executors, who on November 1st had received power to dispose of some of her estates.[2] Richard, on November 12th, prudently acquired permission to do what he would with the wardship and marriage of his son Edmund. Mass was celebrated daily in the Tower for her and an anniversary arranged at Westminster, at Henry III's expense.[3]

Richard was dilatory with his award in the matter of the sheriffs. The question which he was called upon to decide was one of the burning questions of the day, and it was four months before he ventured to give a decision. Action was perhaps forced upon him by his impending visit to Germany, where he was now urgently needed.

This must have come as a surprise to Richard, for he had in October 1260 left the Rhineland no more unsettled than usual, and his prestige south of the Alps had not lessened as a result of his failure to come to Rome. In April 1261 he was elected Senator of Rome for life, but he made no effort to take up the office or use his position in any way, and a couple of years later Charles of Anjou was elected in his stead.[4] If Richard had ever toyed with the idea of using this new dignity as a means of putting pressure on the still vacillating Alexander IV, he was at once disappointed. For Alexander clinched the matter by dying on May 25th and Urban IV, who succeeded him in August, was a man of much tougher moral fibre, prepared to dictate his own terms to both candidates for empire. Clement IV adopted a similar attitude but had even less power to translate his theory of papal supremacy into action. Richard cared little and himself died before the matter could be decided.[5]

While the King of Almain was preparing his award about the choice of sheriffs, he was also building his new castle of Mere in Dorset,[6] advising his brother to widen the road through Windsor Forest,[7] and confirming the appointment of an advocate at Soëst in Westphalia.[8] These are the surviving fragments of what must have been the heavy load of business handled by Mr. Arnold of Holland, who had to deal with Richard's English as well as his foreign affairs.

---

[1] *Flores*, 474.   [2] *C.P.R.*, 193.   [3] *Ibid.*, 195.
[4] See the note by F. R. Lewis in *E.H.R.*, lii, 657-62. The invitation from the Romans is printed in *N.A.*, xiii, 221.
[5] Cf. *infra*, p. 140.   [6] *Cl. R.*, 41. There are signs of much building in 1257 and 1259-1262.
[7] *Ibid.*, 120.   [8] B.F. 5393 (13th April).

I

Henry III was always seeking advice and he now turned to his brother again. He had requested a meeting at Richard's manor of Cippenham, near Windsor, on Friday, May 12th, 1262. For once Richard was too busy to help. On May 9th he wrote, in the formal manner usual in his surviving letters to Henry, that urgent affairs connected with a hasty visit to Germany prevented his attendance, as well as the arrival of further ambassadors from the German nobles. If he ought to have come to Henry about the award with the Earl of Gloucester, his advice is that when it is published Henry ought to do his utmost to keep it.[1] It is likely from this that Henry had arranged the meeting without saying exactly what he wanted to discuss. Conceivably he wanted to hurry up the award. It was at any rate delivered into the wardrobe a few days later.[2]

The urgent messages from Germany — the letter seems to indicate more than one embassy — meant that there had been in April a sudden and dangerous threat to elect Conradin as Richard's successor. Archbishop Werner of Mainz, who was quarrelling with one of Richard's vicars, Philip of Hohenfels, is thought to have appointed a day for the election of a new king. It appeared likely that Conradin would be elected, as is known from a letter of Urban IV to Ottocar of Bohemia. Urban, warned of the crisis by Ottocar, had threatened to excommunicate the Rhenish archbishops if they proceeded to an election.[3] Richard had therefore to visit his kingdom as soon as possible, but it was with no appearance of haste that he left for Germany a third time, more than a month after he had explained the urgent necessity of his journey, on a tour that was to last until February 1263. For the fourth time he was to make his progress up and down the Rhine, treated apparently as a harmless, decorative, and magnificent person who could be relied upon to confirm charters, pardon debts, and spend an infinity of time in settling disputes without knocking together the heads of the disputants. Never, too, was a king who so fully 'lived of his own'. For all this he was tolerated, but not respected.

Leaving London on June 20th,[4] Richard travelled through Flanders to Ghent, where on July 2nd he patched up the age-long quarrel between the families of Avesnes and Dampierre.[5] After arranging a regency in Holland and Zealand,[6] he passed through

---

[1] *R. L.*, ii, 174-5, under wrong date, and printing Leic' for Glouc'.
[2] *Cl. R.*, 126 (May 20th, 1262).   [3] *Reg. Urbain IV*, no. 104; B.F. 4778^c, 5394.
[4] *Lib. de Ant. Leg.*, 50; Wykes, 131, gives June 21st.   [5] B.F. 5395.
[6] *Ibid.*, 5396.

Brabant, where, too, there was a regency, consequent upon the death of his old opponent Duke Henry III. At Aachen, which he had reached by July 13th, Richard left a memorandum of the insignia presented by him to the dean and chapter for use at all future coronations of German kings.[1] There, too, he rewarded by a formal grant to King Ottocar of Bohemia the loyalty and prompt action that had forestalled the election of an anti-king. The alienation of Austria and Styria by this charter of August 6th, 1262,[2] is a milestone in the disintegration of the kingdom which Richard had been elected to preserve. But Richard was a realist and even if he had had the time and opportunity was unfitted by character and inclination to dominate the princes of Germany east of the Rhine. He spent, instead, over a month at Aachen. It seems to have been from here that he wrote to John Mansel, who was deputy-chancellor in France with Henry, to get news of his brother's affairs, asking for a messenger to be sent to him on Friday after the feast of the Assumption (August 18th). Mansel was at or near Boulogne, thinking of the house he had left near Worthing, which he was busy fortifying with a moat and a crenellated wall of stone and lime. He reflects that he is satisfied with the progress of the work and is just on the point of letting the water in. This he reports[3] to his friend Sir Robert de Thwenge, the notorious north country anti-papalist, afterwards one of his executors, and Imbert de Montferrand, another king's knight, suggesting that they send Sir John de Castello, a diplomat *de carrière*, to Richard. Mansel continues that he is doing his best in the parts where he is in the matter of royalist propaganda, and adds 'if the king had preachers for him such as his opponents have, it would be the better for him'. He did not misjudge the situation. He had been thinking of fortifying Sedgwick House for the last four years, and within a year he was limping out of the Tower in flight to France.[4]

[1] The memorandum records his gift to the chapel of S. Mary in the cathedral, to be placed in the treasury in the care of the provost, dean, and chapter, a gold crown decorated with rubies, emeralds, sapphires, pearls, and other precious stones, a set of royal vestments ornamented with his arms, with a sceptre and a gilt 'apple'. They were also to be guarded under the seals of the *scabini* and the communal seal of the city, so that they should be ready for the coronation of all succeeding kings of Germany, and after each such occasion be returned to the treasury (Gebauer, 380-2; *Arch. Journal* (1863), p. 197. Some of these were still there when Bappert wrote in 1905 (p. 63)).

[2] B.F. 5399.

[3] See Appendix Four on the date of this letter, which is tentatively assigned to 1260 in *R. L.*, ii, 157-8.

[4] Sir Robert de Thwenge took the hint and obtained licence to crenellate his own house at Bergh in Yorkshire on August 16th, 1262, a few days after he had received the letter (*C.P.R.*, 1266-1272, App. 729).

If the messenger from England reached Richard at Aachen it did not prevent him from pursuing his journey up the Rhine. Before he set out he received the discouraging news that Urban IV had decided to style both Alfonso and Richard 'king-elect', and had cited them both to appear at Rome.[1]   Passing through Andernach (August 21st), Boppard (August 27th, September 3rd), and Frankfurt (September 17th) he was at Oppenheim (September 27th–28th) or farther south when he received news from Henry himself. Henry was still in France, recovering from the strange illness that had attacked the whole court there, and he writes that he cannot yet provide the support that he had offered Richard before the latter went to Germany, and respecting which Richard had reminded him through Peter of Savoy. In view of the great help he has received from Richard he will see what can be done when he gets home.[2]

The need for this support (*subsidium*) apparently not being urgent Richard continued his journey southwards for another month. He probably misjudged, or was not fully informed about, the situation in England, which was deteriorating rapidly. At Hagenau he mediated with little effect between the citizens of Strassburg and the bishop, who had come to open war — the *Bellum Waltherianum* — on both banks of the Rhine.[3]   About the middle of November he reached his 'furthest South'. Zürich he took under his protection, Bâle, which he may have visited, sent ambassadors, and even Rudolf of Habsburg was at his court. His power in the Upper Rhineland was generally acknowledged, when about the middle of November he turned back. Moving deliberately and surrounded by a number of the German nobility he spent a leisurely three months in returning to England, landing on February 10th, 1263.[4]   From this journey and the manner of his return the conclusion is almost inevitable that Richard cared little for the rest of Germany, and had given up indefinitely the journey to Rome for which he had once

[1] *Reg. Urbain IV*, nos. 358 (August 7th), 350-1 (August 27th), and 2815-18 (August 31st). It was unfortunate that Henry III was at the same time writing to Alfonso, who had again appealed to him for help, that one must recognize as king whom the pope called king. This time Alfonso seems to have been a step ahead in the negotiations (*Cl. R.*, 173, August 16th, 1262). For Henry's earlier letters, which are less abrupt, see *supra*, p. 95, and for 1260 see *Foed.*, i, 397 (May 30th).
[2] *Cl. R.*, 175-6=*Foed.*, i, 421 (September 30th); B.F. 11921.
[3] *M.G.H.*, xvii, 113; B.F. 5416.   The other known dates in this itinerary are: Hagenau (October 16th), Schlettstadt (November 5th), Hagenau (November 18th–21st), Mainz (December 3rd to January 7th), Trèves (January 23rd).   See further Bappert, 68-9.
[4] Wykes, 130.

been so eager. It would be difficult from the events of this third visit to his kingdom to construct any defence against Böhmer's harshly-phrased judgment, 'Dass er die deutsche Krone nur mehr als einem Luxusbesitz betrachtete, mit dem er von Zeit zu Zeit Schaugepränge trieb'.[1]

[1] See B.F. 5289ª.

CHAPTER EIGHT

ENGLAND (1263-1265)

BATTLE OF LEWES; CAPTIVITY

WHILE Richard was paying his third visit to Germany, Henry III was frittering away his time in France, whither he had followed Simon de Montfort in July 1262. With the chief actors abroad, for Edward also was in France, there was no likelihood of an immediate outbreak at home, but the political situation in England was rapidly deteriorating partly through bad luck, partly through bad management. The chief factors in this decline are easy to see. On the death of Richard de Clare, Earl of Gloucester, on July 16th, 1262, his son Gilbert, though he was not yet of full age, hastened to Boulogne to receive his lands from the king. Henry, always punctilious in feudal matters, offended the young man, now the most powerful baron in the country, by refusing his request, whereupon the impetuous 'Red earl' came home and threw in his lot with the Marchers. Secondly, Edward quarrelled with his steward, Roger de Leybourne, over a matter of estate-accounts, so Roger too joined the Marchers. Thirdly, early in September, a strange and fatal epidemic swept through Henry's court carrying off sixty of his followers. The king himself and John Mansel were completely incapacitated, and when he was convalescent Henry insisted on spending a couple of months on pilgrimage in Burgundy, only returning to England in December. Simon de Montfort had taken advantage of his absence to slip back and, it is said, present to a meeting of magnates in London papal letters enjoining strict observance of the Provisions. This may or may not be true: it is a reminder that the barons as well as the king had representatives at the Court of Rome. Finally, in December, Llewelyn invaded the Marches. It is hardly surprising that Henry, still weak from his illness, reissued the Provisions — a feeble gesture — in the second half of January.

From Richard's return in February 1263 until his release from captivity in September 1265, may be regarded as the most unhappy period of his career. Until the battle of Lewes he played an uneasy part. Negotiations with Simon de Montfort and his extremists

118

rapidly became impossible. They had no serious thought of turning to Richard for arbitration. He had dealt successfully with Richard de Clare; but Simon was less easy to handle. Simon de Montfort and the King of the Romans, though not personally at feud, were yet poles apart in temperament. So for the three months of Simon's provisional government (July–October 1263) Richard seems to retire from public life. Whether he was raising an army in Cornwall, or looking after his interests at Berkhampstead, where he was when we lose him in July and where we find him again in October, is not known. He may well have been living quietly in order to recruit his finances.[1]

The high state of public excitement in this period is seen in the comments that greeted Richard's arrival in England. Henry III being ill, it was rumoured that Richard had come back to reign after him.[2] The heir to the throne, still only twenty-four, had no reputation for wisdom. He appeared to contemporaries as a young man whose administration of his own estates both in England and Gascony left much to be desired. His officials were unpopular, his far too numerous household behaved, even in his uncle's home, with outrageous licence, he had himself the reputation of a man of little faith, with an excessive fondness for tournaments. But the story of Richard's ambition to be King of England as well as of Germany has nothing else to support it. Possibly it was with this rumour in mind that some modern writers have assigned Richard to the baronial side in 1263. It may even have been this that allowed the Dunstable annalist to number him among the barons who met at Oxford in April, on Simon de Montfort's return, to renew the oath of 1258.[3] It is conceivable that Richard, keeping up his pose of neutrality, was there to negotiate, but if so he did not meet with the smallest success. The revolt in the Marches had already begun when he returned to London before Whitsuntide.[4] Pierre d'Aigueblanche had been seized, the towns of Gloucester and Worcester were taken, and de Montfort had come to a tacit agreement with Llewelyn. Henry held Dover, but his military preparations were made only

---

[1] He had returned 'exhausto solito more in Teutonicis thesauro suo' (*Flores*, ii, 477). This may be taken to mean that he had spent all his ready money in Germany.

[2] 'R. rex Alemannie venit in Angliam die beate Scholastice virginis pro infirmitate H. regis Anglie fratris sui, ut dicebatur, sed aliud fuit in causa quicquid aliquis sibilaverit' (*Gerv. Cant.*, 219). 'R. . . . venit Londonias cum paucis videre dominum H. regem fratrem suum, qui adhuc tunc temporis non plene convaluit de infirmitate sua; et dicebatur a pluribus quod ad hoc venit ut regnaret post eum, si contingeret humanitus de domino rege' (*Ann. Burt.*, 500).

[3] *Ann. Dunst.*, 221.   [4] *Gerv. Cant.*, 221.

at the last minute and were a failure. Richard was with him part
of the time. They had dined together with the Dominican chapter-
general in London on May 20th[1] and Richard attested on June 11th at
St. Paul's a grant of the Jewry by Edward to the Beraldi of Cahors.[2]
He was at the Tower (about June 24th) when Henry received the
petition of the barons under Simon's seal, transmitted through the
citizens of London.[3] It was about this time that Edward was sent
to rob the bank at the New Temple, to relieve his father's desperate
need of money. This would be very distasteful to Richard as he had,
at Isleworth on June 17th, granted to the Templars in fee-farm the
barony of Castle Holgate in Shropshire and the manor of Sutton in
Hampshire.[4] A few days later John Mansel and some of the distinguished foreigners, including the Archbishop of Canterbury,
fled from England.

Part of this time Richard was at Isleworth by Twickenham.
From here he wrote to Henry that he was proceeding in all haste to
Cippenham near Windsor, with the intention of going on to
Wallingford where he hoped to find the barons in order to treat
with them. Meanwhile he implores Henry to give Edward strict
orders not to attack the barons while negotiations are in progress,
and adds that he has sent to the barons a similar message.[5] Next day
he reports that he had sent a messenger from Cippenham to Simon,
having heard that he was at Reading, urging him to attend a conference at the Loddon bridge, near Twyford, and that although the
messenger reached him at daybreak Simon refused to negotiate,
saying that he could not change his plans.[6] Learning that Simon
had broken camp very early and, by-passing London, had reached
Guildford, Richard changed his mind about going to Wallingford
and returned instead to Isleworth, hoping to meet Henry in London
on the morrow, July 1st. While Simon was securing the Cinque
Ports, Richard retired to Berkhampstead castle, where he probably felt safer than at Isleworth. From here he sent William de
Wolvele, a Trinitarian, his treasurer, and Michael of Northampton,
one of his clerks, as his plenipotentiaries to Henry.[7] On July 10th he

---

[1] *Gerv. Cant.*, 221.   [2] *C.P.R.*, 263.   [3] *Lib. de Ant. Leg.*, 54.

[4] Bémont, 200, n. 6, misplaces the attack by the Londoners on Isleworth. It occurred
in March 1264. Richard had acquired Castle Holgate and Sutton from William Mauduit.
The deeds are in Exch. T. R. Misc. Bk., no. 57, nos. lxxxxiii, cl; cf. *Book of Fees*, p. 1261.

[5] *R. L.*, i, 247.

[6] *Ibid.*, 248, 'quod non posset ullatenus nobis occurrere, neque preconceptum intentionis
sue propositum variare'.

[7] *Ibid.*, 249 (July 8th).

wrote to thank Henry for procuring the release of Henry of Almain, who had pursued Mansel to France and himself been captured there by the royalists.[1]

That Richard's decision to go to Berkhampstead was a right one was shown by the stoning of the queen when she tried to leave the Tower to join Edward and his foreign mercenaries at Windsor. When Richard and Henry sealed the agreement to reissue the Provisions on July 16th and peace was patched up,[2] it was expressly stated in the Patent that it was through the mediation of the Bishops of Lincoln, London, and Chester, not through Richard, that this came about. It is necessary to emphasize this, because the opposite has been stated.[3] Richard's own negotiations had been a complete failure, and the wording of the Patent suggests that he was not even present at the making of this peace. He is not a dissentient, but no more can be said of his attitude than this, that 'the king has procured the seal of his brother R. King of the Romans with his own seal to be attached to these presents'. This is hardly the formula that would have been used if Richard's part had been more than formal.

The peace of July 1263 was a complete capitulation on the part of the royalists, and its first outward and visible sign was the grant under the great seal on July 18th of John Mansel's newly-fortified house at Sedgwick to Peter de Montfort.[4] Simon de Montfort now controlled the administration with the young nobles who followed him, and with the moral support of the populace in London and some other towns, the Marchers, to a large extent the friars and clergy, and, more effective but less vocal, the country gentry. It was a shaky administration. Simon was possibly not strong enough to put in new sheriffs, but appointed *custodes pacis*, who have been likened to major-generals, to take over nearly all the military, police, and judicial functions of the sheriff, leaving the latter as a mere financial agent. It is suggested with much probability by Professor Treharne, that they had been the county agents for Simon de Montfort in the spring rising.[5] The chief events of July-October, the confirmation of the peace in the September parliament, the deadlock in October, with Henry III still claiming to appoint all his household officers, ran parallel with the desertion of Simon by the Marchers,

---

[1] *Foed.*, i, 427; *Gerv. Cant.*, 222; *Ann. Dunst.*, 223.
[2] *C.P.R.*, 269-70; *Flores*, ii, 482; Stubbs, ii, 87, and *D.N.B.*, *s.v.* Richard of Cornwall, 172, make Richard responsible for this. Bappert, 76, ignores the Patent.
[3] *D.N.B.*, *s.v.* Richard of Cornwall, 172.   [4] *C.P.R.*, 269.
[5] Treharne, *The Baronial Plan*, 316, 319.

and the concomitant growth of a royalist party under the leadership
of the Lord Edward, who seized Windsor castle and was joined by
Henry in October.

Though we do not know what Richard was doing during these
months he was certainly not supporting his brother's cause with
heart and soul. He was with equal certainty not openly supporting
de Montfort. His position was ambiguous, and it will be as well to
sum up the case against him at this point, before he reappears in the
royal camp. There had been unpleasant rumours about his return
from Germany, he is mentioned at the Oxford parliament, Henry III
had been forced to release Henry of Almain 'because his detention
will be a cause of inestimable peril to the king'.[1] These facts appear
to be the only justification for Pauli's statement that Richard
'threatened to negotiate independently with the barons'[2] about
July 10th. Until August 15th (presumably from some time in July)
Simon de Montfort lay encamped in Richard's park at Isleworth,
while Henry was at Westminster.[3] On this occasion there is no suggestion of looting or damage. We have also to remember Richard's
subsequent failure to participate in the negotiations preceding the
Mise of Amiens. Even taken together these do not amount to very
much, but they provide a background for the remarkable letter of
Urban IV written on September 16th, 1263, accusing Richard in the
strongest terms of notorious duplicity.[4] Urban writes to this effect:
'The common assertion of the people, and the general opinion of
almost all is that the boisterous fluctuation of the storm, which shakes
the solid foundation of the kingdom of England' has been raised
against Henry 'with your tacit permission, perhaps even stirred up
by you',[5] and that, as Richard's wealth and power is so great that if
he did not permit it no one could raise war against or thwart the
king, the horrid suspicion arises in the minds of all that he approves
this error.

It was not in the interests of the barons that Urban should write
in these terms. Probably the letter was inspired by complaints sent off
by Henry III in July. It was part of Urban's policy to keep Richard
in his place, for he had already (August 7th) announced that both

[1] *C.P.R.*, 269.
[2] *Simon de Montfort*, p. 120. *V.C.H. Berks.*, ii, 129, which goes even further, is perhaps
based on this.
[3] Wykes, 136.
[4] *Reg. Urbain IV*, no. 724. The letter is mentioned by Bappert, 75, n. 2, without any indication of its contents. English writers seem to have neglected it.
[5] 'Te permittente ac dissimulante, nec dicamus promovente.'

claimants to the Empire should be merely 'King-elect' and had cited
them to appear at Rome on May 2nd, 1265.[1] The journey from
Rome could be done in a month, and a day or two after it should
have arrived Richard is again found at court. It is not impossible
that Urban's letter had some effect in helping to persuade Richard
that it was futile to try to maintain his pose of neutrality. Henry had
always been hasty in appealing to the pope for help, and the permanent officials of the curia must sometimes have been hard put to
know how to deal with his correspondence. In this case a difference
may have arisen between the brothers over the behaviour and treatment of Henry of Almain, who, after showing as much vacillation
as his father had done in his youth, did not finally return to the
royalist side until later.[2] Richard's loyalty to Henry III during
Simon de Montfort's first administration must therefore remain in
doubt. More than half his landed wealth was well out of the way of
any *turbatio* that seemed likely; his contract for the Mint had run out;
he had helped his brother in every possible way for twenty years
only to be completely ignored in a vital matter of foreign policy —
Sicily, which he knew personally and had rejected; he had even,
though King of the Romans and *Semper Augustus*, stooped to negotiate with a parvenu who had run off with his sister and now refused
to listen to him. He did not lose his temper, but he could hardly
with dignity remain at court. He had done all he could and he did
not wish to fight. It was best to hold aloof and hope for better times.

On this occasion Richard's patience was rewarded. Almost the
first act of the new royalist government was a grant to him (he was
at Berkhampstead) of the Mowbray wardship.[3] This may be connected with his renewed efforts to negotiate with the barons. The
flight of the archbishop had left the way open for the bishops to take
action, and the initiative may have come from them, but it was
Richard who was in charge of the parleying. Matters had already
gone some distance before he took part. The Bishops of London,
Exeter, and Worcester had already approached Henry with some

[1] *Reg. Urbain IV*, nos. 350-1, 358.

[2] Professor Treharne seems to place this in connection with the events of October. Rish., *de Bellis*, 17, places it in or after January 1264, which is clearly too late, as he was with his father and the king by the beginning of December. Possibly Richard and his son 'came in' together. There is a graphic account of Henry of Almain's secession from de Montfort (*ibid.*) which is probably not far from the truth.

[3] *C.P.R.* The Mowbray wardship was regranted (*ibid.*, 304) when the king recovered the use of his Great Seal, after Simon de Montfort's strange interlude of July-October. For Richard at Berkhampstead on October 17th see *supra*, p. 54.

proposal by October 24th, since next day Henry apologized for not being able to give an immediate answer, which he would give later the same day.[1] By the 28th both parties had agreed to stand to the award of Louis IX and proctors were appointed on Henry's side.[2] The same day the king summoned certain barons to him, saying that he had heard from Richard and the other elected mediators that firm peace was likely to be made very soon.[3] So Richard, having recovered from his set-back in June was behind the first stage of the negotiations leading to the Mise of Amiens. The decision of the mediators was not, however, at this time a final one, for their deliberations must have been disturbed by Henry's march to the coast (November 28th–December 3rd) to secure Dover. This unsuccessful effort, made in company with Richard,[4] who was now continuously at court,[5] may indicate that the negotiations of October had broken down and that the formal submission of both sides to the arbitration of Louis IX in the middle of December represented a new effort at reaching agreement. This time Richard is not mentioned, though he was represented, and he spent Christmas with the king and queen in London.[6] When Henry went to France in January to hear the Mise, Richard remained in England, virtually as regent.[7]

The part played by Richard in the events leading up to the Mise of Amiens is thus obscure. It is as if he had deliberately withdrawn himself after the preliminary agreement in October to submit to arbitration. For though he was at court on December 8th and 25th he was not a party to the formal document drawn up there on December 16th. Henry of Almain witnessed it and Mr. Arnold his 'chancellor' was present when it was drawn up.[8] Richard's abstention was probably deliberate as later in respect of the *Dictum de Kenilworth*. He was a proud man, and preferred to hold himself aloof. This, until it came to fighting, was the strength of his position for a decade after the Mad Parliament, that he had had no part or lot in the making of the Provisions of Oxford, he had only sworn to

---

[1] *C.P.R.*, 292.   [2] *Ibid.*, 294.   [3] *Ibid.*, 296.   [4] Wykes, 137.

[5] Henry and Richard were at Canterbury (*C.P.R.*, 300, December 5th), and Croydon (*Cl. R.*, 371 = *R. L.*, 250-1, December 8th), and Windsor (Wykes, 138, December 16th).

[6] Rish., *Chron.*, 17.

[7] The letters Close and Patent are attested by him between January 8th and February 18th. There are four documents leading up to this Mise, three of them printed in Appendix to Rish., *de Bellis*, from the French archives: (i) the barons submit to arbitration, December 13th (*de Bellis*, 121); (ii) the king does the same, December 16th, at Windsor (*R. L.*, ii, 252 = *Foed.*, 433); (iii) the barons appoint proctors, December 31st, at London (*de Bellis*, 122); and (iv) renewed submission of the king, January 23rd, at Amiens (*ibid.*, 120).

[8] *R. L.*, ii, 252.

observe them at the king's command, and he had so far as we know never quarrelled with anybody about them. Moreover, however much they spoke of him as Earl of Cornwall, he remained the King of Almain, and Mr. Arnold was there to remind them. No one else in England had a prothonotary, and the clerks of the chancery were very conscious of it.[1]

While Henry was on his way to France Richard remained at Windsor, where it fell to him on February 4th to order the destruction of all the bridges over the Severn except Gloucester, the sinking of every vessel and the fortification of fords.[2] For the rejection of the Mise of Amiens was immediate. 'The Londoners, the barons of the Cinque ports and almost all the commonalty of the middle folk of England, who had not put themselves on the King of France's award' rejected it utterly.[3] The situation in the Marches, whither Simon had sent his eldest son Henry, was already such that Richard thought it wise to go there in person. He was at Risborough on January 10th, Berkhampstead on 18th,[4] at Oxford on February 7th, at Worcester on the 10th and a week later at Hereford.[5] Possibly it was at this time that he raised, or caused to be raised, an army in Cornwall which he took with him to the battle of Lewes.[6] Nothing else is known about this or any other contingent that he may have had. The satirist who attacked him after the battle alludes to his German troops, which may in reality have been Flemish mercenaries.

The gathering of the royalist barons took place at Windsor, where Henry held an armed parliament. With hardly explicable folly he had lingered nine days at Canterbury before joining Richard. From this time until they were captured at Lewes the brothers were together. From Windsor they marched to Oxford, which they reached on March 8th. The university, strongly baronial in sympathy, was sent down, and Oxford became for a month the royalist headquarters for the campaign which culminated in the battle of Lewes. From here negotiations were undertaken with the barons. Henry appointed the Bishop of Lichfield and the Archdeacon of Norwich, Mr. Nicholas de Plumpton, as his envoys to treat with the barons in the presence of Sir John de Valentino, who represented

---

[1] *Infra*, p. 128, under May 12, '64.   [2] *R. L.*, ii, 253-4.
[3] *Lib. de Ant. Leg.*, 61; cf. Wykes, 139; Rish., *de Bellis*, 21.
[4] Public Record Office, Anct. Corr., viii, 5, 6.   [5] *C.P.R.* and *Cl. R.*
[6] 'Cornubia ubi Ricardus comes excitavit exercitum, quem secum duxit ad bellum de Leaus' (Blaauw, p. 353, citing Cott. MS. Nero A., iv).

Louis IX.[1] The barons sent the Bishops of London, Winchester, Worcester, and Chichester, who received a safe-conduct to come to Brackley to treat of peace.[2] The bishops had authority to accept the Provisions except the article concerning the aliens, which had become the one insuperable obstacle to peace in the eyes of those on either side who were not in fact willing to forgo the arbitrament of war. The initiative in these negotiations, which continued for over a week, probably came from the bishops, as in the Marshal's rebellion just thirty years earlier. They had got so far as to agree upon a form under which Archbishop Boniface and all exiled clergy English or foreign might return,[3] when negotiations were broken off, probably by the news from London. In any event the return of all the clergy was incompatible with Simon's objection to the aliens, and while negotiations were still proceeding Henry was summoning all the troops he could — knights and freemen — to come with their whole *posse* to Oxford from the south-west and west.[4]

The breakdown of this conference occurred about the same time as a sudden outburst of rioting by the London mob. For some time the power of the merchant oligarchy had been threatened by the populace, who had installed a democratic mayor, Thomas Fitz-Thomas, in 1263. Led by Hugh Despenser, the baronial justiciar, and with their own constable and marshal elected for the occasion, they made straight for Richard's manor of Isleworth, which he had surrounded with a ditch and stockade. They broke the head of the fishpond which he had constructed, at great cost, and destroyed everything that they could not steal. They then razed to the ground his mansion at Westminster and uprooted all his orchards. *Et hoc fuit initium dolorum et origo mortalis guerre.*[5] Richard was by no means the only one to suffer, but he was the first. The manors of William de Valence, Walter de Merton, and Philip Basset are all said to have been similarly treated. King's clerks, barons of the Exchequer, justices of the Bench, all suffered. A little later there was a particularly horrible massacre of the Jews. It was, thought Wykes, a

---

[1] *C.P.R.*, 307 (March 13th). [2] *Ibid.*, 308, and *Foed.*, i, 437 (March 20th).
[3] *Foed.*, i, 438 (March —). [4] *C.P.R.*, 358 (March 20th).
[5] *Lib. de Ant. Leg.*, 61. This account explicitly states that the rioting took place during the 'parliament' at Oxford and implies that a truce should have been observed, during these negotiations (i.e. the Brackley conference). This is the important fact. The precise date is not quite certain. Wykes says the 'first Monday in Lent' (March 10th) probably for the 'Monday after Mid-Lent' (March 31st). Oseney 146 says that many manors of Richard and Philip Basset were looted on St. Mark's day (April 25th), but if this is meant to refer to the same occasion it is much too late. Rish., *de Bellis*, 21, does not date these events precisely.

remarkable display of ingratitude towards Richard, who had so often protected the citizens against the extortions of Henry III. But it was the merchants who had benefited by his protection, and though the 'Cahorsins' and other foreign merchants were attacked, the wealthy burghers do not at this time seem to have suffered. Richard's anger at the damage to his property was great, and he ordered immediate reprisals. *Ab hinc rex Alemannie de feroci factus ferocior.* He sent out his men to seize any Londoners they could find within or without the town (i.e. Oxford).[1] He seems to have felt as keenly about this episode as he had done about the devastation caused by Richard Siward in the 'thirties. This had important repercussions, as Richard, instead of urging moderation upon his brother as hitherto, now joined Edward in counselling stern measures. The royalist army moved straight on from Oxford to Northampton, which was taken by treachery and ruthlessly sacked, then to Leicester and Nottingham, with the intention of going to Lincoln, when the news of Simon's attack on Rochester drove them south by forced marches.

A couple of days before the battle of Lewes Simon de Montfort again allowed overtures for peace to be made through the bishops, probably for the sake of appearances. It appears from three sources that they offered some £30,000 for peace, but the nature of this offer is uncertain. As, however, Wykes,[2] a staunch royalist with a quite unusual knowledge of Richard's affairs, and the contemporary baronial satirist[3] unite in saying that Richard was offered, or asked for a sum of this magnitude, there is likely to be some truth in it. Rishanger, another baronial partisan, has it that the £30,000 was offered by the Bishops of London and Worcester as compensation for war damage.[4] The terms offered are not alluded to in the barons' letter to the king on May 12th, protesting their loyalty to his person and their determination to fight against his foreign and evil advisers. This letter appears to have been brought by the Bishop of Chichester. The king's reply was to defy Simon de Montfort and Gilbert de Clare, and it is possibly at this point that they stepped-up their terms by offering compensation as well. Rishanger, biased but knowledgeable, believed that this offer would have succeeded if Richard of

---

[1] Rish., *de Bellis*, 22. Richard's presence is mentioned at Northampton (*ibid.*, 23) and Tonbridge (*Gerv. Cant.*, 236).

[2] Wykes, 148.

[3] *Pol. Songs*, 69: 'The kyn of Alemaigne bi my leaute
Thritti thousent pound askede he
For to make the pees in the countre.'

[4] Rish., *de Bellis*, 30.

Almain had not instigated the Lord Edward to join him in defying the barons. This he attributed, probably rightly, to Richard's pride and his thirst for revenge. The tone of the letter of defiance sent by Richard and Edward is different from Henry III's purely formal note, and does not suggest that any room was left for compromise. It seems just possible that while the king's letter was a reply to that brought by the Bishop of Chichester, Richard and Edward were replying (for themselves and the other royalist barons) to the second embassy led by London and Worcester, all on May 12th; and that on May 13th the barons at length withdrew their homage.[1] For the withdrawal of homage there is no documentary evidence: it may have been verbal.[2] It should have caused difficulties to Simon after he had captured the king, but he continued serenely to write to himself in the king's name, as to a faithful subject.[3] That this difficulty was borne in mind is seen in 1265 when all had to renew their homage and fealty because the king had defied them before the battle of Lewes.[4]

Since the negotiations of May 12th-13th were unsuccessful, they are of less interest to the general historian than to the biographer of King Richard, for it seems that, but for Richard, there might have been no battle of Lewes, though in that case there would certainly have been one elsewhere before long. But just at this moment the royalists were winning the campaign and they had by far the larger army. Simon was fighting for his life, and he was a good soldier, but he had only to contend with the complete military incapacity of Richard and Henry and the rashness of Edward in pursuit. His dispositions were excellent, in accordance says the Lanercost chronicler,[5] with Vegetius, *De Re Militari*, book iii, but he was lucky to win.

We may imagine that while Edward was planning to ride down a rabble of Londoners who had insulted his mother, the business-like Richard sent for his prothonotary. On the very day of the battle Mr. Arnold composed and wrote out with his own hand a receipt

---

[1] Mr. C. L. Kingsford (*Song of Lewes*, p. 71) placed the embassy of the Bishops of London and Worcester on May 13th, but if he was right in thinking that Wykes, Rish., *de Bellis*, and *Pol. Songs* all allude to the same sum of about £30,000, this would have been offered by the bishops, according to his view, *after* Simon de Montfort and Gilbert de Clare had been given the lie by Richard and Edward.

[2] The *verbalis diffidatio* mentioned in Richard's reply may be glancing at this. The withdrawal of homage 'the next day' (after the exchange of letters) is given in *Ann. Wint.*, 101, and Wykes, 140.

[3] e.g., *R. L.*, ii, 262-3.   [4] *Lib. de Ant. Leg.*, 72.   [5] Lanercost Chronicle, p. 76.

to Louis IX for 134,000 pounds of Tours, being the total received
as the equivalent of five hundred knights for two years according to
the terms of the treaty of Paris. This was done, and subsequently
enrolled, 'without the counsel and consent of any clerk of the
chancery', in the presence of the king's council. It is warranted by
the two kings, their sons Edward and Henry, and Roger de Ley-
burne.[1] This may have been done to reassure Louis IX at a time
when foreign help was being arranged for by the queen and was
eagerly awaited in England by the royalists. Possibly a messenger
was on the point of setting off for France. Could it have been
Mr. Arnold?

In the battle itself Richard and Henry III played but little part.
Richard was forced to surrender by Sir John Giffard[2] and declared
himself Gloucester's prisoner. It is to be feared that this was another
case of *Cito, cito, transferamus nos hinc!* The most charitable view of
the King of Almain's behaviour is that he was withdrawing rapidly
downhill towards the coast with a view to making a junction with
the queen's supporters in France, when he was captured and taken
to a windmill until Simon had time to claim him from Gloucester.[3]

From May 14th, 1264, to September 6th, 1265, Richard was in
captivity. On May 28th, when Simon returned to London, Richard
was lodged in the Tower. Shortly afterwards he was committed to
the care of his sister Eleanor, Countess of Leicester.[4] The Lord
Edward and Henry of Almain, now held as hostages, soon joined
him at Wallingford. His estates were taken over and run by Simon
de Montfort's bailiffs.[5]

In November the royalists were active in the west, and some of
them, led by Robert Walerand and Warin de Bassingbourne, came
at dawn one Friday to try to release the prisoners, but were repulsed.[6]
Some time after this Richard was sent for greater security to

---

[1] *C.P.R.*, 317. The English chancery are still calling him Mr. 'Arnulf'.

[2] Wm. of Newburgh, *cont.*, ii, 543.

[3] For the story of Richard in the windmill, see p. 175.

[4] *Flores*, ii, 498; *Lib. de Ant. Leg.*, 65, states that he was taken from the Tower to Berkhampstead, but this is probably an error for Wallingford; Rish., *de Bellis*, 40; *Ann. Lond.*, 64; *Ann.
Dunst.*, 223.

[5] Wykes, 153; *C.P.R.*, 394 (December 13th, 1264). German writers have said that Richard
retained a measure of freedom in the management of his estates, but this depends upon a misunderstanding of *Cl. R.*, 349 (July 8th, 1264), by which the government (not Richard) settled
the wages of some German miners brought over from the Harz mountains to work in
Devonshire. But Richard, unlike his son Edmund, had nothing to do with mines in Devonshire.

[6] Not in July, as Bappert, 90; Rish., *de Bellis*, 40, cf. Ramsay, *Dawn*, 233; *Robt. of Gloucs.*,
ed. Hearne, ii, pp. 549-50.

K

Kenilworth, with his young son Edmund. It is just to the time of
the attempted rescue that the Melrose Chronicle — there is no other
evidence — assigns his release 'for seventeen thousand pounds sterling
and five thousand pounds of desirable gold'.[1] The suggestion has
been made that he was released and re-imprisoned, like Henry III
and Edward, but it is difficult to believe that Richard allowed himself to be tricked out of such a sum. His imprisonment at Kenilworth
cannot have been uncomfortable, for his sister Eleanor, who was
entertaining a good deal at Dover, sent him from time to time a
considerable supply of spices — dates, ginger, galingale, cloves,
almonds, and raisins, pepper, and sugar — with some wine and
twenty pieces of whale, twelve ells of scarlet cloth for his robes at
Whitsuntide, some satin hoods and a hood of miniver. Edmund
received similar presents. These were sent to Kenilworth between
March 30th and May 9th, 1265.[2] It was perhaps about this time that
Richard wrote to Philip and Werner von Falkenstein that he had
been long in England on account of the war and had been robbed
of all his property and was unable at the moment to meet their
claims.[3] As the letter is the only surviving example of Richard's
(or Mr. Arnold's) German epistolary style, it may be given in full.

Wir Richart Romescher kunig enbieden unserme lieben
getruwen Phil. und Wernher von Falkeinstein unsir gnade
und alles gud. Als ir uns geschriben hait und bruder Wilhelm
ein gra munch von Altdorf uns gesaget hat, des antworten uch,
daz ir under den andern des riches getruwen uns genemer und
lieber seit. Und weren wir uch nit schuldig, wir wolden uch
doch willeclichen unser hant reichen zu uwer schuld zu vergel-
den. Und wir itzunt lange zit in Engellant sint gewest von
criges wegen, unde alles unsirs guds beroubt sin, alse uch unser
lieber getruwer kemerer Phil. von Falk. uwer fader wol sagen
mag. So bitten wir uwer getruwen stedikeid, daz irs nit vor
ubil nemet daz wir zu disen male als wir gerne teden uch nit
genug mogen tun, dan wir wollen kurczlich uch bedencken,
daz ir uch sollent vrowen, daz ir also flizig in unserme dienst
sint gewest.

[1] *Chron. Melrose*, (facsimile edition), 128.
[2] Beriah Botfield, *Manners and Household Expenses*, pp. 8, 14, 23, 25, 26, 31, 67, 71 (there
is no index).
[3] Gebauer, 410; B.F., *Acta*, no. 384.

CHAPTER NINE

ENGLAND AFTER EVESHAM
(1265-1269)

FOURTH VISIT TO GERMANY AND THIRD MARRIAGE WITH BEATRICE OF FALKENBURG

THOUGH Kenilworth castle did not surrender till December 1266, the King of the Romans and his younger son Edmund were released by young Simon de Montfort and the Bishops of Worcester and Chester, on September 6th, 1265.[1] They were set free unconditionally, but the same day, in Kenilworth Priory, Richard drew up letters patent in favour of his sister, promising to be ever true to her and hers.[2] She had helped him while he was a prisoner and his first act was to look to her welfare. Richard was more fortunate in his sister than she was in her sons. However, on this occasion the young Simon behaved correctly towards Richard, who is reported to have said that the garrison would have killed him but for Simon's intervention.[3]

While Henry III went to Winchester to hold a parliament (September 8th) which was afterwards transferred to Windsor, Richard went home and was received with great joy by his household and friends at Wallingford (September 9th).[4] The castle, and Berkhampstead, had surrendered to Edward in August.[5] The same day patents were issued to help him in recovering his estates,[6] and protection was granted for his burgesses of Helston, Truro, Bodmin, and Exeter to export the tin which they had bought from him to La Rochelle and Bordeaux.[7] In the course of the war considerable damage had been done to his property. His park at Beckley, where he had a deer-leap, had been broken into and the beasts driven away;

---

[1] Wykes, 175; *Lib. de Ant. Leg.*, 76.

[2] This Anglo-Norman document, preparatory to a formal patent, has been printed in Bémont, *Simon de Montfort*, 252, n. 2, and elsewhere. Cf. *T. R. Hist. Soc.*, 4th ser., vol. xviii, p. 5, n. 1.

[3] Rish., *de Bellis*, 50-1. [4] Wykes, 175. [5] R. L., ii, 291. [6] *C.P.R.*, 449, 450, 453.

[7] *C.P.R.*, 454. This is noteworthy as one of the very few indications during Richard's life-time of how the produce of the stannaries was disposed of.

his men at Woodstock had been plundered of their cattle.[1] Oakham
Hall in Rutland had been burnt.[2] He lost all his goods in Goswold,
and his stock and valuables at his castle of Eye in Suffolk,[3] and his
woods were cut down after the declaration of peace, in Norfolk and
Suffolk.[4] The greatest damage was at Isleworth and Westminster,
for which the citizens of London had to pay him a thousand marks.[5]
In October 1265 he was allowed, because he had been imprisoned
for a year and more and was now charged with debt, to take an aid
from his tenants.[6] The opportunities for a really wealthy man to
load himself with debt while in prison have always been restricted;
but every properly constructed medieval letter must have its
narratio.

At this time, a couple of months after the battle of Evesham,
parliament decided that all who had been against the king at Northampton, Lewes, and Evesham should be disinherited. That is earls,
barons, knights, free tenants, citizens of London, and burgesses
of Northampton.[7] London made its peace for 20,000 marks.[8]
While the most desperate held out for better terms at Kenilworth,
in the Isle of Axholme, or at Ely, some were brought to bay at the
battle of Chesterfield. The rest had to be dealt with one by one as
they came in. This policy of disherison, already decided upon at
Winchester, was strongly opposed. The King of Almain, the Earl
Marshal, Philip Basset, and other magnates unnamed protested and
withdrew.[9] Their protests were unavailing for years, for the soldiers
who had won the war insisted on making the peace. Their methods
were rough, but by war and peace they subdued the country sufficiently to make it possible virtually to put the monarchy into commission for six years, and for the heir to the throne to go on Crusade
and even remain away as king. A full use of the victories won in
1265 to 1267 was made possible by the loyal co-operation of Richard,
King of Almain. He opposed the policy of disherison, he took no

---

[1] *C.P.R.*, 151 (July 12th, 1267: commission to inquire).   [2] *Rot. Hund.*, ii, 51.
[3] Jacob, *Studies*, 226, citing A. R., 821, m. 2*d*.
[4] In Hawell, Horseford, Boughton in Norfolk and Eye in Suffolk (*C.P.R.*, 493-4, November 3rd, 1265: commission to inquire).
[5] *Lib. de Ant. Leg.*, 94-5.   [6] *C.P.R.*, 495 = *Foed.*, i, 466.   [7] *Ann. of Oseney*, 179.
[8] *C.P.R.*, 530 (January 10th, 1266). Northampton was pardoned for an unspecified sum
in 1268 (*C.P.R.*, 225).
[9] 'Ricardus rex Alemannie nec comes Marescallus, nec dominus Philippus Basset nec alii
magnates assensum prebebant exheredationi eorum' (*Ann. Wav.*, 367); 'quia in judicio illo
non concordabat curia; quoniam majores et discretiores scilicet rex Alemannie et Philippus
Basset et dominus Marescallus et terre ceteri quamplures a curia recesserunt contradicentes et
reclamantes' (Rish., *de Bellis*, 65).

part in drawing up the Dictum de Kenilworth, when Gloucester tried to get better terms for the Disinherited Richard saw to it that he did not suffer by his rash opposition to the government, and in the last year of his life he had the whole policy reversed. But he never made difficulties for the government, and his opposition did not prevent him from benefiting out of the lands of the Disinherited himself, to the extent of 2,000 marks a year.

Consequently, though in close touch with the legate, Ottobuoni, whom he met on arrival (October 31st, 1265) at Canterbury,[1] Richard was until the spring of 1267 little at court. During the rest of 1265 he spent some time with Edward and the legate in arranging terms for Simon de Montfort's widow and children.[2] On October 28th Edward had taken Dover castle and let the Countess Eleanor and her two youngest sons, Richard and Amaury, withdraw to France. Guy de Montfort, a captive at Windsor, was transferred to Dover and thence escaped to France. The young Simon, captured by Edward, was forced to submit to the award of Richard and Edward. They gave him generous terms (December 29th). He was to return to Kenilworth and procure its surrender and then, on condition that he left the country and did not stir up trouble abroad, to receive 500 marks a year from the Earldom of Leicester. As the garrison of Kenilworth would only surrender to the countess in person the award came to nothing and Simon fled to France in February 1266.[3] Further arrangements were made in 1267 whereby he might sell his English lands at the market price and in this matter, too, Richard was to arbitrate, but this was apparently superseded at once by a decision to leave all outstanding matters between the Montfort family and Henry III to the award of Louis IX backed by papal sanctions.[4] It is clear that Richard was as good as his word in endeavouring to help Eleanor and her sons. The de Montforts were offered much better terms than Robert de Ferrers.

Throughout the year 1266 it may be imagined that Richard was working for a more moderate policy in conjunction with Ottobuoni,

[1] Wykes, 179; *Ann. Worcs.*, 455.
[2] On this question see Bémont, *Simon de Montfort*, chap. x.
[3] Rish., *Chron.*, 51; *Dunst.*, 240; Wykes, 181 (giving £400 instead of 500 marks). Richard, Henry III and the queen, and Ottobuoni were all at Dunstable on December 8th and at Northampton for Christmas.
[4] This was a return to a plan already made in 1266, mentioned in Bémont, 259, n. 2. The generous offer of 1267, the subject of a lengthy patent, and the repetition of the decision 'by the whole Council' to leave the award to Louis IX (*C.P.R.*, 1266-1272, pp. 130, 140-2, 216-17) are ignored by M. Bémont. The award was probably never pronounced.

who was of the same mind, *quia in rebus tanta subversione commotis ad reformationem ipsarum opus est clementia, non rigore.*[1] Both of them were trying to mediate the surrender of Kenilworth, where Richard may have been for a short time in July.[2]

Though Richard is not in the chronicles or records at this time the survival of two of his charters shows that he was active in good works. He was at Cippenham[3] on April 18th. Here there was a manor house, much used because on the road to the north from Windsor to Wycombe. Here, a couple of miles north of Eton, Richard granted two charters. By the more impressive of the two he founded the Austin nunnery of Burnham, for perhaps about twenty nuns, the third and last of his religious foundations. The deed[4] was witnessed by Henry III and his court, who were at Windsor on the 17th and turned aside to Cippenham before proceeding to Reading next day. The other charter is to Liskeard, one of seven by which seven Cornish boroughs, later of some importance to the crown, were created.[5] A point of interest in diplomatics is that these two charters, granted at the same place on the same day are attested by wholly distinct lists of witnesses, those in the Cornish charter being exclusively Cornish persons.[6]

On October 8th Richard was at Wallingford, while the court was still at Kenilworth, where the committee of twelve, under the supervision of the legate and Henry of Almain, were drawing up the Dictum published on October 31st.[7] The seeds of future trouble were here sown, since Gloucester was no more pleased with the policy of Henry and the Marchers (particularly Roger Mortimer) than Richard himself, and he was a man to express his feelings in vigorous action.

When Kenilworth surrendered in December, Gloucester and Roger Mortimer, one of Edward's closest friends, had already

---

[1] *E.H.R.*, xv, 107 (Letters of Ottobuoni, ed. Rose Graham).

[2] Wykes, 191; Wav., 371.

[3] Cippenham is often confused with Chippenham in Wiltshire, and is a source of error to foreign writers because, not being a parish it is not easily found. Richard held it from the Abbot of Westminster for 50s. rent. It is in the parish of Burnham, not to be confused with Nun Burnham in Yorkshire (*V.C.H. Bucks*, i, 382, iii, 166-8; *Mon. Ang.*, vi, 545-6, cf. iv, 278-9).

[4] *Cal. Ch. R.*, ii, 99.   [5] *Ibid.* (1327-1330), p. 333.

[6] The other boroughs, whose charters have been analysed in Ballard and Tait, *British Borough Charters*, vol. ii, were Bodmin (1227-1243), Dunheved (Launceston, 1227-1243), Helston (1227-1240 and 1260), West Looe (1227-1243), Lostwithiel (1268) and Tintagel (1227-1256). I have narrowed the dates somewhat. For 1227 it would possibly be better to put 1230, as it is unlikely that Richard granted any formal charters before he came of age.

[7] Confirmation of liberties to the city of Aachen (B.F. 5438).

quarrelled openly over the territorial settlement.[1] Gloucester is not mentioned with King Richard and Philip Basset, who had from the outset dissociated themselves from the policy of disherison, nor did he refuse to serve on the committee set up to frame the Dictum. The point on which he was not satisfied, and on which the Dictum did not touch, was the problem of lands seized or granted away immediately after Evesham. He was professedly attacking the greed of his fellow-marchers in snapping up the estates of rebels, who had no opportunity to redeem their lands. The number of these rebels was swollen by those who rejected the Dictum and so also became Disinherited. It was put forth (according to Wykes) that Gloucester was trying to secure better terms for the Disinherited, but it is not difficult to discover reasons nearer home. Gloucester, like the Earl Marshal in 1233, contrived to work up some degree of feeling in a number of counties in support of what was really a feudal matter. Like the barons before Lewes he protested, on the advice of his lawyers, that his action was not directed against the king.[2] He claimed the fulfilment of promises made to him by Edward before Evesham at Ludlow, demanding the removal of aliens from the council and the castles. But the chancery enrolments tell a different story. Wykes, the royalist, can give us Gloucester as seen from his propaganda, of which Wykes is scornful, and the baronial Rishanger can assure us that Roger Mortimer and the other Marchers were conspiring to kill the earl, but the real causes lay deeper. The Council had decided, at Winchester, that forfeited estates went to the crown *pro hac vice*, saving to the lords their homage and service. This not only left open the question of wardships and reliefs, but planted upon Gloucester, whose support had been decisive at Evesham, a number of tenants whom he may have disliked or of whom he possibly knew nothing. 'Certain lands which were of his fee' were granted to royalists, and though the question of wardships and reliefs was formally decided in his favour, and he was not to suffer in any way, and so forth,[3] he was in fact bound to suffer. A closely-knit and clannish marcher organization could not easily tolerate this kind of intrusion. Gloucester was also allowed to keep the goods seized by him from any of the king's enemies during the war, but with a

[1] Rish., *de Bellis*, 59.

[2] Wykes, 199-200. William de Munchesny, Roger of Leicester, and Harvey de Borham are named. The last was his steward and later a judge.

[3] *C.P.R.*, 532 (January 14th, 1266).

clause saving the king's rights that left scope for friction.[1] The earl had also a personal grievance in the treatment by the crown of his father's castles beyond the Wye, and a wrongful assignment to his mother of dower therein, which became a subject of dispute in the spring of 1266.[2]

These factors explain not only why Richard of Cornwall had refused to have anything to do with the territorial settlement of 1265-1266, but clearly reveal how it was possible for him to intervene so successfully in the settlement of a rising that was less altruistic than it appeared. Gloucester had time to brood over his wrongs, for having withdrawn to Wales, he refused to come to the Christmas court at Oseney, or to the feast of St. Edward in January, and (far worse) would not lend his support to the muster at Bury St. Edmunds in February, against the Disinherited in the Isle of Ely. It must have been realized that his contingent — already a decisive factor in two battles — might have an equally serious effect by its absence in a third.

When he marched up from Wales to London early in April, Gilbert de Clare had 'a large army' according to the chroniclers. He had, that is, in his immediate following three knights, twenty bachelors, and at least eighteen esquires. At least seventy persons (no doubt with their supporters) some of them of considerable distinction, came from 'all parts', chiefly the eastern counties, to support him.[3] To oppose these the king summoned three hundred foreign mercenaries, whose arrival turned the scale in his favour. Henry knew what was afoot at the beginning of March, a month before Gloucester reached London. He dropped the siege of Ely and spent the whole of Lent at Cambridge, where Richard, who was with him throughout the campaign, was lodged in Barnwell Priory.[4] Henry's action, sometimes criticized as a manifestation of his preference for religious observance to military operations, was fully justified. He had to sacrifice his fleet, which was left at the mercy of the outlaws and destroyed, because he had to conserve his forces in view of what he knew. He had to wait for Edward to return from subduing John

---

[1] *C.P.R.*, 533.   [2] *Ibid.*, 273, 592, 663.

[3] Jacob, *Studies*, analyses the 'bachelors' of Gloucester's household. The list of the household as organized for war is in *C.P.R.*, 145-7, where, too, are the names and wages of the king's mercenaries, and, more important, all those who came in as a result of the King of Almain's award. A detailed analysis of this list and of the mainpernors who are also named would throw considerable light on the nature of the support accorded to Gloucester in 1267 (pp. 148-150).

[4] Rish., *de Bellis*, n. 148; *Ann. Dunst.*, 245.

de Vescy in the north and, through Roger Leybourne, to summon foreign help. His alarm at what he had heard is evident in a letter written at the beginning of March in terms of the utmost urgency summoning Philip Basset to his aid in his *supremum periculum*.[1]

The king's alarm was justifiable, for Gloucester had formed a secret alliance with John d'Eyville, the leader of the Disinherited in Ely.[2] There was much inflammable material in the south and east, heaped up by the active propaganda of the last few years, to which the king in a remarkable manifesto issued in January had ascribed the evils of the time.[3] Henry cited as examples of the baseless rumours spread by his enemies a report that he had deprived the Earl of Norfolk of his earldom and that Gloucester had quarrelled with the Lord Edward. Unfortunately the latter was very near the truth. It is possible that Gloucester, who perhaps felt that now that Simon was dead he should take his natural place as leader of the baronage, issued his own appeal. He was not content with bringing his tenants: he had those of 'his fellowship and friendship' as well, and after he had made his peace with the king, it was necessary for him to write to his 'friends and well-wishers' in Oxfordshire and Berkshire (where he had few tenants) to exhort them to behave.[4] He had support, too, in the Isle of Wight where the Countess Isabella de Fortibus, a rich dowager of doubtful loyalty, was accused of harbouring the notorious pirate Henry Poun.[5] Gloucester was welcomed by the Londoners, where the *minutus populus* again set up their own officials. Gloucester had tricked the legate to get into the city (April 9th) and was joined in a few days by contingents from Ely and elsewhere.[6] About the same time Henry sent Roger Leybourne to get help from the Counts of St. Pol and Boulogne.

Meanwhile on April 20th King Richard had been commissioned with Philip Basset to undertake negotiations with Gloucester and his followers, who were given safe-conducts for the purpose.[7] Henry was still at Cambridge on the 25th, but had reached Windsor by the end of the month and remained there till May 5th. By May 9th he had moved to Stratford-le-Bow where he remained in camp for a miserable five weeks, being short of food no less than money.[8] As

---

[1] *Cl. R.*, 367. The letter is undated, but between others of March 1st and 4th.
[2] Jacob, *Studies*, 258.   [3] *C.P.R.*, 653 = *Foed.*, 467.
[4] *C.P.R.*, 144 (June 22nd). The letter is probably a form intended to be sent to other counties as well.
[5] *Ibid.*, 67; *Cl. R.*, 374; Wykes, 203.   [6] *Lib. de Ant. Leg.*, 91.   [7] *C.P.R.*, 55.
[8] Jacob, *Studies*, 259, n. 3.

usual Richard came to the rescue, apparently with considerable
sums.[1] At the same time he and Philip Basset (Henry of Almain is
also mentioned) were daily continuing their talks with Gilbert de
Clare. It was due, no doubt, to this as much as anything that the
armies never met. The earl had fortified the city, but showed no
disposition to fight, and as the south side lay continuously open the
'siege' was a farce. The real siege was that of the Legate in the
Tower, where he had with him the later Boniface VIII, who did not
forget that they had been rescued by the Lord Edward.[2]

After five weeks of discussion Gloucester came to terms. The
final arrangements were made on June 4th, when an embassy of six
persons had safe-conducts for the day to confer with Richard,
Edward, Henry of Almain and Philip Basset.[3] The terms were
drawn up and sealed on June 15th. The Isle of Wight was taken
over for a time by Edward, who then marched off to receive the
surrender of Ely.

Richard's award was simply a return to the Dictum and a general
amnesty for all connected with Gloucester since he left Wales. The
earl had to give security that he would never more raise war against
the king. He offered 10,000 marks, but the actual sum was left
to the decision of the pope.[4] It was prudently arranged that he
should vacate the city before the king entered it. Similar terms were
granted to the rebels at Ely. Those portions of the Provisions which
Gloucester had probably never liked were embodied later in the
year in the Statute of Marlborough. His rising had failed to achieve
anything for himself or for the Disinherited.

The award of June 15th at Stratford was Richard's last great public
arbitration and his most successful. It speaks volumes for his skill as
a mediator that he not only persuaded Gloucester not to fight, but
to yield everything for which he had left Wales. In dealing with
Gilbert de Clare, as with his father, the King of Almain, because
he was more honest and more competent, proved more successful
than either Simon de Montfort or Henry III. The settlement with
Gloucester did not occupy Richard's whole time during the summer

---

[1] Wykes, 204: 'Cui semper ut assolet affluenter pecunia suppetebat.'
[2] T. S. R. Boase, *Boniface VIII*, p. 12, citing *E.H.R.*, xvii, 522.
[3] *C.P.R.*, 143. Gloucester's envoys were: John Fitz John, Robert de Munteny, Robert
de Montfort of Rutland, Hamo Hauteyn, Harvey de Borham, and Mr. Robert de Trillawe.
[4] Clement IV raised Gloucester's security to 20,000 marks, and the handing over of either
Tonbridge castle to Henry of Almain or his eldest daughter to the queen, as a hostage (*Reg.
Clément IV*, no. 569, dated January 11th, 1268), but on July 16th, 1268, the king remitted the
last two securities (*C.P.R.*, 246).

of 1267. He was concerned, too, with the administration of Brabant, and was working under difficulties in camp, whither the perils of war had not allowed him to take his great seal.[1] He tried also to add to his tally of arbitrations by making peace with Llewelyn, but the latter rejected his advances.[2] He is described as present in the preamble to the Provisions of Marlborough of November 18th, but perhaps left the court immediately.[3] For Henry III on November 20th sent him a long and apologetic letter, inviting him to spend Christmas at Winchester, recollecting his promise to provide Richard with 1,000 marks a year in wardships and 2,000 marks' worth of land of the Disinherited, and admitting that he had made peace with the Londoners without consulting Richard, contrary to his promise, *super quo fatemur nos minus bene fecisse.* He concludes that he will urge the pope to help Richard.[4] The final settlement with London was made on March 26th, 1268, at Westminster, when Richard was present,[5] but he still insisted on a separate inquiry into the Isleworth outrage of 1264. This was undertaken in June by Laurence del Broc.[6] On June 9th a further grant to his nuns at Burnham was confirmed,[7] and on July 13th, when he was at his manor of Watlington, he issued a charter to his borough of Lostwithiel.[8] As before, this kind of activity is a sign that Richard is going abroad. His household going with him to Germany received protection on July 10th.[9] The fact that it was a general protection without any list of those going with him indicates that as on his previous journey he travelled with only his personal servants. As his attorneys in England he left Philip Basset, Robert Walerand, and Walter de Merton. On August 4th he left the country.[10]

It would be unnecessary, even if it were possible, to trace the doings of King Richard in Germany from August 1268 to August 1269. It is clear enough that he followed the now familiar pattern of his journeys up the Rhine and made no attempt to visit any other portions of his nominal dominions. He was not in a position to interfere effectively in German affairs except where his interests happened to coincide with those who acknowledged him as king. During his six-year absence the country had almost entirely ignored him, and had perceptibly declined in its respect for law and order.

---

[1] B.F., 5439, 5441; Gebauer, 400.   [2] *R. L.* ii, 312-14.   [3] *Stat. of the Realm,* i, 19.
[4] *Cl. R.,* 407.   [5] *Lib. de Ant. Leg.,* 101-5.   [6] *C.P.R.,* 285.
[7] *Cal. Ch. R.,* ii, 99. This further grant itself is undated.
[8] *Hist. MSS. Comm., Var. Coll.,* i, 327.   [9] *C.P.R.,* 243.   [10] Wykes, 219.

There were fresh tolls, more robbers, and new feuds. Richard had brought no army to cope with the situation, and had no intention of going to Rome, in spite of repeated citations.[1] Since he turned his face towards home in September 1260 the political situation in England had precluded the possibility of getting an army, and the downfall of the Guelfs in Italy would in any case have rendered it useless south of the Alps. He had been content to correspond with Urban IV since August 1263, when, with an elaborate summing-up of the case in his bull, *Qui celum*, the pope had cited both Richard and Alfonso to appear at Rome. But the real importance of this famous document is less in its citation of Richard than in its recognition of the rights of the seven electors.[2] To keep up appearances, and no doubt to explain away his repeated default, Richard sent Henry of Almain to Rome in 1267,[3] and he continued to speak of going there in person[4] in much the same way that Henry III, almost to the day of his death, spoke of going on crusade.

Richard, after leaving London with his younger son Edmund, is next found at Cambrai, with his chancellor, Bishop Nicholas of Cambrai, and Baldwin of Avesnes. He had still the support of the Archbishops of Mainz and Trèves. Engelbert of Cologne was a prisoner of the Count of Jülich. In September he was at Aachen, in December at Cologne. The one outstanding event of his sojourn was not till April 1269, when he held his first and only Diet at Worms. This assembly, drawing its membership only from the Rhineland, passed some sensible decrees abolishing all tolls on the Rhine except the old imperial tolls of Boppard and Kaiserwerth, thus restraining the *furiosa Teutonicorum insania* of the robber-barons in their Rhineland castles, and lowering the price of goods. In the absence of Richard, the Archbishop of Mainz was to be entrusted with the execution of the decrees. At the same time a general *Landfriede* for the Rhineland was instituted, replacing to some extent the Rhenish League of 1254, which had disintegrated at the beginning of Richard's reign.[5] These events form a welcome oasis in the barren wastes of the interregnum. But the impression remains that

[1] Clement IV cited both Richard and Alfonso on May 9th, 1267, for the first day after March 25th, 1268 (*Reg.*, no. 594), and again on May 18th, 1268, for 1269 (*ibid.*, 704).

[2] *Foed.*, i, 430; B.F., 9357; *M.G.H.*, *Const.*, ii, 523, and *Epist. saec. XIII*, i, 545.

[3] B.F., 9775.

[4] *M.G.H.*, xviii, 583 (March 20th, 1269).

[5] Wykes, 222–4; B.F., 5455–7. The way for this had been prepared by a number of local *Landfrieden* instituted during Richard's absence (*C. Med. Hist.*, vi, 125). There was also a church council at Mainz, where Duke Albert of Brunswick was excommunicated on May 8th.

whoever was King of Germany would have to run much faster than this even to remain in the same place.

Richard was at Frankfurt for Whitsuntide, and on June 16th he married as his third wife, Beatrice of Falkenburg (near Liége), a niece of Engelbert of Cologne, at Kaiserleutern.[1] Like his other wives, she was extremely beautiful, and he was passionately in love with her. He could not bear to be separated from her even for a day, and at once brought her home to England to show her his vast possessions in this country.[2] By July 9th they had reached Mainz, and on August 3rd they landed at Dover. Proceeding thence to Gravesend, they were met, it seems unexpectedly, by the Lord Edward, who had come by river from London on the 6th. Edward therefore lodged at Northfleet — having intended presumably to stay at Gravesend — and on the morrow they had a long conference about Edward's crusade and other matters.[3] Edward then proceeded to Dover, and Richard brought his bride to London on the 8th.

---

[1] *E.H.R.*, lii, 279-82 (F. R. Lewis). The Oseney chronicler calls her 'gemma mulierum', and Wykes speaks of her 'incomparabilis forma' (pp. 223-4).

[2] Wykes, 224-5. Richard's detractors professed to see another side to his character: Hic fuit erga omnes mulieres cujuscunque professionis seu conditionis luxuriosissimus, thesaurorum collector cupidissimus et avidissimus, pauperum oppressor violentissimus.

A.D. 1264, feria sexta, videlicet in vigilia Inventionis Sancte Crucis, circa horam sextam decollati fuerunt ccc[ti] sagittarii et xv in Waldia in parochia sancte Marie de Tichesherst, in loco qui appellatur Flemenewelle, coram rege Henrico quarto, qui omnes dolose vocati ad pacem regis per consilium Ricardi regis Alemannie predictam mortem incurrerunt. (Wykes, introd. xxx from Cott. MS. Calig. A. x.) These Welsh archers captured in the Weald were put to death shortly before the battle of Lewes (*ibid.*, 147-8).

[3] *Lib. de Ant. Leg.*, 120.

CHAPTER TEN

HENRY OF ALMAIN AND THE LAST YEARS (1269-1272)

THE departure of Richard to Germany for the last time had occurred at the beginning of a period (1268-1274) during which England was governed by a few magnates to a greater degree, perhaps, than at any time in the century. Henry III, though not old, was in poor health, and more and more the business of the realm fell into the hands of his council. Richard's absence, to some extent, allowed more power to fall into the hands of the three energetic young men — Edward, Edmund, and Henry of Almain.

Richard's eldest son was a man of some personal charm, but impulsive.[1] Though he joined the barons in 1258 he accepted a royalist fee in March 1260.[2] He is listed as one of Simon's young men in the spring of 1263,[3] and in July was captured by the royalists during his pursuit of John Mansel. Through Henry III's intervention he was released,[4] and in August was treating for peace with Wales in company with Walter de Cantilupe and Simon de Montfort.[5] By November 1263 he was firmly in the royal camp, having been given the castle and honour of Tickhill for life by Edward[6] and, rather later, the custody of Corfe and Sherborne castles.[7] He took part in the negotiations leading to the Mise of Amiens,[8] was captured at Lewes, and treated as a hostage.[9] Yet he was sufficiently trusted, in spite of his desertion, to be employed as an ambassador to the French court for some months.[10] It is important to note that he was still in France on May 18th, 1265, and that he is next heard of

[1] When Henry returned from Germany, where his father had knighted him (supra, p. 92), he at once took precedence after the Lord Edward (C.P.R. (1247-1258), pp. 388, 607, 608).
[2] Ann. Burt., 444; Mat. Par., v, 697-8; Treharne, 164, n. 4; C.P.R. (1258-1266), 79, 123. Being acceptable to both sides, he acted for Simon de Montfort as steward on St. Edward's Day (October 13th, 1260) at Westminster (C.P.R., 96).
[3] Wykes, 133; Dunst., 221-2. In February 1263 he was one of the proctors to fulfil the late peace with France (C.P.R., 243). He was with de Montfort in the Marches in the spring (Flores, ii).
[4] Supra, p. 122; C.P.R., 269.   [5] Ibid., 276; cf. 280.   [6] Ibid. (1266-1272), 619.
[7] Ibid. (1258-1266), p. 333; (1266-1272), p. 343.   [8] R. L., ii, 252.   [9] C.P.R., 317.
[10] On September 4th, 1264, he had gone to France from Dover castle, where he was a prisoner (C.P.R., 345). On April 14th, 1265, Henry of Almain and the Abbot of Westminster had letters of credence (ibid., 418). The securities given for this mission were very heavy.

after the battle of Evesham, when on October 15th he was granted the houses of Thomas de Pivelesdon in London.[1] It is generally assumed that he was still in France when Evesham was fought, but the only explicit statement that he was not there comes from an extraordinary French compilation which gives events in their right order but persistently and wildly misdates them, sometimes by as much as fourteen years.[2] In 1266 Henry had charge of the war in Notts., Derby, and Yorks.,[3] defeating Robert de Ferrers at the battle of Chesterfield (May 1266). He was a party to the Dictum and helped to bring Gilbert de Clare to terms in June 1267. When he had fulfilled his mission to Rome, whither Richard sent him later in the same year, he undertook to go to Ireland on Edward's behalf (July 1268).[4] He was back again in October,[5] when his father had already gone to Germany.

While Richard was away Henry made good use of his time. He did not always see eye to eye with his father, and as he was on excellent terms with his cousins Edward and Edmund, he had opportunities for behaving in a way that Richard would not have approved. For Henry and Edward by hard work persuaded the Council to agree to a *Provisio Judaismi* which restricted the manner in which debts might be contracted with Jews (January 13th, 1269). Unfortunately the future 'English Justinian' had his Provision drafted with such ambiguous brevity that the precise limitations meant to be imposed are in doubt.[6] This conciliar provision was confirmed in the Easter parliament.[7] It is very much inferior in workmanship to the formal statute which was necessary to clarify the whole matter when Richard came back. The attitude of Edward to the Jews, thus early revealed, is in strong contrast to the favourable treatment they had learned to expect from Richard.

Just when this Provision was being confirmed Henry of Almain was engaged upon a less public and somewhat unscrupulous transaction on behalf of his cousin Edmund. Henry had captured Robert de Ferrers, Earl of Derby, at Chesterfield in May 1266 and handed

[1] *C.P.R.*, 425, 460. Henry also received the Furnival lands worth about £100 a year (*ibid.*, 582).
[2] *M.G.H.*, xxvi, 517: *Ex Ann. Normannicis.*
[3] *C.P.R.*, 656.   [4] *Ibid.*, 428; cf. 257 (September).   [5] *Ibid.*, 296.
[6] Dr. C. Roth, *A History of the Jews in England*, p. 65, speaks of debts 'on the security of lands held in fee' but the Provision says *dettes ke sunt feez . . . dettes des feez . . . dette de feo* (printed in *C.P.R.*, 376, and elsewhere) and Wykes (p. 221) speaks of *feoda annua*. No doubt the security for most debts was land held in fee. Cf. Ramsay, *Dawn*, 268.
[7] Wykes, 221.

him over to the king as a prisoner. For three years Robert was kept
in prison until on May 1st, 1269, he was taken to Cippenham and
forced to grant away all his estates, or immediately find £50,000
in one payment to redeem them. He was then taken back to prison,
this time to Wallingford, until he was released three weeks later by
the Lord Edward. Henceforth Ferrers, Earl of Derby, is merely
Ferrers of Chartley and his descendants continue to sue in vain for
the lands for nearly a century. The interest of this famous case[1]
here is the fresh light — not too favourable — that it throws on the
character of Henry of Almain. That he was a leading actor in this
legal chicanery cannot be doubted. He is the first of the nominal
mainpernors for Robert de Ferrers. It is in his father's country house
at Cippenham over the river from Windsor that the wretched man
is forced to seal the deed. For reasons best known to themselves,
Edmund and Henry prefer to take their victim back to prison at
Wallingford, not Windsor. Why did they wait three years? Did
they want to be sure that King Richard would not interfere?

A fortnight after this successful piece of villainy Henry married
Constance, daughter of Simon de Montfort's old enemy, Gaston de
Béarn, at Windsor (May 15th).[2] He then went abroad with his
father-in-law and Edward to make arrangements for their crusade,
the date of which had already been fixed. We do not hear whether
he met his father with Edward at Gravesend. It is not to be hastily
assumed, for it is noteworthy that Henry, though admitted by all
parties to have great ability, had not been left by his father as one
of his representatives in England.

Richard had been home three weeks before he joined his brother
at Winchester (August 24th, 1269). Henry III was by this time in
failing health. He held lengthy Great Councils, at which little was
done, the real work falling to Edward, his friends, and a few
professionals. Edward's position was now one of unchallenged
supremacy, and had been formally recognized in November 1268
by a grant to him that appears never to have been enrolled. He was,
according to the Winchester annalist, made Steward of England and

---

[1] The legal aspect of the case is discussed by Professor Jacob in his *Studies*, 217-19. The
case, which came up in 1274, is printed *ibid.*, App. ix. See also Blaauw, 140 *f.* To complete
the story we may add that towards the end of the century John de Ferrers proposed to raise
the 50,000 marks by procuring papal permission to borrow it from the bishops, who, as he
told the pope, were willing to lend. But at the instigation of the king the pope refused.
Robert's heirs were still petitioning the Duke of Lancaster for the earldom of Derby in the
middle of the fourteenth century (Bodleian Library, MS. Dugdale, 18, fol. 13ᵛ).
[2] The contract is in *C.P.R.*, 323.

at Christmas given charge of all the king's castles.[1] This tantalizing statement, which has received as little attention from modern historians as it did from contemporaries, conceals the virtual abdication of Henry III. It is of importance in apportioning responsibility for the government of England during a brief period of Richard of Cornwall's life. The stewardship, after the death of Simon de Montfort, was granted to Edmund with the Earldom of Leicester by a charter of October 26th, 1265, that was prepared and attested but never delivered. It 'remained an escrow'. On the same day, by an amended charter, Edmund received the honour of Leicester without the stewardship, which was eventually granted to him for life, not in fee, on May 9th, 1269.[2] It was therefore, so far as is known, in abeyance from Simon de Montfort's death until it was granted to Edward in November 1268.

The tenurial stewardship in England had never attached to itself any but ceremonial functions. The real work of stewards either in the household or the provinces was done by men appointed (so far as we know) without reference to the officer who functioned at great festivals. The work was more intimate than that of the marshals, much of which was done by deputies appointed by the marshal in fee. But since 1255 Simon de Montfort, who had been *senescallus* in Gascony, deliberately tried to raise the *senescalcia Anglie*, as his family liked to call it, to the status of a great office, as it was for long in France. That he was sincere in his belief that the stewardship of England ought to imply, on a larger scale, the rights and duties of stewards in the households and on the estates of great men, or in France, or even Jerusalem, is seen by his inquiry addressed to the aged Countess Loretta in April 1265.[3] His aspirations served only to shroud the office in a cloak of mystery, beneath which there was in truth very little. But the vagueness of the position made it the more dangerous to grant the office in fee. The immediate resumption of the grant to Edmund, the careful wording of the eventual grant to him in 1269 so as not to bind Henry III's successors, show that Edward was fully aware of the danger, and that his intervention to secure a six months' tenure of the office for himself was meant to

---

[1] *Ann. Wint.*, 107. 'Item xviii kal. Novembris [*for* Decembris] tenuit dominus rex parliamentum suum apud Wyntoniam; in quo fecit Edwardum filium suum senescallum Anglie; et ibidem tenuit rex suum Natale, ubi constituit dictum Edwardum custodem Londonie et omnium castellorum suorum in Anglia.'

[2] L. W. Vernon Harcourt, *His Grace the Steward and Trial by Peers*, p. 138 f. The documents are printed *ibid.*, 154 f., but Mr. Vernon Harcourt overlooked the grant to the Lord Edward.

[3] F. M. Powicke, 'Loretta, Countess of Leicester', in *Historical Essays in Honour of James Tait*.

assert the reigning king's right to dispose of the office as he pleased.

The grant to Edward of 'all the castles' is perhaps to be taken with the grant of the stewardship. We shall see that it meant the counties as well as the castles, and that it was for a term of five years. This made Edward almost a viceroy, giving substance to his position as Steward of England, with authority in that very sphere most jealously preserved, the appointment of castellans, which had not been allowed to Richard of Cornwall and the queen during the regency of 1253–1254.

Richard was not affected immediately by this formal recognition that the political centre of gravity had shifted. He had a comparatively quiet time for some months after his return in August 1269, only emerging for the consecration of the new abbey at Westminster on October 13th.[1] Early in 1270 he was combining the public affairs of England and Germany with the private disputes of Edward and the Earl of Gloucester. He was probably more interested in drafting new rules for drawing up the Pipe Roll than with the sale of the Count of Dassel's rights beyond the Weser to Albert of Brunswick,[2] but the dispute between his nephew and Gilbert de Clare was still more to his liking. This permitted him to lavish two months of his time on a most elaborate Award. Gloucester had again refused to attend parliaments. He professed fear of Edward who was pressing him, no doubt for reasons of public safety, to fulfil his crusading vow. The dispute, submitted to Richard at the Easter parliament, may have had a discreditable origin, not alluded to in the Award, which was published on May 27th.[3] It was less an arbitration than a list of terms to be imposed on Gloucester. The earl was to follow Edward at the first opportunity. If he would help Edward when he arrived the king would give him 8,000 marks

[1] Wykes, 226. On October 15th was confirmed his grant to the Franciscans of Chichester of the Old Castle there to dwell in (*C.P.R.*, 369).

[2] *Red Book of the Exchequer*, iii, 842–4 = *Foed.*, i, 483, the ordinance of the Exchequer drawn up (February 11th, 1270) in the presence of the king, King Richard, the Archbishop of York, the Bishop of Worcester, the Lord Edward, William de Valence, Roger Mortimer, Philip Basset, Henry of Almain, Robert Aguylon, and Robert Walerand. The absence of the Chancellor (Richard de Middleton) and the Treasurer (John Chishull) is noteworthy. For the German business, when Richard was at Wallingford on January 20th, see Gebauer, 408, no. lvii, and Bappert, 121.

[3] Wykes, 228 *f.*; *Ann. Worcs.*, 459. The full text is in *Letters from Northern Registers*, 27–30. It is stated in *Ann. Wint.*, 108, that *all* the crusaders put themselves on Richard's award concerning their expenses, but as they would be paid by Edward or Gloucester there is no substantial difference in this account. It was rumoured that Edward was too familiar with Gloucester's wife (*Flor. Worcs.*, ii, 203). The marriage was dissolved next year (Oxenedes, 217).

towards his expenses and would place at his disposal a suitable ship.
If he refused to help Edward he should have only 2,000 marks. He
was to give security to Richard that he would spend the money on
the crusade. Whether they went or not the earl was not to start a
war or *turbatio* in England. The sanctions for all this were excommunication by the archbishops and bishops all or singly, a
penalty of 20,000 marks, and the handing over of Tonbridge and
Henley castles (*duas non ignobiles munitiones*) until he was at sea in the
Mediterranean. The Award, we are told, was widely published in
French. Gloucester made difficulties of interpretation, but Richard
had reserved to himself the right of interpreting his own award, and
a settlement was reached on June 17th at Reading. Although
Gloucester did not keep the agreement to go on crusade, he went
home and gave no more trouble to the crown for the next twenty
years.

When Edward sailed in August he left five men to look after all
his affairs. Richard thus became the leading member of a committee whose other members were Walter Giffard, Archbishop of
York, Philip Basset, Roger Mortimer, and Robert Walerand, all of
them prominent members of the council.[1] When Richard was
disputing with the barons whether he need take the oath to the
Provisions in 1259, he had claimed to have no peer in England. The
barons realized that in a sense this was true. Simon de Montfort's
partisans might mock him for thinking himself so much better than
other people and calling himself *Semper Augustus*,[2] but as an anointed
king he took precedence even over the bishops, and this must have
been useful in committee, not least when his nephew Edward was
present.

The five commissioners inherited an intricate commercial dispute
with the Countess of Flanders, who had distrained upon the goods
of English merchants for large sums, in satisfaction of pension-rights
which the English government did not admit. Trade between the
two countries was suspended in September 1270, and a licensing
system had to be organized to enable the wool exporters to continue
to deal with other countries.[3] There was bound to be a shortage of

---

[1] *Foed.*, i, 484 (August 2nd, 1270).

[2] The Melrose chronicler who is the source of this information had clearly had access to
some propaganda or propagandist for de Montfort. There was a considerable Scottish
contingent at Lewes (see the Lanercost Chronicle), and as envoys to Henry III in the summer
of 1266 the King of Scotland sent Durand, monk of Melrose, and Henry, a lay brother
(*C.P.R.*, 602).

[3] *Lib. de Ant. Leg.*, 126-7.

cloth, and in October the King of Almain prudently bought for himself 'forty Flemish cloths' from the Riccardi of Lucca. This is the only occasion noted in the whole course of his life on which he had personal dealing with the Italian merchants,[1] but as pointed out in an earlier chapter his merchants from Germany and the Low Countries had a large share in the new licensing system.

By February 1271 Henry III was reported to be dangerously ill. A reshuffle of castles in Dorset, Kent, Essex, Devon, Oxfordshire, and Berkshire seems to indicate some anxiety on the part of Edward's commissioners,[2] less from any present threat to the security of the kingdom than from a fear of what might happen if Henry III died while the heir to the throne was abroad. A letter was sent in the king's name stating that he was unequal to business and urging Edward to come home.[3] It was pointed out also that Richard might at any time be called away to Germany or, if a new pope were elected, be summoned to Rome, but these arguments, particularly the last, do not ring true.

On March 7th, the king being still ill, Richard received a formal commission to protect the realm.[4] Trouble seems still to have been feared, for on March 18th all sheriffs were instructed to take measures to prevent congregations, conventicles, and conspiracies.[5] It may be doubted whether this commission would much have affected Richard's position. There may have been a wish to avoid a formal regency, since on April 16th it was given out that the king had recovered.[6] At the same time further measures were taken to deprive him of any real power. The whole revenue of the country was put at the disposal of the council, *saving to the king only £120 in pennies in parcels*, to give away — 6s. 8d. a day pocket-money. The council was also to have power to make ordinances concerning the king's household. The whole is wrapped up in a somewhat naive way, with formal protestations that the king, after his miraculous restoration to health, was about to go on crusade, for which he would want a large sum of money, so that he must not spend the issues of the land but save them up to pay his debts. By October the council had come out into the open and no longer pretended that anyone but themselves had made this sweeping decision.[7]

Richard had taken advantage of his year of supremacy when Edward went abroad, to have the last word in the matter of the

[1] *C.P.R.*, 487.   [2] October 1270-May 1271. *C.P.R.*, 468, 508, 509, 515, 536.
[3] *Foed.*, 487.   [4] *C.P.R.*, 591-2.   [5] *Ibid.*, 596.   [6] *Ibid.*, 531.   [7] *Ibid.*, 574.

Disinherited, at a parliament of magnates at London in January, when 'by consent' of Richard they were granted their lands.[1] The church had done a little for them,[2] but there must have been many who could not find the price of redemption. Whether this ordinance had any effect or not it is still impossible to say. But Richard's leadership was not unchallenged. He was powerless to protect the Jews. The attack begun in his absence by Edward and Henry of Almain was renewed, and the *Provisio Judaismi* was much broadened and clarified by an ordinance of July 25th, 1271, when Richard was present, forbidding Jews to hold any free tenement. 'At a stroke their status was virtually reduced to that of pawnbrokers.'[3]

Richard's financial interests were not limited to money-lending and the Jews, but his wider commercial activities are more difficult to trace. He had, like every great person, 'his merchants', whom he protected and for whom he sought privileges, sometimes with a definitely political intention. He imported corn when it was most needed, he abolished tolls on the Rhine, he exported tin.[4] Much of his public activity during his last two years is concerned with finance — the organization of the wool trade, the Jewry, the reorganization of the Exchequer, the lay Twentieth, the measures to prevent Henry III from spending. Part of this was due to the crusade, which was just as expensive to launch as any other foreign campaign, but part is a reflection of his interests as the king's first adviser — *in quo preceteris viventibus confidimus* as Henry had once said — at a time when the king was no longer competent to give much effective help in council. The appointment of Richard's own treasurer as Treasurer of England is a fitting conclusion to such a story. Philip of Eye, who had already served his master for twenty-five years, became Treasurer on October 16th and remained in office for two years before retiring to Oseney Abbey, where the chronicler Thomas de Wykes founded a chantry in his honour.[5] The effect of

---

[1] *Ann. Wint.*, 110; *Ann. Worcs.*, 460.

[2] The clerical Twentieth of 1268 was raised nominally on their behalf (Wykes, Oseney, 218-20) and a payment of fifty marks therefrom is noted in *Letters from Northern Registers*, p. 19.

[3] C. Roth, *A History of the Jews in England*, p. 66; *Lib. de Ant. Leg.*, 234 f. This ordinance was passed with difficulty, as there was a pro-Jewish party in the Council. Though passed in June it appears on the Patent Roll only in July, after the Archbishop of York and his brother, the Bishop of Worcester, had written to Mr. Richard de Stanes, the [chief] justice, urging him to secure its enrolment and publication by appealing to the Chancellor, the judges, and other great men of the Court. For the prehistory of it see A. G. Little, 'Friar Henry de Wodestone and the Jews' in *Collect. Francisc.*, ii, 150-7.

[4] *Supra*, chap. iv.

[5] Wykes, 247, 256, 271.

Philip of Eye's appointment was at once seen in a brief and business-like ordinance to free the machinery of the Exchequer from the clogging litigation of persons who found it the best way of collecting debts under the fiction that the king's interests were involved.[1]

Since February 1271 Richard had been comforted by the presence of Edmund of Cornwall, now just twenty-one, who had returned at his wish. But early in April, about the time that the council had determined to assume control of the revenues of the crown, Richard received the appalling news that his eldest son had been brutally murdered.[2]

Henry of Almain and his bride sailed for Gascony about August 15th, 1270, and Henry joined Edward at Aiguemortes in the autumn. In spite of the death of Louis IX they sailed for Tunis on October 3rd at the invitation of the young Philip III of France. Finding nothing to be done in Africa they wintered in Sicily at Charles of Anjou's request, and here, in consequence probably of the official appeal of February 6th from England, Edward determined to send back Henry of Almain. Because 'he was wiser than the others', Henry was chosen to go and arrange for the government of Gascony, proceeding thence to help Richard of Cornwall in England.[3] Philip III was going home for his coronation and Charles of Anjou going to Viterbo to hurry up the work of the cardinals who had long been there in conclave. Travelling under the protection of Charles, therefore, the party reached Viterbo on March 9th. Here Simon and Guy de Montfort were waiting for them, for Guy had become deputy-vicar of Tuscany for Charles. Count Aldebrandini dell' Anguillara 'il Rosso', Guy's father-in-law, was with them.[4]

Early on Friday, March 13th, Simon, Guy, and Count Rosso, possibly with Amaury de Montfort's consent, entered the church where Henry was saying his prayers after Mass, with a crowd of followers and rushed upon him, calling him traitor and, though falsely, murderer of their father. He jumped up and ran to the altar, where they stabbed him, in the church of St. Blaise. Such is the factual statement of Wykes, the most important English authority.[5] All that can be added to it are the statements of Gregory X in his process against

[1] *C.P.R.*, 584.
[2] Richard wrote to the Franciscans from Isleworth on the 24th asking for prayers for Henry's soul (*Lib. de Ant. Leg.*, 134-5).
[3] Wykes, 239-40.
[4] A fuller account of these well-known events is given in Bémont, *Simon de Montfort*, chap. x.
[5] Wykes, 241. See my article in *E.H.R.*, lxi, 157-79, for this chronicle and the author's unique information about Richard of Cornwall.

Guy de Montfort dated April 1st, 1273,[1] and Philip III's letter to Richard of Cornwall.[2] The former gives details of the treatment of the body, and the murder of an attendant priest, and adds that Guy had stood in the doorway gnashing his teeth and crying 'Proditor, Henrice de Alemannia, non evades!' It also tells us that the murder took place in a certain parish church. Philip III's letter states that it occurred in another chapel of Viterbo opposite Henry's lodgings, while the two kings were hearing Mass in the church of the Franciscans.

It is odd that we should be unable to determine with certainty the locality of a murder committed with every possible circumstance of publicity. Philip III, writing on the very day of the outrage, refers it to an unnamed chapel. The pope, two years later, to a certain parish church. S. Silvester is a parish church in the middle of the town near the market-place, and here the murder is placed by some reputable chroniclers, but Wykes is by far the best authority among those who name the place, and his testimony cannot be lightly rejected. He professes to be telling the story of Edward's crusade as he had heard it from those who had been with him.[3] It is unfortunate that in his treatment of this difficulty Davidsohn has completely ignored the version of Wykes.[4] If there was a church of St. Blaise, which seems difficult to verify, it is very likely to have been the scene of the murder. On May 15th the body was brought home and buried on the 21st at Hailes. The heart was preserved in a gilt urn at Westminster, by the Confessor's shrine.[5] Richard must have been sorely tried, but he continued to perform his public duties throughout the summer.[6] On August 1st he suffered another blow

---

[1] *Foed.*, i, 501-2.   [2] *Lib. de Ant. Leg.*, 133.   [3] Wykes, 238.

[4] Davidsohn, *Forschungen*, iv, 201-11, admirable for the later history and repercussions of the case. Blaauw, 234, n. 2, mentions 'the chapel of the confraternity of St. Blaise' giving no authority. If there was a confraternity of St. Blaise at Viterbo, we might expect to find it in the cathedral of St. Laurence, given as the scene of the murder by Rishanger and Walsingham and Trivet. Prof. Powicke in *T. R. Hist. Soc.*, 4th ser., vol. xviii, p. 16, prefers to accept the statement of Guido de Corvaria, who may have been in the city as Pisan ambassador to Charles of Anjou. But this view also ignores Wykes and minimizes the importance of Philip's letter.

[5] *Flores*, iii, 22; *Oseney*, 244; *Wint.*, 110.

[6] *C.P.R.*, 597-8 (June 21st, 1271) and the ordinance concerning the Jews (July 25th). The former is of interest in connection with Richard's action as Regent in 1254, when he destroyed his illegal fish-nets as an example to the other barons. Now, twenty-seven years later, he has a royal commissioner appointed with power to act in five counties and to destroy 'all nets made beyond the assize', and all 'gorces' and weirs in which the opening has been so narrowed that the passage of river traffic is impeded. A subsidiary aim (it is at any rate placed second) was to prevent the flooding of Otmoor and adjacent lands caused by the construction of these weirs lower down. The royal commissioner was William Pasket, and he had been Richard's bailiff, probably of Berkhampstead (*Cal. Ch. R.*, ii, 99 (ii) before 1268), and the flooded lands were those of 'R. King of Almain and other magnates and others'. Thus William Pasket embodies Richard's attempt at Thames Conservancy.

in the death of Edward's five-year-old heir, John, who had been left
in his charge. The boy was buried on August 8th at Westminster, in
Richard's presence.[1] In September, Richard visited Knaresborough,
where he remained at least six days, perhaps to take possession of the
honour and see to the disposal of Henry of Almain's effects there.[2]
But there is no suggestion in any source that Richard was already
failing when he went to the north. The Archbishop of York,
writing to his proctor at Rome on November 3rd, 1271, describes
all the worries of Edward's five commissioners — how money was
short, how Gloucester wanted help against the Welsh, how they
had to be much with Henry III who was not so strong as they could
wish — but there is no hint of anything the matter with Richard.[3]
He had just had committed to him the custody of Rockingham
castle and certain forests which Henry of Almain had had,[4] and the
appointment of Philip of Eye as Treasurer is likely (to say the least)
to have been his work.

Richard was at Berkhampstead on December 11th and next day
authorized a letter of protection for the Abbey of St. Gislen in
Hainault.[5] The same day he was bled, but the following night he
had a stroke, which paralysed his right side and deprived him of the
power of speech. He recovered sufficiently to authorize on February
18th a grant of the regalia to the newly-elected Bishop of Verdun.[6]
After making his will and receiving the Last Sacrament, he died on
April 2nd, 1272.[7] His body was buried beside his son and Sanchia
at Hailes, and his heart in the choir of the Franciscan church at
Oxford.[8]

By his will Richard left 8,000 marks in aid of the Holy Land,[9]
and 500 marks to the German Dominicans.[10] He also left money to
found a college of canons at Oxford, a bequest enlarged by his son
Edmund to found instead the Cistercian abbey of Rewley.[11] The

---

[1] Wykes, 246; *Ann. Worcs.*, 461.
[2] A gift to the Cistercians of Knaresborough is notified to his bailiffs thereof in a writ printed
by Gebauer, p. 408 (September 7th). Other formal documents are noted in B.F., 5478-80.
[3] The archbishop says that Henry III 'non est ita potens corpore sicut vellemus, et ob hoc
stare magis compellimur circa ipsum' (*Letters from Northern Registers*, pp. 39-40). By this
time Burnel had replaced Robert Walerand as one of Edward's attorneys. Burnel had meant
to go on Crusade, and even appointed attorneys, but if he went he must have been sent home
about the same time as Henry of Almain, for he was back by April 1271 (*C.P.R.*, 451, 531,
596), and is described as Edward's attorney in July (*ibid.*, 557).
[4] *C.P.R.*, 581 (October 20th, 1271).   [5] B.F., 5481.   [6] *Ibid.*, 5483.
[7] Wykes, 247-8, where for *sibi fecit muniri* read *sibi fecit minueri*.
[8] Annals of Hailes in *M.G.H.*, xvi, 483; *Flor. Wig. cont.*, ii, 207; *Mon. Ang.*, v, 699.
[9] Bliss, *Cal. Papal Lett.*, i, 621.   [10] *Reg. Peckham* (R.S.), iii, 1027.
[11] *Mon. Ang.*, v, 697-701.

will itself, of which Michael of Northampton was an executor,[1] is not now known to exist. His widow, Beatrice, survived until October 17th, 1277, and was buried in front of the high altar in the Franciscan church at Oxford, near her husband's heart.[2]

The view held by Matthew Paris of Richard of Cornwall's character continually deteriorated after the disappointment of 1238. His final judgment is summed up in a speech which he thought suitable for a member of the baronial deputation that disputed with Richard in 1259 whether or not he could land in England without taking the oath to the Provisions of Oxford. Matthew has the grace to admit that the speech was never delivered: 'We have often appointed you to be our leader in effecting a reform in the condition of the kingdom but, instigated by avarice, you have always cunningly endeavoured to entrap us by suddenly causing the king to recoil from his wholesome resolutions.'[3] Though Matthew knew Richard well personally, his views were coloured by his own political opinions. Consequently by working from the *Chronica Majora* alone it would be possible to construct a more vivid but less favourable (and probably less true) picture than is here presented. In the chronicle of Thomas de Wyke (commonly called Wykes), Richard's personality does not emerge so clearly.[4]

The key to much of Richard of Cornwall's life lies in his poor physique. We are not told that he suffered from any specific physical handicap, nor that he was frequently ill, but simply that he was not really healthy. For this reason he was not a warlike man, and not properly trained in the arts of war.[5] Neither he nor Henry inherited to the full the passionate temperament of their parents. Henry had the petulance of a child, whereas Richard was of equable temper, and was neither litigious nor quarrelsome. He was essentially a proud man, with a strongly developed sense of property, and when once roused could harbour lasting resentment, as he showed over Richard Siward and later over the sack of Isleworth. Though he could talk English he was not popular with lesser people. The London merchants and the Jews were his friends, but to the mob he was 'ever trichard'.[6] He had a weakness for magnificence

---

[1] *Reg. Peckham*, i, 169.   [2] *Ann. of Oseney*, 274.   [3] *Mat. Par.*, v, 733-4.

[4] I have dealt elsewhere with the structure and value of this important source.

[5] *Mat. Par.*, v, 201: 'Tum quia corpore sanus et integer nullatenus extitit, tum quia in armis strenuus nec exercitatus extitit.'

[6] 'Richard tha thou be ever trichard, trichen shalt thou never more' is the refrain of the song on the battle of Lewes in *Pol. Songs*, 68-71.

and vain show — he had his scarlet robes even in captivity — was a lover of pomp and ceremony, and inclined in a harmless way to be boastful, but this is the worst that can be said of him. It has been suggested that he had a 'characteristic infirmity of purpose',[1] but his infirmity was chiefly physical: he would press nothing to the arbitrament of war, but he could be tenacious enough when it suited him. On the whole he was wise and provident, but somewhat lacking in speed of execution.[2]

Richard's moral integrity is only in doubt at certain crises, as perhaps in 1227, more certainly in 1238, perhaps again in 1263, when he withdraws his support from one side or the other at a time when both thought themselves entitled to his favour. This was partly due to his innate love of compromise. He had a zeal for arbitration that amounted almost to a passion. He loved the work for its own sake, would go out of his way to undertake it, and was often successful. Men called him a trickster, and jeered at his love of money, but continued to submit themselves to his award because they knew — Henry III better than any of them — that he was fundamentally honest. He was businesslike and had a flair for finance, but was not mercenary. Henry was indebted to him over a period of years for thousands of marks, and Richard could have obtained, had he wished, a complete stranglehold on his brother's finances. But he asked for no interest on his loans. As far as can be seen he lent only to his relatives and friends,[3] for as he told the citizens of Vienne, he was no merchant. Nor was he a miser. He spent most lavishly on Wallingford castle and Hailes abbey, and if he received much from the unprecedented papal grant of the redemption of crusading vows, he paid much back not only by bequest but in his lifetime.[4]

Though much trusted by Henry III, particularly in the later years of his reign,[5] he never hesitated to criticize his brother's incompetence and instability. He made a small fortune for them both out of the Mint, Henry's contribution being a beautiful but useless gold

---

[1] *D.N.B. s.v.* Richard of Cornwall.

[2] Some of his awards were long in coming, and each time he went to Germany he spent far too long in preparation.

[3] i.e. to Henry III, Peter of Savoy, Boniface of Savoy, Edward, Edmund, Richard de Clare, and Hugh Bigod.

[4] Apart from the 8,000 marks bequeathed by will Richard sent £1,000 to the Holy Land in 1245 *ex innata sibi munificencia.* Cf. *Mat. Par.,* v, 411; 'Qui de statu Terre Sancte plus aliis sollicitabatur.'

[5] In 1267 Henry wrote to him 'sicut de vobis pre ceteris viventibus confidimus' (*Cl. R.,* 407).

coin. For Henry was an artist to his finger-tips, while in Richard's career there is no hint even of literary interests or patronage. His private life was not immaculate, nor was he a man of many friends. With the exception of Peter of Savoy they were probably the friends of his youth — the Marshals, the Bassets, his stepson Richard de Clare, and perhaps Hugh Bigod.

In Germany as in England he would have gained immense favour with the magnates 'if he had been as vigorous in war as he was prudent and circumspect in his counsels'.[1] This was to expect the impossible. The political centre of gravity in medieval Germany was always shifting from one place to another with the demesnes of the ruling house, and it might have been better for the country if Richard had had a Rhineland demesne and had stayed there to rule it. But he lacked the martial qualities, as well as the material resources and the opportunity to achieve this formidable task. In England he did an immense amount of public work during the last thirty years of his life, and did not ask for an excessive reward. Taken as a whole, it is a period of prolonged and loyal co-operation in everything possible with his weaker brother, and latterly with his brilliant nephew Edward. If Henry had followed his advice more consistently at home, or taken it at all in matters of foreign policy, more than anything perhaps over Sicily, the explosion of 1258 might never have occurred and Richard might have gone to Rome.

[1] *Mat. Par.*, v, 695: 'Si armipotens extitisset in viribus, sicut fuerat in consiliis prudens et circumspectus.'

RICHARD OF CORNWALL'S LOANS TO THE KING AND OTHERS

9.6.1240	£100	Order to pay this sum lent by him to the king.	*C. Lib. R.*, i, 472.
10.8.1242	200 marks	*do.* lent in Gascony.	*ibid.*, ii, 154.
1243	£300	Lent to the Earl of Gloucester, guaranteed by Tewkesbury Abbey.	*Ann. Theok.*, 134.
8.2.1244	1,000 marks	Lent to the wardrobe.	*C.P.R.*, 419, 426, cf. *C. Lib. R.*, 238, 298.
19.3.1244	500 marks	*do.* for the Gannock campaign.	*C.P.R.*, 421, 481.
8.12.1244	1,000 marks	Lent to Boniface, Archbishop-elect of Canterbury.	*C.P.R.*, 446.
July 1245	3,000 marks	Lent to king on security of bezants, bars, and spangles.	*C.P.R.*, 456.
17.8.1245	[2,000 marks	Bond to Richard in this sum, being 1,750 ms. lent for the Welsh campaign and 250 ms. for his terminal fee. Probably including February 8th and March 19th, 1244, above.]	*C.P.R.*, 459.
23.4.1246	—	Unspecified sum lent to Peter of Savoy, to be a first charge upon his estates if he dies saving 100 ms. a year until 1,000 ms. have been paid which he owes to the king.	*C.P.R.*, 479.
5.2.1247	—	Order to pay him 2,000 ms. by the Quinzaine of Easter, the 300 ms. of gold which he had as security (see July 1245) to be returned.	*C. Lib. R.*, 105.
22.2.1247	—	To have 300 ms. at Easter to complete the 2,000 ms. for the payment of which he betook himself to the Jewry (? see August 1245).	*C. Lib. R.*, 109.

27.7.1247	10,000 marks	Acknowledgment of his loan which has been applied for the utility of the realm (i.e. the recoinage).	*C.P.R.*, 505, 511.
1.10.1247	—	Order to pay him 1,000 ms. in lieu of a like sum lent by him to the king.	*C. Lib. R.*, 142.
5.2.1248	—	Order to pay him 2,000 ms. at Easter and 2,000 at Michaelmas and so on till the 10,000 is paid.	*C. Lib. R.*, 166.
3-4.8.1248	1,000 marks	Bond to him in this sum, being 500 ms. loan and 500 ms. of his fee.	*C.P.R.*, 23. *C. Lib. R.*, 195.
12.3.1249	5,000 marks	Keepers of the Bishopric of Durham to let him have all the issues until he has been paid this sum.	*C.P.R.*, 38.
3.11.1249	500 marks	Lent to Peter of Savoy. On March 12th, 1253, it is repeated that Peter's debts to Richard are to be a first charge on his estates at his death (*C.P.R. 181*).	*C.P.R.*, 54.
27.5.1250	—	To have amercements of Lincoln Eyre, until all debts, etc.	*C.P.R.*, 66.
		do. of Salop and Staffs. in part payment, etc.	*Cl. R.*, 285.
14.7.1250	—	Order to pay 300 ms. to his use in part, etc.	*C. Lib. R.*, 295.
24.7.1250	—	Order to pay 5,000 ms. out of the issues of the Exchange in part, etc.	*C. Lib. R.*, 296.
7.10.1250	200 marks	Lent to Richard de Wyche, Bishop of Chichester.	*C.P.R.*, 75.
27.10.1250	—	Has had £2,020 out of the issues of the Bishopric of Durham.	*C. Lib. R.*, 307.
29.12.1250	—	To have 250 ms. of his fee and 220 repayment of loan, out of the Norfolk Eyre.	*C. Lib. R.*, 325.
16.1.1251	—	Has had £700 out of the last eyre in Somerset and Dorset.	*C. Lib. R.*, 327.
20.1.1251	—	To have 500 ms. as his share of the issues of the Mint.	*C. Lib. R.*, 329.

*c.*5.2.1251	—	To have £236 10s. 7d. at St. Edmunds at mid-Lent, from the Norfolk and Suffolk Eyre for arrears due for exchanging old coin.	C. Lib. R., 332.
8.7.1251	2,000 marks	Lent by him for making new money and maintaining the change in Ireland.	C.P.R., 101.
12.3.1253	4,000 marks	Lent by him for affairs of Gascony on gold security, repayable at All Saints.	C.P.R., 364.
30.6.1253	2,000 marks	To deliver the king's jewels as soon as he has received 2,000 ms.	C.P.R., 204.
6.7.1253	1,000 marks	Lent by him on security of tallage of Jewry.	C.P.R., 209 Cl. R., 386.
7.7.1253	6,000 marks	Bonds for 6,000 ms. and other sums lent to the king for 700 ms. of gold which he had as security. (The calendar is ambiguous.)	C.P.R., 236, cf. 210.
18.7.1254	—	[Richard to be asked to lend £10,000 to the king in Gascony, on security of the whole issues of the exchequer.]	C.P.R., 311.
31.8.1254	—	[The king is so indebted that he cannot leave Gascony: the treasurer to borrow 6,000 or 7,000 ms. from Richard or someone else.]	C.P.R., 326.
9.10.1254	[6,000 marks] 4,000 marks	Grant to Richard, who has respited till February 1255 the payment of 6,000 ms. lent before the Gascon expedition and of 4,000 ms. lent since then, that if the king does not pay, Richard may make his profit of the gold pledged to him. On November 4th, 1256, ratification of delivery to Richard of 1,207½ ms. of gold pledged to him when the queen was regent (*C.P.R.*, 528).	C.P.R., 373.
24.2.1255	5,000 marks [3,000 marks]	Lent by him to the king on the security of the whole Jewry, repayable at Wallingford or the New Temple. To receive 8,000 ms. back, of which 3,000 were to be in part payment for the money in which the king is bound	C.P.R., 400-401.

		to the earl for his jewels pledged to the earl at another time. If the Jews default they are to pay 500 ms. on each occasion. See *C.P.R.*, 439-44 for details of the collection of £3,000 5s. 4d., and cf. 464.	
20.6.1255	£1,000	Promise to Richard, from whom Edward, the king's son, has borrowed £1,000 payable at Christmas 1255 at Wallingford, that it shall be a first charge upon his goods.	*C.P.R.*, 413.
April 1256	£1,000	Lent to Peter of Savoy, to be a first charge on his estates or chattels.	*C.P.R.*, 469.
8.5.1256	—	Richard to receive 750 ms. arrears of his fee at once.	*C.P.R.*, 472.
[*c.*1.11.1256	4,000 marks	Said by Matthew Paris to have been lent to Edward for his campaign against Wales. Matthew also states that a second application was refused.]	*Mat. Par.*, v, 593, 597.

Counting from October 9th, 1254, there is a total of 25,000 marks out on loan, and a profit of about 2,000 marks to be had from the 1,207½ marks of gold called in on November 4th, 1256. The coincidence in date between the calling-in of the gold and the conclusion of the intrigues leading to Richard's election as King of the Romans casts doubt on the accuracy of the very circumstantial story in Matthew Paris of the 4,000 marks lent to Edward.

1266	£250	Hugh Bigod admits a debt of £250 to Richard payable at Michaelmas.	*Cl. R.*, 239.
3.2.1268	2,000 marks	Request to the legate to pay out of the tenth to Richard 2,000 ms. in which the king is bound to him. (Probably for the Ely campaign of 1267: see Wykes, 204.)	*C.P.R.*, 187.
15.5.1268	—	King acknowledges 2,687½ ms. debt to Richard.	*C.P.R.*, 229; *Cl. R.*, 470-71.
July 1268	—	Order to Sheriff of Norfolk to pay half, and Sheriff of Yorkshire the other half.	*Cl. R.*, 161-62.

Nov.-Dec. 1269	—	Richard has only received £140 of the 2,687½ ms. The rest to be charged on the eyre in Devon.	*C.P.R.*, 364.
6.3.1271	—	King owes Richard 2,306 ms.	*C.P.R.*, 520.
20.6.1271	2,000 marks	Lent to Edward, repayable out of the Jewry.	*C.P.R.*, 545.
26.6.1271	3,000 marks	Lent to the king, repayable out of the Bishopric of Salisbury.	*C.P.R.*, 543-44, 547.
3.8.1271	1,000 marks	Lent to Edmund, the king's son.	*C.P.R.*, 567.

It was perhaps in reward for his financial and diplomatic services in 1267 that Richard received a promise (*Cl. R.*, 407, November 20th) of 3,000 marks' worth of land, i.e. 1,000 marks in wardships (of which the Mowbray wardship was in part satisfaction) and 2,000 marks of land of the Disinherited (of which the lands of Adam of Newmarket were in part satisfaction). By February 3rd, 1268, nothing had been done about the wardships, but Richard is to be satisfied before anyone else is paid. It is not yet decided whether the Mowbray wardship, which he has farmed for 400 marks a year, should form part of this settlement (*C.P.R.*, 187). On April 24th, 1271, he received the Mauduit and Huntercombe wardships (*C.P.R.*, 533) and on June 28th the remaining third of the Hastings wardship (*C.P.R.*, 546) as part of the same settlement.

M

APPENDIX TWO

THE ESTATES AND THEIR ADMINISTRATION

The records are few. There must have been some kind of central financial organization, but almost nothing is known about it. Of Richard's treasurers, stewards, or chancellors little can be said. Two of them have become notorious. Nicholas Danne (de Anna, de Enna), described by Matthew Paris in his exuberant way as the earl's clerk, special counsellor, and treasurer, died in 1246 after falling off a horse while drunk and breaking his neck.[1] Sir John Bretasche, his accomplice — he was really steward of Berkhampstead[2] — was with him at the time and suffered the same fate. Nicholas may be identical with 'Nicholas the clerk, chancellor of the Earl' who attests in 1240 and before 1243.[3] Another chancellor, John, is mentioned by Paris because he was present when a long news-letter addressed to the Queen of France was read out describing the battle of Mansourah and the capture of Louis IX. John passed on the news to Earl Richard who was sitting at the Exchequer when it arrived on August 1st.[4] Richard's council is nowhere mentioned.

In a general way it may be said that the estates were divided up into bailiwicks according to the system found in operation under his son, and it is therefore unnecessary to recapitulate the facts as marshalled by Miss Midgley, but there are three important points in which Richard's arrangements differed from those of Edmund of Cornwall.

In 1296-1297 the nine stewards of bailiwicks and the keepers of the works of Wallingford castle, each with his clerk, went to Berkhampstead and there, as I see the procedure, these clerks (since the account of each bailiwick is written in a different hand) drew up the fair copies of their receipts and expenses. When the account of a bailiwick had been balanced the scribe went on to list (i) the *allocaciones* or allowances to the steward for salaries, expenses connected with the audit, money paid over to the earl or his officials, debts which for one reason or another they were theoretically but not in practice liable, and (ii) a series of precepts to the steward concerning the treatment of individual estates or general rules for his guidance, or precepts concerning the form of account, e.g. in 1297

---

[1] *Mat. Par.*, iv, 588.   [2] *Abbrev. Plac.*, 112; *Cl. R.*, 1241, p. 270.
[3] *C.P.R.* (1381-1385), p. 264. Both attest a charter to Selborne Priory (before 1240), Magd. Coll., Oxon., Hants i, Bromdean 13; *C.P.R.*, 1327-1330, p. 333.
[4] *Mat. Par.*, v, 147, 165-9.

rents or services alienated by the earl's charter were in future to be deleted from the accounts.

The two surviving bailiwick accounts of Earl Richard's time deal with Berkhampstead (1269-1270) and Wallingford (1270-1271).[1] These show (i) no heading *Allocaciones* after the *summa*. What was later put under this head was at this time put under expenses; (ii) no precepts to the stewards. To put the matter briefly, these important differences seem to justify the belief that in the last years of Richard's life the administration of his estates was far less centralized than it had become by 1295 and that there is no evidence of any conciliar control. The third point of difference is that the administrative centre in 1270 was Wallingford, not Berkhampstead.[2] This is in keeping with what would suggest itself for other reasons, but it would be unsafe to assume that because the annual audit took place in 1270 at Wallingford it therefore had taken place there in every preceding year since the Jews were moved thither in 1242. It is likely, however, that it frequently, even usually, did.

Richard's estates were worth to him about £5,000 to £6,000 a year, Cornwall and the stannaries, Wallingford, Knaresborough, and Sanchia's marriage-portion providing £4,500 of this.[3] Berkhampstead and Isabella of Angoulême's dower, plus Haughley, Lydford and Dartmoor and Eye produced another £900. The total is not much more than half the appanage assigned to the Lord Edward.

I give below a table to show the growth of this great agglomeration of lands, followed by notes, alphabetically arranged, concerning chiefly the demesne manors. There is no attempt at completeness: the list is rather to serve as a directory, and for further information under most of the heads reference should be made to Miss Midgley's work, even where it is not cited.

1. Cornwall and Poitou during pleasure   1225
   Cornwall as earl   1227
   Cornwall and the Stannaries in fee   1231

2. Berkhampstead and the Dower of Isabella of
   Angoulême during pleasure, with St. Valery
   and Eye   1227

---

[1] P.R.O., Ministers' Accounts 863/2, Geoffrey de Helpestone's account as steward of Berkhampstead for 1269-1270, and Min. Acct., 1095/5, Geoffrey de Leukenore's account as steward of the honour of Wallingford and the honour of St. Valery for 1270-1271. This Geoffrey had been steward the year before (Min. Acct., 1118/17). Sir R. de la More was Constable of Wallingford.

[2] 'In expensis . . . venientis ad Waling' ad compotum suum reddendum cum tribus equis per tres dies veniendo, morando, et redeundo 10s.' (Min. Acct., 863/2). The account is incomplete and not wholly legible.

[3] These figures are for the most part really valid only for the last years of the century, and can in any case give only the roughest idea.

The same, with St. Valery and Eye, in fee   1231 (4 Feb.)
The same, with the same, and Rutland in fee   1231 (24 Aug.)

3. Wallingford, and Manor of Watlington   1231

4. Haughley   1234
   Knaresborough   1235
   Kirton-in-Lindsey   1235
   Lydford and the forest of Dartmoor   1239

5. The marriage-portion of Sanchia of Provence, 500 librates, made up as follows:
     (i) Mere, Corsham, Fordinton, Newport   1242
    (ii) Glatton, Risborough   1243
   (iii) Bensington   1244
   (iv) Bradninch   1244
    (v) Oakham and Lechlade   1252
   (vi) Langborough, Barford   1256

Cornwall itself had been practically a palatinate under William of Mortain, Reginald of Dunsterville, and Earl John, none of whom accounted at the Exchequer. This was not so under Richard of Cornwall or his son Edmund. They appointed their own sheriffs — Richard uses the style 'steward and sheriff'[1] — and 'received the full revenue of the shire'.[2] But the sheriff was the king's officer. The king's writ ran in Cornwall and his justices held their eyres there. From time to time Richard was granted the profits of the eyre. Under John, the men of Cornwall paid 500 marks for the privilege of electing their own sheriff.[3] They later claimed the right of election by virtue of a charter of King John, and stated that Richard of Cornwall had deprived them of this liberty.[4]

The Cornish estates were increased in 1270 by a purchase from Roger de Valle Torta in fee tail of the castle of Tremerton and the Manor of Calstock with 60½ knights' fees in Cornwall and Devon, for £300.[5] As the estate was worth at least £40 a year in 1297-1298 this looks like a very

---

[1] Three of Richard's sheriffs were: Walter de Therbyn (*Mon. Ang.*, old ed., ii, 901), Stephen de 'Meym', 'steward of Cornwall' (*Cal. Cl. R.*, ii, 25, dated November 7th, 1259), John Beaupre, 'our steward and sheriff of Cornwall' (*Cal. Ch. R.*, iii, 479, dated July 1268; and *Anct. Deeds*, v, A.10843, *c.* 1270 as 'Steward of Cornwall'). The P.R.O. *List* gives Stephen de 'Heyra' 1256, but 'Meym' and 'Heyra' are probably Stephen Heym, as in *Anct. Deeds*, v, 10843 and Exch. T. R. Misc. Bk., no. 57, fol. 3.

[2] S. Painter, *Feudal Barony*, 112-13.

[3] *R.Lit.Cl.*, i, 457.

[4] W. A. Morris, *The Mediaeval English Sheriff to 1300*, 183, from *Rot. Hund.*, i, 56. For Edmund's sheriffs see Midgley, xxix.

[5] *Anct. Deeds*, v, A.10842-3; cf. Exch. T. R. Misc. Bk., no. 57, no. 28.

good 'buy'. His other three castles in Cornwall were Launceston, Tintagel, and Restormel; and the other demesne manors included Helston-in-Kerrier, Stoke Climsland, Helstone in Trigg, Liskeard, Tybista, Penknight, Tywarnhail, Tewington, Penlyne, Moresk, and Rillaton.

ASTHALL (Esthalle), co. Oxon., demesne manor of the honour of St. Valery, worth £10 in 1237. *Bk. of Fees*, 613. Held of the king for half a fee. *Cal. I.P.M.* i, no. 808. Given to Richard of Cornwall, son of Earl Richard. *Cal. I.P.M.*, iii, 482, 483, 487, 488.

BARFORD ST. MARTIN, co. Wilts. Granted to R. in 1254 as £10 6s. 4½d. p.a. in part payment of the marriage-portion of Sanchia of Provence. *Cl. R.*, 13. Charter of April 25th in Exch. T.R. Misc. Bk., no. 57, no. cxxxvii. Late *Terra Normannorum*. By 1297-1298 there was only 40s. rent. Midgley, 82.

BEACONSFIELD, co. Bucks., near Burnham, with which it was assessed for the carucage 1237-1240. *Bk. of Fees*, 1447. R. granted a market at his manor of, February 6th, 1255, Exch. T.R. Misc. Bk., no. 57, no. cxxxv.

BENSINGTON, co. Oxon. The manor and four and a half Chiltern hundreds granted to R. and his heirs by Sanchia, October 17th, 1244, *Cal. Ch. R.*, i, 280, cf. *Cl. R.*, 229, 372. The demesne was farmed out to the twenty-five tenants by charter alleged in *Black Prince's Register*, iv, 19, 21-3.

BERKHAMPSTEAD, co. Herts. The honour, comprising 22 and a fraction of the little fees of Mortain (five-eighths the normal fee) in Herts., Bucks., and N'hants. (*Red Bk.*, 363, 498, 733), was granted to Richard in 1227 as part of the dower of Isabella of Angoulême. It was taken back by Henry III on September 29th, 1227, as it had only been granted during pleasure, *Pat. R.*, 145. Granted in fee in 1231, *Cal. Ch. R.*, i, 129. To be part of Sanchia's dower if she survived him, January 4th, 1244, *Cal. Pat. R.*, 414. Granted with the castle and honour, and the county of Rutland (*q.v.*) and all the lands which ISABELLA (*q.v.*), etc., in fee simple for two fees, August 24th, 1246. Exch. T. R. Misc. Bk., no. 57, nos. ccxiii, cxxxiii.

Richard added to the castle a three-storied tower covered with lead in 1254, *Ann. Dunst.*, 191.

BLACKTHORN in Ambrosden, co. Oxon., demesne manor of the honour of St. Valery, worth £20 in 1237. *Bk. of Fees*, 613.

BOULOGNE, honour of, *see* Kirton, Glatton.

BRADNINCH, in Devon, the manor with twenty fees appurtenant granted to Richard and his heirs by Sanchia, November 11th, 1244, *Cal. Ch. R.*, i, 281; Midgley, xxii.

CIPPENHAM in Burnham, co. Bucks. Held of the Abbot of Westminster by 50s. rent. There are earthworks there on the site of 'Cippenham Palace', which was probably only a moated manor house, *V.C.H. Bucks.*, iii, 166-8. *Cal. I.P.M.*, i, p. 274; iii, p. 464.

CORSHAM, co. Wilts., an ancient demesne manor granted to Richard and his heirs by Sanchia, December 25th, 1243, *Cal. Ch. R.*, i, 276, but he had possession in 1242, *Cl. R.*, 81. Most of the demesne he farmed to the customary tenants in fee for 110 marks a year. The charter (1242-1257) is reproduced in Sir Harold Breakspear's paper on 'Corsham' in *Wilts. Arch. and Nat. Hist. Mag.*, vol. xliii, pp. 511-39. In 1246 Richard had 20 oaks for the construction of his houses there, *Cl. R.*, 471.

CRANBOURNE, co. Dorset. Richard had the castle moat there stocked with bream in 1241, *Cl. R.*, 281. The custody of some of Richard de Clare's estates was in his hands until 1243 (*Cl. R.*, 287; *Ann. Theok.*, 131), probably those which he had acquired through Isabella Marshall, Countess of Gloucester, his first wife. For Richard de Clare's wardship see F. M. Powicke in *E.H.R.*, October 1941, pp. 539-46. Gilbert Marshal was given the custody of the Clare lands in Wales in 1235 (*Ann. Theok.*, 96).

EXNING, co. Suff. In 1235 Henry III ordered Richard's bailiffs of 'Desinges' to send him at once a cask of their master's better wine from this manor (*Cl. R.*, 59). There was land here of the honour of Boulogne (*Bk. of Fees*, 389).

EYE in Suffolk. Richard I gave the honour to Henry, Duke of Lorraine of the house of Louvain (*d.* 1235) with the niece of William de Warenne, who had held it at the beginning of Henry II's reign, *Bk. of Fees*, i, 137-8; Pirenne, *Hist. de Belgique*, i, 437-8. In 1212 the duke still held it, but in 1215 it was held by a *custos*, having perhaps been taken back by John after Bouvines, *R. Lit. Pat.*, 1467. On July 3rd, 1221, it was granted to Richard the king's brother during pleasure, with Falkes de Bréauté *tamquam senescallus* to answer to Richard for the issues *R. Lit. Cl.*, i, 605, 621; *Pat. R.*, 294. On January 2nd, 1225, it was again granted to the Duke of Louvain (*R. Lit. Cl.*, ii, 10[b]) and he still held it in 1226 (*Pat. R.*, ii, 27) but in 1229 Hubert de Burgh had it (*Cal. Ch. R.*, i, 101). On January 28th, 1230, Earl Richard had it during pleasure (*Cl. R.*, 287, cf. 332) and in 1231 it was granted to him in fee, *Cal. Ch. R.*, i, 129.

The honour of Eye normally paid scutage on 90½ fees, of which over 70 were in Suffolk. In 1237 the 'manor' was said to be worth £160 a year. *Bk. of Fees*, 460, 619; *Red Bk.*, 477.

FORDINGTON in Dorset, an ancient demesne manor granted to Richard and his heirs by Sanchia, December 25th, 1243, Exch. T. R. Misc. Bk., no. 57, no, ccxv. The Enrolled Charter omits this manor. *Cal. Ch. R.*, i, 276.

GLATTON, co. Hunt., granted as Fordinton. Held of the king as of the honour of Boulogne for 4½ fees. *Cal. I.P.M.*, iii, 461.

HAMBLEDON, co. Bucks., part of the marriage-portion of Richard's first wife, Isabella Marshal (*V.C.H. Bucks.*, iii, 47), with Henley, Sundon, and Thornbury (*q.v.*) and possibly other manors.

HARWELL, co. Berks., held by Richard in 1228, *de ballio domini regis* as *Terra Normannorum*, worth £13 5s. od., of the honour of St. Valery (*q.v.*). *Bk. of Fees*, 385; Midgley, xxi. See also *Cal. I.P.M.*, i, no. 808; *V.C.H. Berks.*, iii, 485 *ff*.

HAUGHLEY, co. Suff., *caput* of the honour of Haughley, was granted during pleasure without the fees, March 6th, 1234, *Cl. R.*, 385. The charter dated March 14th is in Exch. T. R. Misc. Bk., no. 57, nos. ccviii, cclxviii. The manor, which had belonged to Hubert de Burgh, was worth £30 in 1235, *Bk. of Fees*, 403, and see the important account *ibid.*, 1457-1459.

HEMEL HEMPSTEAD, co. Herts., ancient demesne of the honour of Berkhampstead. *Cal. I.P.M.*, i, no. 808; Midgley, x, xiii.

HENLEY, co. Oxon., acquired in 1231 as Hambledon, *Cal. I.P.M.*, i, no. 808.

ISABELLA OF ANGOULÊME'S DOWER granted to Richard, in fee with the lands of Count Robert of Dreux (Drewes, Druis, etc.), that is the honour of St. Valery (*q.v.*) and the lands of the Duke of Lorraine, that is the honour of Eye (*q.v.*), all of which he had formerly held *de ballio regis*, on February 4th, 1231, *Cal. Ch. R.*, i, 129. The dower in England as committed to Thomas of Cirencester in July 1227 (*Pat. R.*, 135) consisted of Exeter★, Lifton, Kenton★, Greatweek in Devon (granted to Richard, December 13th, 1228, during pleasure, plus Addiscot★ (Eilrichescot)★ *Cl. R.*, 137), Ilchester, in Somerset, Wilton★, Malmesbury★, in Wiltshire, the town of Rockingham but not the castle or honour, Waltham in Essex, Queenhithe in London (various grants of 1228 show Richard in possession of these, plus Chichester in Sussex, Winterslow in Wilts., *Pat. R.*, 191, *Cl. R.*, 24, *Lib. R.*, 100). Berkhampstead★ (*q.v.*) was committed to Raymond de Burgo, July 12th, 1227, *Pat. R.*, 134. The county and vill of Rutland were granted separately. Those marked (★) were ancient demesne. Litton was alienated by Richard to Andrew de Cancellis before 1242 (*Bk. of Fees*, 757). This family of Chanceux, proscribed in Magna Carta, frequently attested Richard's charters. Other lists of Richard's ancient demesne manors are found in *Cl. R.*, 1242, p. 404, 1252, p. 110, 1268, p. 463.

ISLEWORTH in Middlesex, may have been part of Berkhampstead. Richard was in possession in 1231 when he was granted a fair there, *Cl. R.*, September 8th, p. 556. For details see 'Thomas de Wykes and his Chronicle' in *E.H.R.* It was worth about £130 in 1297-1298.

IVER, co. Bucks., held of the honour of Wallingford (*Bk. of Fees*, 116) was granted by Edmund to his half-brother, Richard of Cornwall, Midgley, xx.

KIRTON in Lindsey, and the soke, had been held by Hubert de Burgh, as of the honour of Boulogne in 1227, *Pat. R.*, 130. Granted to Richard for two fees on February 13th, 1235, *Cal. Ch. R.*, i, 193. See Midgley, xvi, xxii.

KNARESBOROUGH, co. Yorks. The manor, castle, and honour were granted to Richard and the heirs of his *uxor desponsata* on January 28th, 1235. Exch. T. R. Misc. Bk., no. 57, no. ccxv. A highly privileged honour, with its own justices (S. Painter, *Feudal Barony*, 114) held for two fees. Midgley, 186-94, 200-1 shows it to be worth about £350 in 1297-1298.

LANGBOROUGH, co. Gloucs., the manor, late of Hugh Mortimer, granted to Richard as part of Sanchia's marriage-portion, in 1254, *Cl. R.*, 67. The charter in Exch. T. R. Misc. Bk., no. 57, no. cxxxvii, is dated April 25th, 1256. See Midgley, xi.

LECHLADE, co. Gloucs., granted with OAKHAM (*q.v.*) as part of Sanchia's marriage-portion in 1252. The statement in Lewis's *Topographical Dictionary* that Richard founded a house of Black Canons here probably refers to the hospital, the patronage of which fell to him with the manor. See *C.P.R.*, 1261, p. 181; *Cl. R.*, 1254, p. 5; *Cal. Cl. R.*, i, 440.

LYDFORD in Devon, with the castle and the forest of Dartmoor in fee, October 10th, 1239, £10 a year, Exch. T. R. Misc. Bk., no. 57, no. cxxxi; *Cal. Ch. R.*, i, 247. Worth about £60 a year in 1297-1298.

MARLOW, co. Bucks., ancient demesne of the honour of Wallingford (*Bk. of Fees*, 1450). John, Richard's first-born son, died there in September 1232 (*Ann. Theok.*, 89).

MERE in Dorset, granted as part of Sanchia's marriage-portion, with Corsham (*q.v.*) on December 25th, 1243, *Cal. Ch. R.*, i, 276, cf. i, 283. Richard had licence to build a castle on the hill above Mere, July 5th, 1253, Exch. T. R. Misc. Bk., no. 57, no. lxxxxiii. Between 1257 and 1262 he was given a total of 200 oaks for this purpose. *Cl. R.*, *passim*.

NEWPORT in Essex, granted as MERE (*q.v.*). *Cal. I.P.M.*, i, no. 808.

OAKHAM, co. Rutland (*q.v.*) as £116 15s. 5d. worth of Sanchia's marriage-portion on May 16th, 1252, *Cl. R.*, 92; *Cal. Ch. R.*, i, 392, dated June 5th; Exch. T. R. Misc. Bk., no. 57, no. ccvi, dated May 31st, with LECHLADE (*q.v.*). The hall was burnt in 1264, *Rot. Hund.*, ii, 51. Richard enclosed Flitteris Wood (now Park), *C.P.R.*, 1252, p. 147, and may have converted the manor house into a castle, *V.C.H. Rutland*, i, 111, ii, 8; *C.P.R.*, 1263, p. 290.

QUEENHITHE (*Ripa Regina*) in London, part of the dower of ISABELLA OF ANGOULÊME (*q.v.*), farmed by Richard to the City of London for £50 a year on October 13th, 1246, Exch. T. R. Misc. Bk., no. 57, no. x, ratified by Henry III, February 26th, 1247, *ibid.*, no. ccix. The rent was later reduced to £21; see Midgley, xix.

RISBOROUGH, Prince's, co. Bucks., granted as part of Sanchia's marriage-portion, December 25th, 1243, as MERE (*q.v.*), with the park, held in chief for one fee, *Cal. I.P.M.*, i, no. 808.

RUTLAND. Richard presumably received the county by grant of 1227, as part of Isabella's dower, but it is not known what rights he thus acquired. He did not hold the forest. The P.R.O. *List of Sheriffs* gives 1227, Geoffrey de Rokingham, 1248, Ralpe de Grenham (who was steward of the honour of Eye in 1247, *Cal. Ch. R.*, ii, 378, and chief steward of Isabella de Fortibus in 1266, Denholm-Young, *Seignorial Administration*, 75, n. 3), 1257 Anketinus de Martival (and 1258 to 1272 Treharne, *op. cit.*, 208, n. 6).

SHOWELL, near Swerford, co. Oxon. Richard was granted 33 oaks for building a house there in 1252, *Cl. R.*, 138, 139. Tenure unknown.

SUNDON, co. Bedf., part of the marriage-portion of Isabella Marshal, Midgley, xx.

THORNBURY, co. Gloucs., ancient demesne, part of the marriage-portion of Isabella Marshal. Grant of yearly fair, July 20th, 1239, *Cal. Ch. R.*, i, 244. Houses there in 1236, *Cl. R.*, 262.

TITBURST, near Aldenham, co. Herts., held by Richard of St. Albans. See *V.C.H. Herts.*, ii, 155, citing Exch. T. R. Misc. Bk., no. 57, no. cxlix.

TREMATON, town and castle, and manor of CALSTOCK in Cornwall, with 60½ fees bought by Richard in 1270 from Roger de Valle Torta for £300. See *Anct. Deeds*, v, A.10842-3; Midgley, xxiii.

ST. VALERY, chiefly in Oxon. The honour descended from Bernard of St. Valery (*d.* 1190) with his granddaughter to Robert, Count of Dreux, of Brittany, and was granted to Richard, August 21st, 1227, *R. Lit. Cl.*, ii, 198. In 1237 the demesne manors were Beckley, Willaston, Blackthorn in Ambrosden, Asthall, and Yarnton, together worth £68, *Bk. of Fees*, 613. See Ault, *Private Jurisdiction in England*, 177-208, for the 24⅔ fees, also *V.C.H. Hants.*, iv, 656, and *V.C.H. Bucks.*, iv, 243-4. At Beckley, the *caput*, a favourite residence, Richard was allowed a deer-leap in 1230. The Lord Edward stayed there in Richard's absence, June 23rd, 1258. *C.P.R.*, 13.

WALLINGFORD

1216(-1218) Castle and honour committed to Richard, the illegitimate son of King John, *not* Richard of Cornwall, *R. Lit. Pat.*, 185.

1227 The honour committed to Philip d'Aubigné. *Pat. R.*, 140.

1229 (November 1st) The castle and honour committed to Richard of Cornwall, until May 1231, with the town also in May 1230. *Pat. R.*, 313, 434; *Cl. R.*, 258.

1231 (May 12th) The castle and honour committed to Geoffrey de Craucombe, *Pat. R.*, 434.

1231 (August 10th) The same to Richard of Cornwall in fee, *Cal. Ch. R.*, i, 139. On May 27th, 1232, the town was added, *Cl. R.*, 568.

The history of the honour to 1212 is in *Bk. of Fees*, 117-18, and *The Boarstall Chartulary* (Oxf. Hist. Soc.), ed. H. E. Salter, 295 *ff.* Watlington (*q.v.*) was 'seemingly the honour's only demesne manor'. Ault, *Private Jurisdiction*, 209-39, esp. 224, n. 74. The honour comprised about 120 fees. *Ibid.*, 210.

WALTHAM, co. Essex, was ancient demesne, part of the dower of Isabella of Angoulême (*q.v.*). The farm was regularly paid to Richard direct from the Exchequer, and so would not perhaps appear in the estate accounts. It is missing in 1296-1297. *Cal. Lib. R.*, i, 100, 116, 150, 236.

WATLINGTON, co. Oxon., of the honour of Wallingford (*q.v.*). Richard was granted a market there, with free warren in all his demesnes throughout England, June 20th, 1252. Exch. T. R. Misc. Bk., no. 57, no. ccxiv.

WESTMINSTER in Middlesex. Richard granted 30 oaks from Windsor forest for his houses there, April 8th, 1234, *Cl. R.*, 409.

WILLASTON, co. Oxon., hamlet of Mixbury, demesne manor of the honour of St. Valery (*q.v.*), worth £7 in 1237. *Bk. of Fees*, 613.

WILTON, co. Wilts., part of the dower of Isabella of Angoulême (*q.v.*). In 1230 the town paid £30 farm, but contrast Midgley, 74 *f.*, where it yields only about £7 in 1297-1298.

YARNTON (Erdinton), co. Oxon., demesne manor of the honour of St. Valery (*q.v.*), held of the Bishop of Lincoln for two fees. *Cal. I.P.M.*, i, no. 808.

WITHAM, Croultone, and Losmere, held in chief for two fees, *Cal. I.P.M.*, i, no. 808.

ARMS AND SEALS

The known seals of Richard are:

1. As Count of Poitou, April 1227. The seal has RICARDI FI[LII] . . . SIGLLM, and on the reverse . . . [PIC]TAVIENSIS. There seems to be no room for Cornwall in the legend. (D'ouët d'Arcq, *Inventaires des Sceaux*, no. 10188. See *Layettes*, no. 1926). The seal is attached to the truce with France.

2. As Earl of Cornwall and Count of Poitou, attached to a deed of *c.* 1240 in Magd. Coll. Oxon. archives, Hants. vol. i, Bromdean 13. *Obverse*: the earl on horseback with sword drawn, 'Sigillum Ricardi comitis Pictavie'. *Reverse*: a shield bearing a lion rampant within a bordure charged with fourteen bezants, the shield within a floreated border, 'Sigillum Ricardi comitis Cornubie'.

The arms should be 'argent, a lion rampant gules crowned or in a border sable bezanty'. For these see *Mat. Par. Addit.*, vi, 471; A. R. Wagner, *Historic Heraldry of Britain*, p. 42, pl. iii, 15, who says that Planché took the bezants as Poix for Poitou. Others say they are for Cornwall. The crown on the lion has nothing to do with the fact that Richard became King of the Romans. These arms are found in the Franciscan church at Bordeaux, the south aisle at Westminster, the east window at Bedall church in Yorkshire, Richmond, Great Malvern, St. Albans and elsewhere.

The seal should have been changed when the style 'Comes Pictavie' was dropped.

3. As King of the Romans, enthroned in majesty. See *Brit. Mus. Catal. of Seals*, vol. vi, nos. 21, 158 and 21, 159, plate II; cf. D'ouët d'Arcq. *Inventaires*, no. 10890 and *Layettes*, no. 4413. There is a plate in Sandford, *Genealogical History*, p. 95.

THE DATE OF JOHN MANSEL'S LETTER TO SIR ROBERT DE THWENGE AND IMBERT DE MONTFERRAND, IN *ROYAL LETTERS*, II, 157-8

In this letter Mansel states that the King of Almain has asked for a messenger to be sent to him on Friday after the feast of the Assumption to inform him as to the state of the king's affairs. Mansel directs them (or one of them) to send Sir John de Castello. He tells them of the progress of the building operations at his house at Sedgwick, which he is crenellating, of the weakness of the king's party in propagandists, and his own efforts in that direction. He sends greetings to his friends Gerard de Rodes and Alenard de Seningham.

Shirley's note is helpful only in its opening sentences: 'This letter was written apparently in August, and after the distinct organizing of the baronial party. This and the death of the writer limit us to the years 1259-1264.' It is also obvious that any date after the end of June 1263 (Mansel's flight from the Tower) is excluded, narrowing the limits to 1259-1262. The rest is a matter of weighing probabilities.

If both Richard and Henry had been in England, this elaborate procedure for finding out how the latter's affairs stood would have been unnecessary. In August 1259 and August 1261 they were both in England, but in August 1260 Richard was at Worms and in August 1262 at Aachen. There is something to be said for the former of these dates because Richard mentions John de Castello as one of his envoys to Bologna in a letter probably sent in August 1260. That is, he might have been sent out by Mansel to Worms and thence on to Bologna by Richard. There are three obstacles to this view. Worms is a long way from England, and yet Richard can fix a day for the arrival of a messenger from overseas. This implies that, in writing to Mansel, Richard knew where he would be in a month's time. This is perhaps not a serious difficulty, but the phraseology does not sound natural for such an arrangement. The second point is that Mansel, who seems recently to have been at Sedgwick near Worthing, writes *in partibus ubi sumus* to two of Henry III's household knights, closely associated with the court, without knowing which of them it will reach. This suggests that Mansel and his correspondents are a considerable distance apart, that the court is split. Again, a more direct way of proceeding could have been adopted in 1260.

The third point is far more substantial. Mansel speaks of the approaching completion of the fortifications at Sedgwick: 'opus nostrum de Seghwyc dei gratia bene procedit ita quod in brevi poterit aquam tenere'. He received licence to crenellate it on March 12th, 1262 (*C.P.R.*, 206; an earlier licence of November 4th, 1258, was presumably not used), and by July 1263 it had been fortified (*ibid.*, 269, 279, 381). As mentioned in the text, Thwenge got licence to crenellate just after the date proposed for letter — August 1262. At that time Henry III had gone to France with John Mansel in charge of the Great Seal. Robert de Thwenge and Imbert de Montferrand either went with him or followed him there. All were at or near Boulogne in August (*C.P.R.*, 1266-1272, App. 726-9) and Richard was only two or three days' ride away at Aachen, where he spent some time. Alenard de Seningham was also at Boulogne (*C.P.R.* 152). He and Gerard de Rodes came over to England with the Count of St. Pol in 1261, but had been paid by Henry III since June 1260. It is suggested that Mansel was with Henry and that the others had not yet arrived.

THE BLOOD OF HAILES

Edmund of Almain, later of Cornwall, went with his father to Germany in 1268 and brought back with him the relic that was to be famous for centuries at Hailes. The annalist of Hailes writes: 'Et Edmundus filius regis Alemannie per instructionem quorundam virorum de nobili viro et domino de Dilaunde adquisivit nobilem portionem sanguinis domini nostri Jesu Christi cum innumerabili quantitate reliquiarum' (*M.G.H.*, xvi, 483). This is wrongly entered under 1267. It is usually stated that Edmund divided the blood between the abbey of Hailes and the college of Bonhommes which he himself founded in its honour at Ashridge in 1283. But the glory went to Hailes 'as surely as God is in Gloucestershire', and there remained until 'the rough chemistry of Henry VIII's commissioners detected it to be the blood of a duck' (further sixteenth-century details are in Blaauw, *The Barons' Wars*, pp. 351-2).

Henry III, as already mentioned (*supra*, p. 72), was very up to date in the importance he attached to the ceremony in honour of the blood made annual by him in 1247. The cult of the body of Christ had been instituted at Liége only in 1246, as the result of a vision seen by St. Juliana of the moon (signifying the church) with a black spot on it (signifying the lack of this cult). In 1264 the cult of Corpus Christi was legalized for the whole of the Western Church by Pope Urban IV, who had been Archdeacon of Liége. From the origin of this cult and the impetus given to it in 1264 it seems likely that the Dilaunde of the chronicle is really Zealand. Observance of the feast was compulsory. The office was written by Thomas Aquinas.

APPENDIX SIX

RICHARD OF CORNWALL IN THE WINDMILL

The Mill near Lewes is mentioned in the London Chronicle (cited in Rish., *de Bellis*, notes p. 135), in *Pol. Songs*, 69, and in the following passage from the Melrose Chronicle (facsimile ed. with an introduction by A. O. Anderson), p. 128:

Ex hoc bello frater regis Henrici, Ricardus vero comes Cornubie, qui ante paucos dies diffidarat barones ad bellum appellans illos regis et regni proditores, metu mortis perterritus fugit in molendinum quod vi ventorum dicebatur molere, claudens hostium super se. Ad quod inclinato die belli ad vesperam accesserunt barones valide contra ipsum acclamantes, 'Descende, descende, pessime molendinarie! Egredere, egredere, molendini magister instante!' Set et timiditatem eius et vecordiam ulterius exprobrantes adjungunt, 'Quid tibi opus erat fieri molendinarium, per maximum infortunium, qui nos pauperes barones nuper diffidati ad bellum, qui etiam non minori nomine dum nos diffidares voluisti te appellari quam Regis Romanorum et Semper Augusti?' Fuerat enim paulo ante rex Alemannie, propter quod vocavit se Semper Augustum et Regem Romanorum. Egreditur ergo Ricardus de molendino et abducitur a baronibus vinculis cathenatus in firma custodia detinendus. Ex qua, quia pecuniosus erat valde, liberatus est post quinque circiter menses pro redempcione plurima, viz. pro xvii milibus libris sterlingorum et quinque milibus libris auri desiderabilis.

INDEX

Index